AMITAV GHOSH'S THE SHADOW LINES

CRITICAL ESSAYS

AMITAV GHOSH'S THE SHADOW LINES

CRITICAL ESSAYS

Edited by

Arvind Chowdhary

ATLANTIC

PUBLISHERS & DISTRIBUTORS (P) LTD

Published by
ATLANTIC
PUBLISHERS & DISTRIBUTORS (P) LTD
7/22, Ansari Road, Darya Ganj, New Delhi-110002
Phones : +91-11-40775252, 23273880, 23275880, 23280451
Fax : +91-11-23285873
Web : www.atlanticbooks.com
E-mail : orders@atlanticbooks.com

Branch Office
5, Nallathambi Street, Wallajah Road, Chennai-600002
Phones : +91-44-64611085, 32413319
E-mail : chennai@atlanticbooks.com

Printed in India at Nice Printing Press, A-33/3A, Site-IV, Industrial Area, Sahibabad, Ghaziabad, U.P.

For my parents
and for
Somya & Snigdha

ACKNOWLEDGMENTS

Acknowledgments are due to my contributors who have made this book possible, to my wife for painstakingly going through the entire manuscript, to Prof. Sisir Kumar Das for his perceptive and encouraging response to my own article, to my colleagues and friends in different colleges of Delhi University for generously sharing with me their literary insights into the novel, to my student, Deepika Jain, for making a good job of the proof-reading of the manuscript. I must thank Mr. A.N. Sharma for computer typing it and Siddhartha and Devesh for rendering the necessary secretarial help to me.

I also take this opportunity to thank Atlantic Publishers and Distributors for their full cooperation in bringing out this book.

PREFACE

Rubek:

> You have no conception, really, of the way
> an artist's mind works.

Maya (smiles and shakes her head):

> Good heavens. I don't even have any conception
> of the way my own mind works.

–Henrik Ibsen, *When We Dead Awaken, II*

The Shadow Lines is a novel in which Amitav Ghosh has been able to realise his artistic conception through an art form, which is cohesive. However, it remains somewhat incomprehensible to some readers; they are, particularly, mystified by its non-linear mode. Consequently, they are not able to make up their minds about its structure, and various techniques that have gone into its making. The present volume of critical essays on *The Shadow Lines* is being presented in the hope that it will enable the reader to gain an insight into the meaning and structure of the novel. In the first part of the book, the contributors bring out the various aspects/elements of the novel. Ultimately, these essays put together answer the questions: *What* vision of life has been created in the novel, and *how* it has been created, though some of the contributors even venture to answer the question, *how well* Amitav Ghosh has done it. The second part has five essays, which look at the novel from some current critical perspectives, but the emphasis of these essays is upon practice, and not theory. The idea is that the reader will learn about a specific approach by seeing it applied to *The Shadow Lines.*

Works of literary art are usually not comparable as they create different elements in their respective fictional worlds, even though they employ some of the common traditional devices along with the innovative ones. Moreover, we cannot really compare them as we are not possessed of a sure principle of literary judgment — personal and social factors are bound to creep in. However, it is fruitful to inter-relate works by the same author. Aditya Bhattacharjea has done exactly that in his significant essay, '*The Shadow Lines* in Context.'

The chronology of events in the novel needs to be discerned for a fuller understanding of the novel. It has been painstakingly researched by the editor and is provided at the end of the book. Angelie Multani has prepared a 'family tree' for three generations of Indian characters in the novel (British characters have been left out for the purpose), and rightly so, because the focus of the text is, essentially, on the Indian situation. The advanced reader is expected to look up notes and references given at the end of each article for getting suggestions for further reading on a specific topic.

As the art of novel is multiform and complex, this book of critical essays reflects discriminating judgment in terms of breadth of appreciation. The book seeks to provide various 'entry-points' to the novel. The purpose, ultimately, is to make it more lucid to the reader and enrich his understanding of the text. Though 'Critical Essays' is primarily addressed to the student, the common discernible reader, lay and academic, may find it useful and interesting.

ARVIND CHOWDHARY

CONTENTS

CONTRIBUTORS

Dr. Aditya Bhattacharjea is Reader in Economics at the Delhi School of Economics, Delhi University. He is the co-editor (with Lola Chatterji) of *The Fiction of St Stephen's* (Ravi Dayal, 2000), a collection of essays on recent Indian novels in English.

Dr. Alka Kumar is Reader in English at Shyama Prasad Mukherjee College, University of Delhi. She writes on gender and literary theory, and on themes relating to Canadian Studies. She is the author of *Doris Lessing: Journey in Evolution.* (New Delhi: Book Plus, 2001)

Alpana Neogy is Reader in English at Ram Lal Anand College, Delhi University. She writes on Indian Fiction.

Angelie Multani is currently teaching at Gargi College. She writes on gender issues. She has published articles on Moliere, Shakespeare and Mahesh Dattani in leading academic journals, including, *Seagull Theatre Quarterly.*

Dr. Arvind Chowdhary is Reader in English at Ram Lal Anand College (Evening), University of Delhi. He writes on aesthetics of poetry and fiction.

Manjula Saxena is Reader in Philosophy at Indraprastha College for Women, Delhi University. She writes on literary aesthetics.

Meenakshi Malhotra is Senior Lecturer in English at Hans Raj College, Delhi University. She writes on gender and literary theory.

Dr. Minoti Chatterjee is Reader in Political Science at Gargi College. She has researched on Political Ideology, in relation to pre-partition Bengali Theatre.

Dr. Nivedita Sen is Reader in English at Hans Raj College, Delhi University. She has extensively worked on children's literature in Bengali.

Premindha Bannerjee teaches English at Jesus and Mary College, Delhi University. Her field of interest includes Modern European Drama.

Dr. Promila Garg is Reader in English at Daulat Ram College, Delhi University. She has published a work, entitled *The Freedom Movement in Indian Fiction in English* (Ashish Publishing House, 1993).

Dr. Rita Joshi is Reader in English at Lady Shri Ram College, University of Delhi. Her doctoral thesis is on Lawrence. She was sponsored by Charles Wallace Trust to research on Indian Fiction in English at Cambridge. Her papers have been published in leading academic journals, including *English Language Notes* (University of Colorado) and *Indian International Quarterly.*

Dr. Roopali Sircar is Reader in English at Sri Venkateswara College. She holds a Ph.D. in African Literature, and is the author of *Twice Colonized: Women in African Literature* (New Delhi: Creative Books, 1995).

Rudrashish Chakraborty teaches English at Kirori Mal College, Delhi University. His field of interest includes Renaissance Historiography and Literature, and Marxist Literary Theory.

Someshwar Sati teaches English at Kirori Mal College, University of Delhi. His field of interest includes post-colonial theory and literature.

Introduction

ARVIND CHOWDHARY

The Shadow Lines is a highly innovative, complex and celebrated novel of Amitav Ghosh. Published in 1988, it received the prestigious Sahitya Academy Award in the following year. Not only literary critics but also some noted litterateurs have acclaimed it for what it has been able to achieve as a work of art. Its focus is a fact of history, the post-partition scenario of violence; but its overall form is a subtle interweaving of fact, fiction and reminiscence. Its multi-layered complex structure makes it a difficult text, which demands perceptive reading for a richer experience. It is, principally, organised through the weaving together of 'personal lives and public events.' The finished form, ultimately, excavates personal and social history *vis-à-vis* the racial riots in some parts of East Pakistan (now Bangladesh) and, mainly, Calcutta in India. Its wider appeal is to be found in its contemporaneity. But it is about any place and any time that has known violence, death, memory and pathos.

I

In this section I may trace out how the novel originated. Ghosh tells us that he was greatly upset by the riots that followed Indira Gandhi's assassination, and that his novel came out of the turmoil of that moment. The incident revived his memories of 1964 riots in Calcutta, Dhaka and and elsewhere, 'an enormous crevasse had opened.' It was when he was living with a 'conflict,' or we may say, having 'a quarrel with himself,' that he felt impelled to write the novel.[1] Though *The Shadow Lines* is mainly about 1964, it is about 1984 as well. Rather, it is a continuous narrative, which replicates the pattern of violence, experienced in the 11th September incident of America.

Henry James said that 'it is art that *makes* life, makes interest, makes importance.'[2] And Amitav Ghosh's text precisely does that. It creates a piece of 'virtual life' which is *significant*. That is why, 'it speaks to the world' and satisfies the parameters set by the 'works' of literary art — parameters, say, of organisation and clarity as manifest in an art form, which is at the same time, the delineation of some vital aspect of life — in this case, a socio-political reality of our times. But, though Ghosh's novel 'shows the realistic novelist's capacity to catch the telling and placing details of the appearance of things, and an acute ear for speech and dialogue,'[3] he is aiming at something more profound: a 'poetic truth' which is really deeper and more comprehensive than the mere fidelity to fact which we expect in the work of the historian.[4]

'The artist's work,' as Goethe admirably says, 'is real in so far as it is always true; ideal, in that it is never actual.'[5] It is in the light of this profound observation that we may view 'the achieved vision' of Ghosh's text. It is rooted in reality and yet it looks beyond.

II

In his essay "The Intrinsic Sociology in Fiction," Brent Harold observes that there is no conflict between the experience of reading a literary text as an art form and the view that it may yet be taken to have a social or political intent. He argues that 'the structuring elements of the work are words, the very quality of which is to evoke life outside the work.'[6] Now, if we agree to adopt this point of view in respect of Ghosh's novel, it may be said to make a socio-political statement, by virtue of the very elements it integrates as its structure. This implicit statement may be put thus: all borders, the physical ones in particular, not only distinguish but tend to divide what they distinguish, say, the nation states. As against these boundaries, individual memories cannot be divided, that is, they defy limitations to any particular region, religion or community. Would it therefore not be duly human if we followed the logic of memory and maintained mutual amity in spite of physical divisions? I see this suggestion as a corollary of the 'statement.'

Some eminent critics however refuse to grant to Ghosh's *The Shadow Lines* any relevance to life and reality. One of them even alleges that Ghosh, the author, evades the historical reality.[7] I leave it to the reader to judge if this critical attitude is warranted by the way the characters in the novel are made to behave. Are they not seen to grapple with, and chafe at the alienation of hearts that followed the division of land? How can one ignore the fact that at least some people in Ghosh's fictional world risk their own lives in daring to save innocent people on both sides of the border? Humanness here overruns the man-made boundaries, making the inexorable appear a little shadowy. Be it noted that the novelist does not quite wish away the borders. Nor does he suggest that the people are the same everywhere. Differences must persist, but they should not breed hatred or violence. Yet at no point is the ideal made to jut out.

Thus, it should be clear that Ghosh's engagement is with the real world. This real engagement accounts for his interest in sociology and anthropology in actual life. We may safely infer that his keen study of these disciplines has lent credibility to his fiction.

III

Though Amitav Ghosh's novel is based on historical reality, it creates a complete piece of fiction. There is nothing in it, which is not entirely created. All its details get integrated into the fabric of the novel. We may trace out such integration at the level of characterization. Ghosh, as we know, has invented an extraordinary but slightly whimsical character in Tridib. He acts as the organising principle of the novel. He lives a fuller life at the level of mind, through his creative imagination. His credo is to perceive the multiform reality by using 'the imagination precisely.' He is a very original character, as he does not allow himself to be appropriated by a master-narrative like nationalism. His life is governed by higher-order needs such as creative thinking, understanding and love. He is guided by none but himself and he guides the narrator, being his mentor. May, in the novel, seems to complement him. The other characters like Ila, the Shaheb and Nick Price are presented as striking contrasts to Tridib. Although Tha'mma and Robi share the depth and sensibility of Tridib, they are different from him, as they are constrained by such divisive ideologies as nationalism.

It is not difficult to see that through the first two categories of characters, Ghosh presents a binary division: life of imaginative thinking or contemplation *versus* the life of the senses. The narrator shares with Tridib the life of creative thinking, whereas characters like Ila and the Shaheb represent the life of the senses. Since *The Shadow Lines* is Amitav Ghosh's second novel, it is natural that some biographical details have gone into its making. But it will be preposterous to identify Tridib or the narrator with Amitav Ghosh himself, though they are his spokesmen. The novel is certainly not a straightforward autobiography. And even if we concede for the sake of argument that the 'I' is modeled on the author himself, 'the author-as-character' is still an 'invented figure.' 'The author as a voice is only a function of his own fiction, a rhetorical construction, not a privileged authority but an object of interpretation.'[8]

That brings us to the question of the nameless narrator. It does not make a difference if he does not have a proper name. He does not become 'faceless' on that account. His name is 'I.' He grows and develops in the novel and acquires a literary status as a full-fledged character. Tridib wanted him to use his imagination precisely when it came to interpreting reality. Equipped with such a faculty he is able to relearn the meaning of space and time, in the context of the violence in Dhaka and Calcutta, much later after Tridib's death. Tridib had shown him the path and he follows him essentially, but that does not make him less original. It is in the light of this observation that we may read the criticism that he does not live his own life, or that he lives in the 'story' of Tridib.

There is some truth in the criticism that his men characters tend to be more complex and interesting than his women characters; and that he has made his characters, particularly, Ila, go through some really painful experiences. However, Amitav Ghosh's own position on the issue is that 'his men characters are as much conflicted as his women characters.' But Ghosh is not a 'cruel' writer. He treats his creations with respect and affection. It is very much true of Tridib, though his relationship with Tha'mma is somewhat ambiguous. He has done both these characters, more or less, lovingly, though Ila has been criticised for her superficial cosmopolitanism. It may be mentioned here that since the focus is on the main characters — namely, Tridib, the narrator and May — some of his minor characters — especially British, including Mrs. Price, have been created as marginal. We have to bear in mind that such characters may be full-blooded characters in actual life, but in a piece of fiction, their place is determined by the overall structure of the novel. Thus, there is no substance in the charge that they do not come to life. The artistic design demands that they be presented in a fairly summarised form. Probably, *The Shadow Lines* is neither a novel of character nor a novel of plot but 'a novel of ideas.' And the characters subserve the chosen purpose of projecting some vital ideas in the text.

IV

David Lodge in his essay "Novelist at the Crossroads" observes that the modern novelist is in a privileged position as he can avail of an astonishing variety of styles. The 'aesthetic pluralism' of the times allows him to make use of 'traditional as well as innovative styles, minimalism as well as excess, nostalgia as well as prophecy.'[9] But it needs to be pointed out that each literary artist, worth his name, uses the same device in his own way. Thus, when Amitav Ghosh uses traditional realism he does not merely conform to it, but brings a questioning attitude to such reality and looks at it afresh from an entirely new perspective. This is how he understands time and space as virtual entities, in the context of racial violence. Similarly, nostalgic strain in the text does not merely recreate the past — the glory that was but which resides in memory now and forever — but showcases the contrasting dark and poignant social reality.

The arranging of episodes and of digressions, the art of foiling; the use of symbols, metaphors and tropes as structural elements — all this indicates a conscious purpose that yields an extraordinary symmetry of form.

As it happens to be a memory novel, the narrative is wrought in non-linear mode. It moves back and forth, in utter disregard of our conventional notions of time and space. This technique enables Ghosh to make the narrator subsume and appropriate the memories of other characters, and make them a part of his own memory and consciousness. Some incidents, belonging to different times and different places, even coalesce to give the narrator an insight into some vital aspects of reality — which is rather innovative.

V

This quest for form and meaning makes it a modernist text. But it is post-modernist in at least two senses. One, it seeks knowledge or meaning by dissent, that is, by putting into question existing paradigms, and by inventing new ones, rather than assenting to the so-called universal truth or agreeing to a consensus. For instance, the idea that violence gets driven to the borders, once new nations are carved out of a single state is a myth, which gets questioned in the novel. The experience tells the narrator that remote areas like Srinagar and Khulna and not-so-remote areas like Dhaka and Calcutta seem to draw closer because of a spate of violence triggered by a single incidence of the theft of a relic, belonging to the Prophet Mohammed. Here space is being understood not as extension, but space as it draws closer through mutual discord and mutual concern, or space as it moves apart through mutual indifference. Two, the fragmented, disjointed and discontinuous mode of experience, which is delineated in the text, is characteristic of post-modern subjectivity. To illustrate, different characters experience Tridib's death in the novel in a disjointed and discontinuous manner. Its fuller implications are understood when different characters bring their partial perspectives on this very painful and poignant incident.

VI

Language is not only an important aspect of the novel, it is 'the whole thing' — as it is through language that the artist creates the fictional world — its situations, characters, atmosphere, etc. Now, for analysing the language of a novel, a significant approach is the one proposed by Bakhtin and later on developed by David Lodge. According to this approach, we take into account the 'many styles' or the 'many voices' of the created world for making any statement about its language. Lodge rightly observes that for the literary artist 'the world is full of other people's words,' and that he is supposed to orient himself to such world before he selects the language, which will suit his literary purpose. And it seems that Ghosh inadvertently follows this practice, for it seems that he has chosen his words with care. To suit the somber subject matter of his novel, he has essentially used four styles: analytic, figurative, nostalgic and prophetic. The narrator of the novel, for instance, turns nostalgic when he reminiscences about Tridib, but his language becomes analytic and even figurative when he is trying to find meaning into the personal and social history. Ila, on the other hand, uses plain simple language to express her facts about 'the world as it is.' Tridib sounds precise and technical when he talks about various topics, relating to different disciplines of knowledge, but his language becomes metaphorical, even prophetic when he deals with such abstruse subjects as the perception of reality. What apparently look like 'banalities' and 'conundrums,'[10] in his case, are actually words of wisdom, couched in a peculiar language, which is associated with artists and imaginative thinkers. As for Tha'mma, she uses plain, simple language in her day-to-day conversations and dealings, but she becomes nostalgic in the context of her memories of Dhaka. May, too, uses plain and simple language, for the most part, but she sounds prophetic towards the end of the novel. Like the narrator's, Robi's language is quite analytic, even figurative, for analysing the question of 'freedom,' but for rendering his nightmarish experience, he uses the highly charged, symbolic and condensed dream-language. It is through these 'polyphonic medley of styles,' or voices, that the somber reality is evoked.

VII

In the context of this grave reality, elements of humour provide gentle and sympathetic laughter, which serves to cement human bonds in the novel. But, mainly, it is the other kind of laughter — intellectual and derisive, which we associate with 'wit,' that is interspersed through the novel. To illustrate, when the narrator fondly remembers Tridib's Gastric — not as a condition of indigestion, but as an organ peculiar to Tridib, he seems to be striking afresh, though imaginatively, a kind of close kinship with Tridib, which he had with him when he was alive. But humour serves a moral purpose in the context of Ila's belief that 'the world as it is' is real. She is virtually being scoffed at for her preoccupation with 'the present.' This kind of humour — which evokes an intelligent and derisive laughter, Bergson saw as a kind of weapon which was meant to chastise a rigid kind of behaviour.[11] Ila's behaviour is one such example.

VIII

Ghosh has received adverse criticism for some sections of his novel from critics and the lay readers alike. Take for instance, the pornographic letter, which May received from Tridib; and the other, of course, is the novel's ending, which I shall come to later. Even May thinks only a 'mad' man could have written such a letter. We can justify this action of Tridib only if we take the broad view that he had been in love with May for many years and that the letter was intended to convey to her, though indirectly, that he keenly desired her. But we will have to qualify our statement with regard to Tridib, as desire in his scheme of things, essentially meant reaching forth towards 'the other,' and not mere gratification of physical desire. By writing such a letter Tridib, unwittingly, seems to have created a temporary wedge between May and himself. But this 'wedge' functions as a 'slide' for her when she actually meets him, as she is instantaneously won over by him because of his endearing qualities. Similarly, the incident in which May allows the narrator to get physically intimate with her — though earlier on, she had successfully repulsed his advances towards her when he was drunk — at the face of it, appears to be an incredulous act. But, it, too, serves as a step towards the 'bonding' between the narrator and May, towards the end of the novel: It becomes easier for May to turn to the narrator for emotional relief, love and understanding, after the earlier incident. It is only in such an intimate moment that she shares with him her most personal and private experience relating to Tridib: a revelation that Tridib died a sacrificial death.

As for the 'ending,' it rounds off the inner form of the novel — that is, it completes the protagonist's journey towards himself. He has come to understand, eventually, an aspect of reality which, he found heterogeneous and confounding. In the context of the riots and the killing of Tridib in one such riot, he has learnt a new meaning of time and space. And, assisted by May, he has had the glimpse that his mentor, Tridib, 'gave himself up'; it was a 'sacrifice.' It is not as if the reality is going to change after the 'sacrifice' has been made, and is experienced as such by the two-some, namely, May and the narrator. As Lukàs puts it, 'after such self-recognition has been attained, the ideal thus formed irradiates the individual's life as its immanent meaning; but *the conflict between what is and what should be has not been abolished* and cannot be abolished in the sphere wherein these events take place — the life sphere of the novel; only a maximum conciliation — the profound and intensive irradiation of a man by his life's meaning — is attainable.'[12] And the narrator in Amitav Ghosh's novel seems to have achieved this objective.

IX

Amitav Ghosh's singular distinction lies in his original perception of reality, which he translates through an art, which is at once intuitive, conscious and deliberate. In *The Circle of Reason* he is seen struggling to create a form which does not really get realised, but in *The Shadow Lines* he seems to have arrived. There is almost a general consensus that *The Shadow Lines* is an adequately structured book, one in which he has found 'his own distinctive voice-polished and profound.' Like his story, *The Imam and The Indian,* it highlights 'cultural displacements, but also inter-culture connections.' With its thrust upon 'cultural displacements,' *The Shadow Lines* creates 'the brave new world of disorder, of rootless histories and selves,'[13] which is a post-modern phenomenon. But, at the base of it, is the quintessential theme of the quest for 'home,' which makes it timeless.

X

An eminent Indian critic thinks that Indian writers in English are 'cut off from the experiential mainstream, and from that common cultural matrix [...] shared with writers of all other Indian languages.'[14] One implication of his remark is that such fiction is inauthentic and that it does not really represent the Indian voice. But we should not forget that Amitav Ghosh is quintessentially an Indian, a Bengalee, who was born in Calcutta and raised in Dhaka and Colombo. But he came back to study at the University of Delhi. Subsequently, he studied at the universities of Alexandria and Oxford, but again came back to India to teach in the Sociology Department of Delhi School of Economics. Of course, he has been abroad for many years now, having taught at the universities of Virginia and Columbia, but he keeps returning to India to revive his cultural links with the country of his birth.

I have, briefly, traced out the biographical details of Ghosh to point out that he, essentially, belongs to the Indian cultural matrix. As for his movement across four continents (he is widely travelled in South Asia, Europe, Middle East and North Africa), we may say that it has helped him in formulating his diasporic consciousness, which is reflected in his various works. Though *The Shadow Lines* does not deal directly with contemporary Indian diaspora, Ghosh's experience of travelling has gone into the making of his 'London' in the novel, which is peopled by a global diaspora. But his experience of travelling, it seems, is better utilised in depicting the subcontinental reality against a western perspective, which forms the core experience of the novel.

XI

As Shashi Tharoor rightly says the writers really 'live inside their heads and on the page,' their addresses do not matter; what matters is that they create fiction which appeals to 'readers irrespective of their ethnicity.'[15] Amitav Ghosh's fiction has tremendous appeal for the reader. His very first novel, *The Circle of Reason* (1986) was highly acclaimed and appeared in Italian, Swedish, French and Danish translations. It was recognised as the first important novel produced by an Indian after Sulman Rushdie's phenomenal success. Though critics found it 'overwritten and inadequately structured,' it managed to get the Prix Medices Estrangere. His next novel *The Shadow Lines* (1988) was a remarkable success and it won the 1989 Sahitya Academy Award.

Ghosh's *In An Antique Land* (1993) is a 'hybrid of history, cultural investigation, and travelogue'[16] — a remarkable book 'that reaches back into the twelfth century as it touches on the dilemmas of our times.' It has received roaring reviews: 'Like the best travelogues, this book is also an intellectual and historical journey;'[17] but with the significant difference that 'Ghosh is an engagingly humble and receptive traveller,' which is 'a refreshing reversal of the usual power relationship between the observing (European) travel writer and his indigenous subjects.'[18] His next important novel is *The Calcutta Chromosome* (1996), 'a novel of Fevers, Delirium and Discovery.' It is essentially a 'medical thriller,' which won the prestigious Arthur C. Clark Award.

His '*Dancing in Cambodia, At Large in Burma*' (1998) is another masterpiece of travel writing. It has three pieces: the first one evokes the first ever visit by Cambodian Dancers to Europe in 1906; their performances had inspired Rodin to do his celebrated sketches. This section also contains Ghosh's interpretation of 'Pol Pot Years' from 1975 to 1978 — a regime which ravaged Cambodia and reduced it to near destitution. Ghosh happened to visit Cambodia in 1993; he met some members of Pol Pot's family and travelled to that village where he was born — all this is recorded in the first part of his book. The second section presents Angkor Wat, 'awash in stories,' and what it symbolised for Cambodians. The last section mainly brings out the recent history of Burma from the death of Aung San in 1947 to his daughter Suu Kyi's current struggle for the restoration of democracy in her country. It is based on Ghosh's two visits to Burma in 1995-1996.

His next work *Countdown* (1999) is a short piece of non-fiction, which questions the wisdom of politicians in following nuclear programmes in the subcontinent. He warns of the dangerous consequences of pursuing pro-nuclear policies. He says, 'the bomb has become the weapon with which the rulers of the subcontinent wish to avert whatever is ahead. The pursuit of nuclear weapons in the subcontinent is the moral equivalent of civil war: the targets the rulers have in mind are, in the end, their own people.'

Ghosh's latest novel *The Glass Palace* (2000) is a monumental work which has received rave reviews. One review says that '*The Glass Palace* is an epic novel written with an unerring skill. It grasps the rise and fall of empire across the twentieth century, even as it maps the geographies of the heart.'[19] Ghosh has himself said that writing this novel was like 'fighting a war.' According to another review, Ghosh is one of the few post-colonial writers who has expressed in his work 'a developing awareness of the aspirations, defeats and disappointments of colonised peoples as they figure out their place in the world.'[20] Ahdaf Soueif says: 'This is the East as seen by its own people, described by a writer whose allegiance is simply to the human. Ghosh is one of the most sympathetic post-colonial voices to be heard today.'

Ghosh says that although the (colonial) past cannot be changed, it is our duty to examine it and to interrogate our role in it; and this is exactly what he has done in *The Glass Palace*. As Meenakshi Mukherjee puts it, it is 'the most scathing critique of the British Colonialism.' It was not unexpected of Ghosh to have declined the nomination for the 2001 Commonwealth Writer's Prize. His explanation sounds quite convincing. He says: 'I would be betraying the spirit of my book if I were to allow it to be incorporated within that particular memorization of Empire that passes under the rubric of the Commonwealth.'[21] As a literary artist he thinks that 'the value of a literary prize should be in the first instance, in celebrating literature — not in valorizing a particular view of the past or present, nor in creating, as it were, a literary block.'[22] This should put at rest the criticism that he is an anglophile.

XII

The Shadow Lines is organised at various levels. Take for instance, the 'story' within the story of this novel, the story of Tristan the hero who 'was a man without a country, who fell in love with a woman-across-the-seas' (183). It is significant that

Tridib 'received' this story from Snipe as a birthday gift. Tridib was particularly fond of it, and had told it to the narrator before he (Tridib) left for Dhaka where he met his death. In a sense, it is a 'legacy,' which the narrator inherits from his mentor, Tridib. This universal story figures in cultures of different nations. Interestingly, Tristan was a knight who fell in love with Iseult, his uncle's bride, after drinking a love potion. The narrator of *The Shadow Lines*, towards the end of the novel, too, secures a kind of bonding with his uncle's 'love,' May, by developing love and understanding with her. (The ending may sound unconventional and quizzical to some. But it should be clear to the reader by now that *The Shadow Lines* is a highly organised text, and that it has to be read closely). The significance of Tristan-Iseult story can be brought out further thus: This is Tridib's story and the narrator's too. It makes it possible for us to imagine a world which was not divided by boundaries, where one did not have to give up one's 'home' because of political upheavals — a place where one experienced the 'stillness' and the quiet of the earth.

XIII

Ghosh has not written as a literary critic or theorist, but his art indicates that he is keenly interested in fictional form. *The Shadow Lines* is an apt illustration of this. Now, in order to unfold this form, we need to pay a close analytical attention to its various parts and see them as integrated to its organic structure. In other words, we treat the novel as 'a unique order of words as a poem.' Surely, it demands close attention to 'the words on the page' as a poem does. As the novel has an intricate non-linear form, it is desirable that we turn the pages back and forth, after we have done the first reading. It will help us in refreshing our memories about what we already know, that is, what has happened and to come, so that 'we can think of the whole text spread before us.'[23] Alongside, we can follow the 'spatial approach' to the novel, which implies that we trace the key images and motifs, interspersed throughout this novel. If we look at the text in this way, we shall find that its parts *Going Away* and *Coming Home* function as tropes, as do 'maps' and 'mirrors' in the novel: They project the sub-continental reality against a western perspective and are woven into each other. Whereas *Coming Home*, essentially, deals with things Indian, *Going Away* provides the necessary background.

XIV

Ghosh has been publishing since 1986. So, it is not unnatural if he has not received adequate critical attention. But whatever little that has been written on him shows a general lack of perspective on his work. Either it is too laudatory or too critical. A discriminating evaluation of his work is called for. In the first part of the present book an attempt has been made to bring together essays which look at the various aspects/elements of the novel. The contributors are aware that, though they are dealing with a particular aspect or element of their choice, the aspect/element in question is inextricably blended with the novel. The second part of the book has some essays, which look at the novel from some current theoretical perspectives *demanded by the text*; but no attempt has been made to bring in Theory or 'isms,' unnecessarily. The last section has a single, but significant essay, which relates *The Shadow Lines* to Ghosh's other works, both fiction and non-fiction.

It is appropriate that the book opens with an investigation of the nature of *The Shadow Lines*. In her essay '*The Shadow Lines* as a Memory Novel' Manjula Saxena maintains that memory is the stuff of which this novel is essentially made. But memory in the novel appears in its aesthetic form or as Langer calls 'virtual memory,' which is 'the primary illusion' of all successful works of literary art. During the course of her discussion, Saxena makes a fine distinction between actual memory and 'virtual memory' in terms of Kant's concepts of noumenon and phenomenon. The main thrust of her essay is, that though memory has been used in the novel as its 'efficient' and 'material causes,' its final cause or purpose is to create an image of a personal and social history — which is a non-memory goal. Her essay ends up with an interesting observation that even if the events in the novel were imaginary, it would still be considered as a memory novel, as all such events are created in the 'experiential' or 'mnemonic mode.'

Premindha Banerjee in her essay 'The Narrator and the Chronicling of Self in *The Shadow Lines*' argues that the text is not essentially historical, and that the organising principle of the various memories, namely, the unnamed narrator is central to the narrative. Her contention is that in the act of chronicling and conferring meaning upon the historical events, the narrator narrates himself and acquires identity and meaning. However, for the elucidation of the text's total meaning we have not only to depend upon his experiences, but also the experiences of various other characters. Banerjee seems to suggest that the narrator is not an 'unreliable narrator,' but we need to take him, with a little reservation, which is in itself a tribute to Ghosh's narrative — it does not sound 'authorial.'

In her essay 'Tha'mma My Grandmother: Imaging The Elderly in *The Shadow Lines*' Roopali Sircar thinks that those who should have been depicted as the voices of wisdom and authority — 'the ageing others,' have not merited Ghosh's attention. Either they have been summarily dealt with or rendered in negative and pathetic terms. Tha'mma, for instance, is a point of significant reference for the narrator, but she represents anything but herself in the novel. Even the relationship between Tha'mma and the narrator is presented as need-based. As for the last phase of her life, she is presented as a senile 'dodo.' Likewise, Jethamoshai is depicted in altogether pathetic terms. Sircar's thesis is that as in life so in fiction justice has not been done to the elderly, even though they have rare qualities of head and heart. It is strange that Tha'mma is made to fail in her chosen mission towards the end of the novel, 'despite her courage, despite aeons of memory and despite deep wells of warmth and affection.' By contrast, the dreamers — Tridib and the narrator, are valorised.

However, what is denied or negated in literature *gets created*, as contrast. It is in this light we see Tha'mma and her brand of militant nationalism in the novel and in the two complimentary essays on the 'nation.' Nationalism is a thing of the past; it is relegated to the background. Thus Someshwar Sati's article seeks to read Amitav Ghosh's *The Shadow Lines as* 'an interrogation of a political consciousness baptised in the crucible of national division.' What emerges in the foreground in the text is a subjectivity which is expressive of 'a new civilisational ethos' conditioned, primarily, by 'the overwhelming dynamics of gobalisation.' Ghosh is deconstructing the nation, primarily, as 'an endless source of wanton brutality and violence.' Sati makes a salient point when he observes that 'in an age of agnostic individualism, a homogenising narrative of national consciousness tends to erase the individual in its entirety.' That is why the narrator is trying to reconstruct his personal history. It is not surprising that the narrative of national history is at odds with personal history. In such a scenario, Ghosh posits the concept of a world beyond nations in history, which is inherently utopian, Sati rightly maintains, and of which Ghosh himself is aware.

Alka Kumar's essay 'Nation As Identity' brings out the inherent difficulty involved in treating an unstable and complex concept as the nation. We can talk about the nation only in a tentative way. However, we may look at the issue from a cultural perspective. At least, Tha'mma's nationality and individual identity may be constructed through such an approach, but our hope is belied, as towards the end of the novel, Tha'mma is seen trying hard to understand her predicament. To her chagrin, she discovers that her place of birth is messily at odds with her nationality. So, nationalism is on the way out. It is in this light we understand Kumar's view that though 'the nation is crucial to the conceptualisation, scope and structure of *The Shadow Lines,* somewhere along the way it becomes an elusive and shadowy entity, as the principal protagonists in the drama are unable to make sense of its resonant contradictions.'

To the question of nationalism and nation is connected the question of political freedom. It was expected that freedom won in 1947 would create a perfect order, but, unfortunately, it has generated animosity and hatred in our polity. In the name of freedom what has got created are the shadow lines or the barriers between the communities and the nation-states. It has led to 'displacement and dispossession' and large scale communal violence; even the individual and national identities have got messed up. In such a bleak scenario, freedom appears as a 'mirage.' Alpana Neogy brings out all this in a cogent way in her essay 'The Shadow Lines between Freedom and Violence' Freedom means different things to different characters in the novel. For Tha'mma, of course, it was freedom *from* the colonial rule, but in the post-partition scenario violence masquerades as freedom. Thus there is communal violence, even marital violence. At the root of it all is the question of identity. But Neogy ends up her essay on an optimistic note: 'the tenderness and concern that the narrator feels for Tridib, Ila and his grandmother; the strength of the narrator's mother and her loving and caring attitude; the bonding and affection between the Prices and the Datta-Chaudhris — these vignettes of hope and love endure throughout the novel.'

Amitav Ghosh has used many devices to structure and organise his novel. One significant device is the trope, *Going Away* and *Coming Home*. Nivedita Sen in her essay, entitled 'Going Away and Coming Home: *The Shadow Lines* and The Travel Motif in Children's Fiction,' takes the aspects of 'going' and 'coming' as a travel motif. She gives linguistic and metaphorical interpretations to the idea of coming and going, in the context of the novel, which, as she says, delineates a critical historical moment. But she also foregrounds her discussion in the context of some specimens of Bengali children's literature, where the motif of journey is used, though in a much less intricate way than in Ghosh's novel. Sen locates the novel within the genre of *bildungsroman*. But her exhaustive treatment of the ideas of 'going' and 'coming,' in the context of the subcontinental reality, and her viewing of the figurative 'coming home' of the narrator to the foreigner, May, make it look like an Inter-national novel. This kind of 'home-coming,' she says, is, ultimately, a tribute to the 'Tridibs' of the world, who remain 'peripheral to the memory and imagination of the people.'

There are various other tropes and images which enrich the novel by their subtle shades of meanings and nuances. Rita Joshi has made an intensive study of some of the major images and related them to the individual characters and the overall thematic structure of the novel. She gives an 'ironic' interpretation of the two major tropes, namely, 'maps' and 'mirrors.' Whereas maps, which are supposed to be representative of a corporeal reality, are seen as 'illusory,' the 'mirrors' are seen as reflective of the 'true self' and hence are to be regarded as 'substantial.' Since *The Shadow Lines* happens to be a memory novel, 'photographs' are very significant images, as they reflect 'the past which influences the present through memory.' Then there are sets of images, which signify individual and social identities. For instance, Tridib's spectacles and the cigarette smoke coming from his cloistered room signify his insights and dreams, and his 'Gastric' portends 'disorder'; and western clothes in the context of Ila signify a donned social identity. Joshi gives an extensive interpretation of Magda the doll. Magda acts as a metaphor for Ila's various experiences. 'It will be correct to say that Ila rewrites her own story when she makes Magda undergo experiences similar to hers, but with a different ending.' Interestingly, Joshi has fresh interpretations to offer for apparently simple images as the lizard and the snake. The images are so powerful that they function as 'characters' in the novel. Collectively, these images give expression to the theme of 'illusion and reality,' Joshi opines.

But all this happens in the fictional world of the novel. It is essentially constituted of time and space, and what happens in it. Time and space, as we know, are essential dual, mode of our existence, and so are they of the fictional characters. Time is essential for a novel because of its story. The story is the basis of a novel, a 'narrative of events arranged in their time sequence,' as E.M. Forster puts it. But we do not live by time alone; we live by 'values.' And, so, a novelist may pick and choose some intense moments and try to recreate them in his fiction. The fact is that our memory is not interested in 'Father Time' or clock time. It is much more so in the case of modern novelists, including Amitav Ghosh. (Novelists like Bronte, Sterne, Marcel Proust do not take the time sequence seriously. They write their novels in the mode of memory.) Ghosh is influenced by Proust in his conception and delineation of time in the novel. It is 'the inseparableness of us from the past,'[24] particularly, which he shares with Proust. But 'it is never possible for a novelist to deny time inside the fabric of his novel: he must cling, however lightly, to the thread of his story [...] otherwise he becomes unintelligible [...]' says E.M. Forster. And Ghosh seems to observe this principle.

Arvind Chowdhary in his essay 'Time and Space' brings out this duality of time, in the context of *The Shadow Lines*. As Ghosh's novel is 'located in a subjective consciousness, he rightly strikes a balance between time experienced subjectively and mechanical or scientific time.' It is a right kind of combination which allows Ghosh 'to locate his novel in a historical and geographical reality and at the same time become aware of the richness of subjective experience' — an experience which is 'liberated from time by memory and imagination,' Chowdhary maintains. 'Time-shift' is a very handy device in creating such experience; it gets 'naturalised' in Ghosh's novel as 'the operation of memory.' But there is also the transcendence of the profane world in the novel, in and through whose texture the prophetic shows itself to the aesthetically inclined reader.

Time, admittedly, is more encompassing than space, observe Chowdhary but space is no less vital, as an integral dimension of our experiential reality. Ghosh, being a sensitive literary artist, is keenly aware of this. He has given us a vivid and varied account of how space is experienced by the different characters in his novel. There are no 'neutral, impersonal places' in Ghosh's *The Shadow Lines*. As Tridib says: 'a place does not merely exist but it has to be invented in one's imagination.' But for Ila, a place just 'exists,' and is no more than a utility. But this exploration of time and space, through memory and imagination, is eventually to be taken as the narrator's *a la recherche du temps perdu*. 'By defamiliarising himself with the world in which his mentor lived, and died a sacrificial death in a riot, he makes himself aware of the consciousness of the times and its meaning for human existence,' Chowdhary concludes.

XV

The second section of the volume has five essays, out of which four are devoted to the following contemporary theoretical perspectives: the feminist, the post-colonial and the historicist. There are two essays, which represent the feminist approach, and there is an essay each for the other two approaches mentioned above. There is another essay, which looks at the novel from a purely Indian point of view and brings out the *Bengalee* in *The Shadow Lines*.

Meenakshi Malhotra in her essay 'Nationalism and the Question of Freedom in *The Shadow Lines*' looks at the crucial questions of freedom and nationalism from the viewpoint of gender. She brings in globalism in her discussion as Ghosh interrogates the nation from the perspective of globality. Malhotra points out that in the recent times, which have witnessed the collapse of different political blocks and nation states, nationalism has been discredited and reduced to an outmoded 'grand narrative of history.' It is a legacy of the colonial political heritage that has continued to trouble us: a legacy that post-colonial writing continuously seeks to dismantle and erase. Ghosh, likewise, in *The Shadow Lines* through his interrogation of borders and boundaries, questions the relevance and the continued validity of the concept of 'nationhood.' Malhotra brings out the different versions of freedom in the text. Thus, while the narrator's grandmother's idea of freedom is tied up with freedom *from* the colonial power and attaining nationhood, Ila's concept of freedom is, basically, a struggle for personal identity or a quest for personal freedom in a post-colonial, post-modern context. As against these versions of freedom, the narrator's idea of freedom under the influence of his mentor Tridib, assumes an intellectual cast, so that he is able to perceive the shadow lines that intersect our lives—as individuals, as a community and as a nation. Malhotra thinks that *The Shadow Lines* embodies an implicit phallocentricity, which shows up in its conceptualisation of women. The author, for instance, openly denies Ila the privilege of inheriting Tresawsen's legacy of selfless action; that privilege is meant only for the visionary Tridib and the reflective unnamed narrator. The women are made the locus of only the problematic aspects of militant nationalism, Malhotra affirms.

Anjali Multani in her essay 'Lines and Shadows: A Reading of Gender Roles in Amitav Ghosh's *The Shadow Lines*' looks at both male and female characters with a view to ascertaining how they are constructed in the text as well as how the reader is led to approach the text in certain ways which influence the meaning constructed. She points out that the elements, which are described for the male characters are the ones when they are in face to face contact, whereas the elements for the female characters are those when the character is portrayed as *an object to be seen*. Thus the female character gets immediately located outside the reader and is projected through a male perspective. This is how a sexually conditioned response is evoked from the reader with regard to May when Tridib mentions her at Gole Park to his *adda* acquaintances. It is unfortunate that Robi and the narrator take Ila's desire for freedom as sexual transgression — a desire that needs to be curbed by the family/ society. Multani in the course of her essay makes an interesting observation that the non-conventional male attributes — say, the academic bent of mind of Tridib or the narrator, are valorised, while some of the most fundamentally negative 'feminine' characteristics as jealousy, spite, destructive activity are reinforced through the representations of Ila and the grandmother. Multani closes her essay by taking a balanced view that whereas alternative views of history and freedom, developed through the insights of male characters are invaluable, the representation of the female characters and of their gendered behaviour and attitudes is biased in favour of the privileged male narrator and leaves much to be desired.

Post-colonial texts not only embody colonial ideologies but also militate against them. They demand perceptive readings. Such texts often evoke either strong criticism or unqualified appreciation. Silivia Albertazzi, for instance, seems to lavish praise upon *The Shadow Lines* when she says that the text deals with 'all post-colonial concerns of our period,' including, 'the search for identity, the need for independence and the difficult relationship with colonial culture,' etc. But she does not really tell us what is Ghosh's attitude towards colonial ideologies, in the context of his exploration of the post-colonial concerns. While giving a post-colonial interpretation of *The Shadow Lines*, Promilla Garg maintains that Ghosh is a 'first-world' writer who considers the world to be a 'global village,' where men and women of different nationalities should be trying to reach towards one another, irrespective of their culture and race. So far, so good. But her objection is that in the process one should not forget one's culture and take to the western ways. Unfortunately, Ghosh's main characters — Ila, Tridib and the narrator — are too much anglicized, which makes Garg observe that 'independent India is culturally colonized still.' Garg's main thesis is that Ghosh's vision is not rooted in ethnic India, and that the novel is more a study of cross-cultural relationship between India and England than anything else. In the course of her essay, Garg outlines two types of post-colonial understanding in the novel: one represented by social elites like Mayadebi and the Shaheb and the rootless Ila, and the other by the grandmother. The latter would like Indians to act and achieve their own identity and not waste time in aping the west. Garg strongly feels that Ghosh seems to be enamoured of the colonial masters and their culture, as is reflected through his novel. Probably, we need to look to Ghosh's latest novel, *The Glass Palace* for a critique of the Empire. *The Shadow Lines* has a different focus altogether: it primarily brings out the post-partition trauma in the context of a violent incident in a race riot and raises relevant questions relating to such violence.

Rudrashish Chakraborty in his essay 'Violence in *The Shadow Lines*: National Rhetoric and Historical Silence' explores the gaps and fissures in the treatment of history in Ghosh's *The Shadow Lines.* Chakravarty argues that history is hardly narrated in the novel but suggested through 'cryptic phrases, monologues, sudden burst of energy, image formation etc.' He thinks that the narrative voice betrays a sense of personal vindication rather than a compelling political awareness in the context of an apparently fact-finding mission of some seemingly isolated case of violence which, in fact, is integrated to larger issues of nation-formation and discourses of nationalism. He suggests that the authorial voice cannot be taken as authentic in its treatment of history. Chakravarty maintains that Ghosh's claim that his earlier novels deal with 'castaways of history,' is belied by *The Shadow Lines.* Ghosh's protagonist Tridib, who is represented as upholder of a global vision, fails to comprehend the grim reality/realities asserted by the accounts of the grandmother, the old senile uncle, Khalil the rickshaw-puller and Saifuddin. Chakravarty sums up his essay by observing that the text neither intends nor attempts seriously to explore partition history and the subsequent sub-continental politics.

Minoti Chatterjee's essay '*The Bengali in The Shadow Lines*' starts on a very sentimental note. She says that there is 'a generation of Bengalees whose collective memory still makes them believe that borders have a tenuous existence and that not even a history of bloodshed can make them real and impermeable.' They are *Probashis* — the Bengalees who live outside Bengal. Such *Probashis* include Bengali-Hindus and Bengali-Muslims on both sides of the border. But she, subsequently, through her unbiased reading of political history, accounts for the artificial divide between the Hindus and the Muslims of Bengal. A substantial part of her essay is devoted to bringing out the *Bengalee* in *The Shadow Lines*. The essay goes on to establish that the text is essentially rooted in Indian ethos. She takes the stand that despite his anonymity, the narrator of *The Shadow Lines* is a 'a firmly rooted Bengalee.' Minoti states that the characters in the novel are Calcutta-centric or Dhaka-centric, though there are characters like Ila who try to dissociate themselves from such culture. Minoti seems to pay a tribute to Tha'mma by saying that Tha'mma embodies the attributes of the Bengalee *Bhadralok* and nationalism both. There are two strands in Minoti's essay: one is the celebration of The Bengalee in *The Shadow Lines* and the other is the highlighting of 'war between oneself and one's image in the mirror' — that is, an acute awareness of the ghastly reality that stares one in the face that 'spaces that surround one, the streets that one inhabits, can become suddenly without warning, as hostile as a desert in a flash flood.' But Minoti ends up her essay with the satisfaction that Ghosh's political insights do not impede his wonderful quality of story-telling and his sense of humour and the *Bangalee* in him — these elements are manifest in the text in large measure.

XVI

Aditya Bhattacharjea's essay 'The Shadow Lines in Context' adopts a broader perspective, examining *The Shadow Lines* in relation to Amitav Ghosh's other writings, both fiction and non-fiction. It begins with summaries of the plots and structures of four of his other books, for the benefit of those who have not read them. In the course of this, he draws attention to Ghosh's versatility in handling very different genres, as well as some of the themes, techniques and the autobiographical details that recur in his work. He goes on to challenge the views of critics who, on the basis of just *The Shadow Lines,* accuse Ghosh of celebrating a vacuous cosmopolitan hybridity or of being a loyal admirer of English society. Bhattacharjea points to distinct anti-imperialist element in Ghosh's other books and their highlighting of the close historical ties between India and her neighbours to the east and west. He shows how the central motif of *The Shadow Lines* —the blurring of boundaries, and the binaries home/away and coming/going — is worked out in the other novels, despite the very different forms the author adopts. He also argues that Ghosh's treatment of exile is very different from that of other Indian novelists writing in English. The novelist's enduring objective is to remind his readers of the historical closeness of Asian societies, transcending barriers of ethnicity. Although Bhattacharjea appreciates this effort, and defends Ghosh from what he regards as misplaced criticism, he argues that this treatment of ethnic conflict is simplistic and naïve.

Let me conclude this brief introduction to the book of critical essays on *The Shadow Lines* by quoting David Lodge: 'In the last analysis criticism claims our attention, not as sets of data nor as sets of conclusion, but as human discourse.' This discourse, of course, aims at interpreting and evaluating literature, and is likely to be different for each individual as she/he brings her/his own experiences and understanding of life to it.

Notes and References

1. Amitav Ghosh shared this information about the inception of *The Shadow Lines* with the audience in February 2002 in an interactive session at Gargi College, Delhi University.
2. Cited by Bernard Bergonzi in his introductory book David *Lodge* in

the context of the latter's appreciation of James. (Northcote House in association with the British Council, 1995), 60.

3. David Lodge's remark cited by Bernard Bergonzi in the context of the former's preoccupation with 'reality.' This can be extended to Ghosh's realistic mode of representation in *The Shadow Lines.*
4. William Henry Hudson in *Introduction to the Study of Literature* (London: George G. Harrap and Co. Ltd., first published 1910; reprinted 1944), 166.
5. *Ibid.* 167.
6. Cited by Margaret Church in *Structure and Theme, Don Quixote to James Joyce* (Ohio State University Press; Columbus, 1983).
7. A.N. Kaul, "A Reading of The Shadow Lines" in *The Shadow Lines,* Educational Edition (Delhi: Oxford University Press, 1988), particularly, 309.
8. David Lodge in *After Bakhtin,* 43.
9. David Lodge (Novelist *at the crossroads* 209) cited by Bernard Bergonzi, op.cit., 150.
10. A.N. Kaul, op.cit., 308.
11. Bergson gives laughter a function, as a social corrective. According to him, a humorist is 'a moralist disguised as a scientist.' See his *Le rire: essai sur la signification du comique* [Laughter: An Essay on the Meaning of the Comic (1900:128)]. For a brief discussion of his concept of humor, see Rutledge Encyclopedia, 735.
12. Georg Lukàcs, *The Theory of The Novel,* first published 1963 trans. Anna Bostock (London: Merlin Press, 1971). Lukacs explains this idea further thus: 'The immanence of meaning which the form of the novel requires lies in the hero's finding out through experience that a mere glimpse of meaning is the highest that life has to offer, and that this glimpse is the only thing worth the commitment of an entire life, the only thing by which the struggle will have been justified' 80.
13. James Clifford in "The Transit Lounge of Culture" in the context of Ghosh's 'The Imam and the Indian,' *Times Literary Supplement,* no. 4596 (May 3, 1991): 7-8. His remarks can be applied to *The Shadow Lines.*
14. Harish Trivedi in "The St Stephen's Factor" in *The Fiction of St Stephens* ed. Aditya Bhattacharjea & Lola Chatterji (New Delhi: Ravi Dayal, 2000), 7.
15. Shashi Throor in his article "Bedevilling Question in the Cadence of English" in *The Hindu,* Sunday, August 5, 2001.
16. *The New York Times* book review.
17. *Washington Times* review.

18. *The Guardian* (London) review.
19. Introductory remarks for Amitav Ghosh's *The Glass Palace* (Delhi: Ravi Dayal Publisher and Permanent Black, 2000).
20. *The New York Times* review of *The Glass Palace* by Pankaj Mishra.
21. This is his answer to the question as to why he declined the nomination for the Commonwealth Literary Prize 2001.
22. This reflects his attitude towards literary prizes in general.
23. David Lodge's approach towards the reading of fictional prose, as indicated in his *Language of fiction* (1996), mentioned by Bernard Bergonzi in his book *David Lodge,* op.cit., 49. It can be safely applied to Ghosh's *The Shadow Lines.*
24. But when Amitav Ghosh creates the illusion of 'simultaneity' in *The Shadow Lines,* his treatment of time seems to be closer to Bergson's concept of time. According to Bergson, time as an order of succession has its roots in the mind. There is neither past nor future in space; and things in the external world are perceived as simultaneous. See Bergson's *Time and Free Will,* 120.

PART I

1

The Shadow Lines as a Memory Novel

MANJULA SAXENA

To determine whether Amitav Ghosh's *The Shadow Lines* is a memory novel or not, we will have to answer two questions. First, what is memory? What are its distinctive features? And second, are these features present in *The Shadow Lines*? One allied question that must be answered would be, that even if a few distinctive features of memory are present in the novel, have they been retained in their original form or have they been changed or modified? And, finally, if they have been modified, what all has taken place during the process of modification? To put it very simply, in what form or dimensions, does memory figure in *The Shadow Lines*? To answer this, we will very briefly look at what memory has done to the work in question. Is it actively making the novel or is the novel just a collection of memories?

Let us get back to the first question: What is memory? We all understand it rightly to be a psychological process as much integral to our consciousness as thinking is. We are rational because we think, and also because we memorize. We use these faculties consciously when we learn our lessons for taking examinations, or subconsciously when different experiences leave their impressions on our minds, without our becoming aware of this. So, both thinking and memory are the very essence of our rationality; they contribute equally to our learning. But, then, they are not identical. Memory is both rational and emotive — pertaining to the cognitive and the affective parts of personality. Thinking, on the other hand, even as understanding and not as mere awareness is purely rational — completely devoid of feelings, emotions and sentiments, which are the components of our affective life. Memory, therefore, is perhaps more gratifying than the purely objective, disinterested kind of thinking. Literary artists, poets and novelists alike have acknowledged the presence of emotive element in memory. No wonder, the famous poet Shelley alludes to memory in these words:

> *We look before and after,*
> *And pine for what is not*
> *Our sweetest songs,*
> *With some pain are fraught.*
>
> (*Ode to Skylark*)

The word 'pain' here is indicative of the emotion accompanying memory. Similarly, Ghosh, the novelist makes the narrator of his novel recall his own experiences with a fondness — another emotive element. Take for instance, the narrator's following recollection of an incident, pertaining to Tridib:

> When I was about nine Tridib once stayed away from his haunts for so long that regulars began to wonder what had happened to him [...]. Then, one evening I heard that he had surfaced at Gole park again. I [...] found him [...] and heard him say 'I have been to London [...] I have English relatives through marriage'[...]. It was then [...] that I cried: Tridibda [...] you made a mistake. You were in your room, smoking [...]. There was a howl of laughter and a chorus of exclamations: You fraud, you liar [...] you haven't been anywhere [...] another sharper voice broke in and said [...] the fact is that he is a nut he has never been anywhere outside Calcutta[1] (12).

The narrator 'was furious with himself for having exposed Tridib to their ridicule [...] shouting he told them the truth as he knew it: that Tridib had been to London, with his parents, many years ago when he was a boy' (12-13). The point to be noted here is that in recalling his attempt to undo the damage to Tridib's reputation, the narrator feels relieved and happy. Now, happiness, undoubtedly, is a state of emotion.

Memory of experiences, unlike that of facts is *either happy or sad but never indifferent*; thinking, on the other hand, is definitely non-emotive as when I think about an abstract concept like 'space,' or my solving a mathematical problem. I do these activities by exercising my mind or rationality alone; but, memory, I may repeat, is both rational and emotive. That is why, it is an apt instrument and sustainer of the creation of a work of literary art.

Socrates long ago mentioned some important features of memory, which we need to discuss in the context of *The Shadow Lines*. Here is what Socrates said to Theaetetus about memory:

> Imagine, then, for the sake of argument, that our minds contain a block of wax, which in this or that individual may be larger or smaller, and composed of wax that is comparatively pure or muddy, and harder in some, softer in others, and sometimes just the right consistency. Let us call it the gift of the Muses' mother, Memory, and say that whenever we wish to remember something we see or hear or conceive in our own minds, we hold this wax under perceptions or ideas and imprint them on it as we might stamp the impression of a seal-ring. Whatever is so imprinted we remember and know so long as the image remains; whatever is rubbed out or has not succeeded in leaving an impression we have forgotten or do not know.[2]

This statement by the great Socrates contains the following truths about memory:

1. Memory, like all knowledge begins in perception or experience. Before sense-perception, or as the philosopher would insist, before the *determinate* kind of perception begins, mind is a 'blank slate' or *Tabula Rasa* as Hume calls it; it does not have the traces of memory on it.
2. Experiences leave some kind of a trace, which goes into the formation of the fund of memory. Now, I ask, is not *The Shadow Lines* also an organised structure of

memories? Just as the table is made of wood and nails and adhesives, similarly, Ghosh's novel is apparently, at least, made up of the narrator's memories relating to Tridib, his relatives and acquaintances. There are memories of various characters, like the narrator's grandmother's, of Mayadebi's, the narrator's cousin Ila's and of Mary's — the acquaintance of both Tridib and the narrator, and so on. Then, there are memories of the normal or stylized behaviour of these characters. Referring to the grandmother, the narrator says: 'For her, likes and dislikes were unimportant' or 'She [grandmother] would pretend to dismiss him with a toss of her head' (6). Then, in this fund of memory there are memories of places. The author recalls the grandmother's observation, namely, 'Tridib living in that crumbling house' (6) or the stall at the corner of his lane where Nathu Chaubey sat, or the place at the far end of the garden of Queen Victoria's house in Sri Lanka where the thala-goya, seeing a snake thrashed at the end of its rope, 'battering the tree it was tied to' (28) — all these instances are the memories of the places. Further, there are memories of conversations among different characters, even memories of recognition, say, 'We recalled how quickly we had taught ourselves to distinguish the shapes of their aircrafts from ours' (22), and of the character's reactions like 'Trigonometry!' in the context of the grandmother's observation that her uncle did not let any Muslim come within ten feet of his shadow in his younger days or 'playfully, he [the old man] waggled his head' at May and she smiled back (213). In other words, innumerable memories of different kinds, have gone into the making of the novel, serving as the matter (and not the subject matter) of the work. Moreover, all memories are traceable to perceptions in the fictional world. This is in accordance with the Socratic view that memory begins in perception.

3. The next important idea implicit in the statement of Socrates is that there are individual differences in memory. This is especially significant in the context of

the works of literary art, of which *The Shadow Lines* is a brilliant example. We may recapitulate what Socrates tells Theaetetus, '[...] Our minds contain a block of wax, which in this or that individual may be [...] pure or muddy, and hard in some, softer in others [...]. Here, the 'hard' is the less sensitive, and 'softer' is the more sensitive receptivity of an individual which results in shallow or deep memories, respectively. I am sure, that like all artists, Ghosh/his narrator is also blessed with a 'softer' memory. Otherwise, how could he remember so much in such minute and vivid detail? Remembering May Price exactly as she had looked seventeen years ago, the narrator says:

> Her hair was still cut exactly as I remembered it from the time she had stayed with us in Calcutta: falling thick and straight to her shoulders, mantling her head and the sides of her face; but where I remembered it as dark and glossy, it was streaked now with strands of gray which shimmered when they caught the light (14).

Or, when he recalls hearing, even in the drunken state, 'the sound of feet pounding heavily after him' (155), or the vital fact mentioned in the letter that was written by Maya Debi to the narrator's grandmother — 'Maya Debi wrote that she had not been able to visit their old house yet [...]' (189-90). Without a softer, that is, more alert sensitivity, how could the narrator remember that his grandmother gasped with disappointment and nostalgia on seeing the courtyard of her ancestral house. 'A workshop [...] inside our courtyard! What's become of the old jackfruit tree?' (190).

There is no doubt that the more sensitive people have a 'softer,' more impressionable memory, but not all such people are artistic in temperament. Equally true is the fact that all artists, literary or performing, have a 'softer' memory as the material cause for their creative endeavour. They also store and retain their experiences for longer periods, to be used purposively later — in fact, more purposively than a layman does. Impelled by their inherent tendency to use up every possible memory for the creation of some or the other work of art, artists receive almost every impression more fully and this they can do only with the softer memory material. This softer memory material does not allow, in their case, events to just happen and pass them by. Rather, in their case, impressions of all events are deliberately gathered up and then remain dormant in their memory till such time as the retainer finds the occasions for their actual use. Then they are recollected and transformed, at least, by literary artists like Ghosh into the materials of narratives.

Such memories are, necessarily, invariably accompanied by the artist's awareness and understanding as to how he is going to use them effectively in the creation of a work of art. I clearly see this happening in *The Shadow Lines.* Possessed of a highly refined sensitivity, Ghosh's main fictional characters, retain, may be unconsciously, their experiences, and relate them to the experiences of the other characters in the novel, directly or indirectly, immediately or remotely. Ghosh, the literary artist, has woven them all into an organic unity, befitting a successful novel. He has done it through narrative devices with the help of which the raw material *i.e.* memories, have got organised and become a major component of the novel.

Let us now very briefly discuss the implication of the next idea in the statement by Socrates. It is this: in our psychological life, forgetting occurs and may occur at different times for different reasons. One is the biological reason, which affects everyone — the mental faculties become weak in old age and one starts forgetting. The other reason for forgetting is that one tends to forget that which one does not like. Generally, the pleasant and the useful are remembered and the unpleasant is forgotten. This characteristic of memory, that is, its being selective, is also quite evident in *The Shadow Lines.*

> When the narrator tells Ila how he 'longed to Visit Cairo, to see the world's first pointed arch in the mosque of Ibn Tulun, and touch the stones of the Great Pyramid of Cheops [...]. She clicked her fingers, gave herself a satisfied nod, and said aloud, inadvertently oh yes, Cairo, the Ladies is way away on the other side of the departure lounge (20).

Here the narrator remembers and recalls Cairo, for its beauty and interesting historical architecture. In contrast, Ila remembers 'the Ladies' and only the Ladies — a utility. The rest of Cairo has been either forgotten or it simply does not get registered on her mind. Ila's memory is clearly selective in *The Shadow Lines.*

Coming now to the third question, that is: In what form is memory present in the novel? Let us, for a moment, suppose that the majority of incidents, narrated in the novel, never actually occurred. Historical events like the two riots and biographical facts of the author's own life can, of course, not be denied. But supposing that the author has only imagined the rest of the events, can the work be still called a memory novel? Here we will have to take note of a fact. Very often it is maintained that memory belongs to the past and imagination to future. Should we then presume that in a narrative, imagination plays no part? Further, is it proper to hold that memory and imagination are so exclusive of each other that they can never interact, not even in a narrative? The answer is a firm 'no.' In fact, the two not only coexist but also, more often than not, work together in unison. For example, while narrating the September 11 incident of America, do we not even today imagine some of its details to make it a complete account? We do. We recall the actual attack as we watched it on news channels but we also imagine some of the consequences that were never shown — the ones, we know for certain, have taken place. Not only the narration of the incident but also our memory of it is bound to include the merely imagined details of the incident. The point is that memory is imaginative and imagination can fabricate memories. This is exactly how memory and imagination function in unison in Ghosh's work. *The Shadow Lines,* to be sure, is interplay of imagination and memory — memory recalling certain incidents and imagination weaving memories. Tridib's Gastric mentioned in *The Shadow Lines* is a recollection of a fact but it also includes the narrator imagining it as a special organ — peculiar to Tridib. It is a clear case of memory and imagination interweaving effectively to create an artistic element in the work (5).

Creative or aesthetic memory is a device as integral to artistic creation as actual memory is to learning. The famous aesthetician S.K. Langer calls it the 'virtual memory' or the 'semblance' of memory. Distinction between actual and 'virtual memory' can be likened to the one that the German philosopher Kant draws between noumena and phenomena — so basic to his theory of knowledge. Noumenon, according to Kant, is the thing-in-itself; and phenomenon, is the thing-as-it-appears to us. Only the latter, in Kant's view, is the true object of knowledge. We know a thing, as it appears to us generally as existing in space and time and arranged in a causal order. For example, fire and smoke are two separate events but we know them generally as each other's cause and effect and as occurring in space and time. Space and time as well as causal relation are, for Kant, mental categories, which we necessarily impose onto the object of perception. That these categories are mental, Kant argues by saying that being infinite, they cannot be parts of the finite outer world. So, in every perception, space, time and the causal relation are imposed on the thing-in-itself by the mind, thus converting it into 'phenomenon.' Similarly, aesthetic memory is actual memory as it has been acted upon by the creative imagination of the artist when he uses it. This modification of memory is necessary. As S.K. Langer says:

> [...] Whereas actual experience is a welter of sights, sounds, feelings and, physical strains, expectations and minute undeveloped reactions, memory sifts all this material and represents it in the form of only distinguishable events. Sometimes, the events are logically connected [...] but most events are recalled as separate incidents and can be dated only by being thought of in a causal order [...].[3]

Further, Langer referring to memory in the context of narratives says: 'Narrative is a major organizing device. It is important to literature as representation is to painting and sculpture.'[4] Putting the two quotations together we understand that narration, which is integral to a novel or a story and in fact to most of the literary arts, necessarily, organizes the diverse elements of the work, so that memory or imagination even as the material cause of the literary work becomes different from the original memory.

Clarifying the distinctive nature of this memory for narratives, Langer says:

> Sometimes the memories of different places and activities [...] are so incongruous that we have to recall and arrange a series of intervening events before we really feel convinced that the two such diverse situations belong to the same life. Especially when memory is very vivid it has no continuity. The deeply impressed incident seems to rise out of the past all alone with such extraordinary detail that it suggests an experience just passed [...].[5]

Finally, about the distinctive feature of narratives of which *The Shadow Lines* is a striking example, Langer says, 'narratives of memories always have semblance of memory more purely than actual history.' In the context of the art of poetry she observes that 'the poet makes a semblance of events that is experience-like, but universally accessible; an objectified, depersonalized 'memory' entirely homogenous, no matter how much is explicit and how much implicit.'[6] However, in a lyric this 'semblance' is that of a very limited event, whereas in a sustained narrative, say, a novel, this semblance is comprised of a series of events.

Langer's main idea pertaining to memory is fourfold: first that recollection, particularly of the narrative type necessarily organizes memories in various ways. Second, that in the nexus of memory, a single memory may stand out for a variety of reasons, so much so that it appears almost self-complete. Thirdly, two radically opposite events can be seen to belong to the same life by recalling the relatively minor intervening detail, and finally that in narratives 'virtual memory' is present in its purest form, unaffected by actual memory. Now let us see whether these features of 'virtual memory' are present in Ghosh's work or not.

The narrator in *The Shadow Lines* relates different kinds of events and experiences in different ways. For instance, he interrelates the two political events, namely, the war of 1962 and the riots of 1964, differentiating them from each other and then in the same breath mentions a cricket match that was played during the same period as the riots. He remembers this disparate detail in the context of the riots. Subsequently, it helps him to notice a headline in the newspaper, which says: 'Twenty-nine killed in riots' (222-23).

Similarly, the event of the CBI recovering the Mu-I-Mubarak, with people of Srinagar rejoicing at its recovery, assumes importance in the context of a significant event: 'When I was reading through that short report for the fifth time, it struck me suddenly, like a slap in the face, that May, Tridib, and my grandmother must have left for Dhaka the day before' (226). We notice that, through such examples, Ghosh is not only relating different events, he is even dating them in a causal order. When the narrator notices that Malik is getting a little impatient with him and not paying attention to what he is telling him, he feels impelled to act so as to interest him. Noticing Malik's inattention is the cause of what the narrator does next. He frantically tries to find evidence in support of his contention that the riots of 1964 did happen and claimed many lives. He remembers all this vividly. Similarly, the recovery of Mu-I-Mubarak and the accompanying celebrations help him mark the day of the departure of May, Tridib and his grandmother. All these memories get directly or indirectly related in different ways to build up the novel.

The second important point in Langer's concept of 'virtual memory' is this: an event may stand out among other events because of its sheer emotional impact. I may illustrate this with the help of the following excerpt from the novel:

> Ridiculous though he was, I was alarmed by the tone of his voice [...] as he said, 'we have received information [...]. that you have been visiting prostitutes in houses of ill repute [...].
>
> I was so taken aback that I managed to say: who has given you this information sir?
>
> Your own grandmother [...] you can see for yourself. The writing was unmistakably my grandmother's [...] I was so shaken by the sight of her resurrected hand, reaching out to me after her death. I have never understood how she learnt of the women I had visited a couple of times, with

> my friends nor do I know how she saw that I was in love with Ila so long before I dared to admit it to myself (92-93).

The incident can be seen to stand out due to its sheer emotional impact. It is a finished, discrete, incident, with an absolute identity of its own. That is why it lingers on in the narrator's memory without ever leading him to the next memory in the series, in the narrator's mind. Nor does it refer to his memory of the incidents prior to it. It is a self-complete entity and it not only gets retained in the protagonist's mind but also dominates it.

Yet another idea of Langer about aesthetic or 'virtual memory' is that 'sometimes [...] we have to recall and arrange a series of intervening events before we really feel convinced that two such diverse situations belong to the same life.'[7] I may cite the following example from *The Shadow Lines* to illustrate it:

> When we were fourteen, she [Ila] once pointed to a picture of a boy who, to me, already looked like a grown man with a face like an American film star [...]. His name is Jamshed Tabrizi, she said, he is a fencing champion and this year his father gave him a BMW sports car for his birthday [...] and as soon as he gets his license, we are going to drive down to the beach at Pattaya [...]. And then, in a rush, looking at me sideways, she added, he is my boyfriend (23).

But a few lines later, 'he was [...] with his arm thrown around the shoulders of two laughing blonde girls [...] and [...] Ila herself on the edge of the back row [...] standing with a book under her arm.

She saw that I had noticed this, and when I came upon that yearbook again a week later, I discovered that the page had been torn out' (23).

The memory of Ila tearing out a page from the yearbook helps the narrator relate definitely two separate incidents to Ila's life — her claim of being intimate with a so-called boyfriend and her subsequent isolation in a foreign land. They are seen as related to the same person by the narrator because of his recollection of the intervening incident of Ila tearing the page.

Finally, to explain what Langer means by saying that narratives always have semblance of memory 'more purely than actual history,' I may cite the following example:

> That house, that one, just down the road, over there, [...] is called Lymington mansions [...] an incendiary bomb fell on it, and burned down two floors. That was on the 1st of October 1940, two days before your uncle died (56).

A bomb falling on a building can be an event recorded in history, accessible to all but it is not presented there as an experiential event; it does not get recalled by anyone, in particular. So, strictly speaking, this incident has not been acted upon by anyone's mind and, therefore, is not a case of 'virtual memory.' Not being subjective or experiential, it is not an example of a 'semblance' of memory. But in the piece of narrative above, a particular memory — namely, that the Lymington mansions have been partly destroyed, is being remembered as an event. The memory of this event has remained imprinted on the mind of the narrator, because it is experienced with sadness as a personal loss. Subjective factors, integral to 'virtual memory' creep in. That is why, it is being recalled so vividly and it remains inextricably bound up with his life. Such a recalled or imagined incident is also accessible to all but it necessarily evokes emotive response in them. It may be noted that an incident created in a work of literary art, and the same incident recorded in a book of history, will be received differently. Whereas the former may evoke an emotional or aesthetic response, the latter will be received as a piece of objective history. In the former it is the presentation of memory as semblance or phenomenal memory, and in the latter it is the gathering of pure, objective kind of information, like the one which a reader gets while reading a book on current affairs. Only the disinterested and dispassionate understanding is involved in reading such a factual book.

To conclude, Ghosh has used memory in all its dimensions not merely as the 'efficient' but also as the 'material' cause of the novel. Just as the activity of the carpenter is the 'efficient' cause of the table, similarly the act of recalling done by the author/narrator is the 'efficient' cause of the novel. Further, the content of recollection is the 'memories' of which the narrative is composed. Such memories are the 'material' cause of the work in the same way as wood is the 'material' cause of the table. However, the final purpose of the novel is to create an image of personal and social history, which is a non-memory goal. Yet to achieve this objective, Ghosh has made maximum and effective use of memory in almost all its dimensions and forms. Even if the novel were constituted of imaginary incidents, cast in the mnemonic mode of 'virtual memory,' it would still be considered as a memory novel.

Notes and References

1. Amitav Ghosh, *The Shadow Lines* (New Delhi: Oxford University Press, 1995), 12. All subsequent quotations from the text refer to this edition, and their page numbers are given in the parentheses.
2. Socrates' views about memory in an extract from Plato's *Theory of Knowledge* in F.M. Cornford Trans. (1935), 121.
3. S.K. Langer in *Feeling and Form*, Chapter 15, "Virtual Memory" (London: Routledge. & Kegan Paul, 1953, Third impression 1963), 263.
4. *Ibid.* 261.
5. *Ibid.* 264.
6. *Ibid.* 265.
7. *Ibid.* 264.

2

THE NARRATOR AND THE CHRONICLING OF SELF IN *THE SHADOW LINES*

PREMINDHA BANNERJEE

The opening of *The Shadow Lines* draws attention to the presence of the narrative voice and establishes the close correspondence between the realms of memory and lived experience. The conventional narrative method of linearity and chronological sequence is subverted by the narrative voice, which as an implied author is separate and distinct from the real author. While recognizing the autobiographical impulse behind the narrative, a reading of *The Shadow Lines* raises questions about the narrator's autonomous existence as a character and the reliability of his narrative stance. As a narrative device the narrator seeks to unify and integrate the divergent strands of the stories, the different voices and characters that constitute his memory and his limited knowledge of events. As the memories and experiences of other characters filter through his consciousness, and as he re-presents and renarrates them, the reader is made aware of the multiple levels of narration and the absence of a univocal narrative.

To what extent is the narrator implicated in the events he recounts? What makes him select and present the various stories, as he does, from his perspective and position? And how central is he to the story that he unfolds through his narration? These are some of the vital questions that need to be answered.

Much has been written about the narrator, whose growth from childhood to youth and the understanding that he gains therefrom, is seen in terms of a bildungsroman in which the motif of the journey facilitates the exploration and understanding of the self.

The story is interwoven around actual historical occurrences, but the text in itself is not historical. The centrality of the narration inheres in the manner in which the narrator constructs himself through the act of narration so that in the act of chronicling and conferring meaning, he is also narrating himself and acquiring identity and definition.

Set against the outbreak of the World War Second (1939) and the post-partition communal riots of 1964 in some parts of India and Bangladesh (erstwhile East Pakistan) in its foreground, the fictionalised narrative is interwoven with history and validated by actual experiences in the lives of the major characters. It is this intersection of the public and the private domain, which enables the narrator to adopt an interrogative mode and speculate about the premises on which historical events can be known and accessed.

The shifting veil of narration reveals to us a young boy in a well-defined economic and social setting (middle-class Bengali *Bhadralok*), bound in a web of family ties and relationships that straddle two cultures. The story of Datta-Chaudhuris and the Prices, set in colonial India and England at the onset of World War Second, provides the author with the launching pad to present issues of contemporary relevance, such as the quest for freedom, nationhood and its implications, and the role of the insubstantial lines that demarcate and distinguish different states. In order to project this, he evokes some post-colonial and cross-cultural encounters. His narrative weaves a complex web linking the historical and the imaginary.

The narrator makes detailed references to the houses, lanes, and cities, locations that resonate with personal and cultural significance. Cairo, Addis Ababa, Algiers, Stockholm, are not just faceless cities identified by the location of the 'Ladies,' as they are to Ila, but places testifying to the narrator's creative and imaginative self. At times the specificity of time and place posits a reality which is knowable only through a detailed topography, an amassing of factual details.

The matrix of extended family relationships and associations spanning three generations, firmly locates the young narrator and depicts the indelible impact that his relatives, particularly, the grandmother, Ila and Tridib leave on him. His own parents appear peripheral to his journey of discovery and self-knowledge. For the most part they just seem to provide him with a secure middle-class background and the opportunity for further studies in London. At home it is his grandmother who wields utmost influence on the narrator through her stories of life in Dhaka, and the freedom struggle in Bengal, and her ideas of nation building and through her hostility and opposition to Ila.

The grandmother's response to the notion of freedom and nationalism raises questions about the meaning and desirability of nationalism. Her narration of her personal memories of the terrorist movement in Bengal reveals her secret desire to have been part of the militant resistance to colonial power and her understanding of the nation is rendered in terms of baptism through bloodshed:

> They know they are a nation because they've drawn their borders with blood. Once that happens people forget they were born this or that, Muslim or Hindu, Bengali or Punjabi they become a family born of the same pool of blood.[1]

But after the riots in Dhaka, her understanding of the nation changes. It becomes anarchic and produces a split between the imaginary 'us' and symbolic 'them.' The narrator as a child, undergoes a similar response, when during a riot, the sudden awareness of the 'difference' poses a threat, and he denies knowing Montu who now represents the intangible 'they.' But as the narrator grows up, he recognizes and admits the fallibility of his earlier beliefs — the illusory nature of 'nations and borders.' Thus the centrality of the narration lies in the narrator's developing consciousness, a consciousness that registers, records, participates, re-presents and recounts. Also when we view him as the 'hero' of the novel, the description 'hero' is to be taken more in the structural rather than the thematic context, as the novel seems to jettison the traditional notion of a hero.

The narrator's identity takes shape in and through his responses to the characters he engages with and the responses he elicits. Otherwise the narrator remains unnamed, there are no references to any distinguishing characteristics or physical traits in his case, yet it is through his reconstruction of events that meaning and significance is inferred by the reader.

However, the focus of action in *The Shadow Lines* is not the narrator, he is only the central point of reference, an unobtrusive participant and not an agent of influence or change. He evolves through his participation in the stories narrated to him, yet his uncritical response on different occasions remains a point of concern. Take for instance, this incident. When Robi, Ila and the narrator visit a nightclub, and Ila wants to dance, Robi asserts his authority and states that he will not allow her to do so. In the face of this masculine assertion, Ila challenges Robi and gets up to dance. The narrator pleads with Ila to sit down, but when Robi physically stops Ila from dancing, saying, 'girls don't behave like that here,' the narrator offers no resistance and in doing so, he tacitly endorses the patriarchal and cultural values that Robi ascribes to Indian culture. It is this documented experience which the narrator recounts to the grandmother when she makes her scathing remarks about Ila and questions her decision to reside in London. But the narrator makes no reference to his own position and views on this episode.

The narrative incorporates epistolary memories, oral stories and newspaper accounts. The narrator himself is structured by the experiences that invite the reader's participation. In this creative relationship between the narrator and the reader, the reader infers meaning and significance, according to his own ideological context even as he is drawn into the charmed circle of the narrator's unstated beliefs and assumptions.

Memory plays a major role in shaping the narrator's consciousness and the ambivalence of this factor is constantly emphasized. One is at a loss to understand the intention of the narrator when he states, "I remember" along with "I don't remember." The sharpness of the narrative is contingent upon the mnemonic ability of the narrator who as a child confesses to a certain confusion and incertitude, and as he grows up realises that memory need not necessarily provide clues to understanding and enlightenment.

The narrative at times appears disparate and fragmented, but each story has its autonomous existence till it becomes a part of the larger narrative and the consciousness of the narrator.

Published in 1987 *The Shadow Lines* presents historical dates going back to 1939.[2] The dates are significant not for an examination of historical events, but for the reconstruction of the events of public history and their shaping discourses on the narrator. The narrator's enlightenment also coincides with the recovery of history through personal memory — a memory, which had remained buried in the interstices between the domain of public knowledge and private understanding. This history includes immediate personal experiences. To illustrate, when the narrator visits the Prices in England, he demonstrates his familiarity with the people and the material objects because he has imaginatively encountered them all through Tridib's stories. Another example that can be cited is the photograph of Dan Mike and Francesca, which encapsulates a moment in time. It validates the existence of a history that is reconstituted through the narrator's memory and retrieved through this text. History is thus documented and foregrounded through personal perceptions and memories. Tridib, lla and the narrator — all pursue disciplines like archaeology and history. So, these characters are supposed to have a historical sense. But the elucidation of the text is largely dependent on the perception and conferral of meaning by the narrator himself.

Nearly all the major characters — Tridib, lla, and the grandmother, are encrypted in the stories they invent and narrate. But Tridib asks the narrator to guard against the danger of being appropriated by another's story. It is Tridib who enables him to recognise the liberating power of the imagination. He insists upon him to construct his own stories. The narrator who implicitly trusts Tridib's narratives imagines and acts at different points as if he were Tridib himself.

The narrator's first visit to London is almost a literal replication of Tridib's own visit to London. Each experience relating to this journey comes alive to the narrator as Tridib had already narrated it to him in great detail. The vividness of Tridib's description is so much ingrained in his memory that it refuses to be consigned to oblivion. The narrator is thus able to locate precisely the places that Tridib had mentioned. The collapsing of distinctions between the narrator and Tridib's consciousness is related to the narrator's desire to be seen as Tridib. It is very much evident in the ending of the novel where the narrator gets intimate with May, his uncle's beloved.

It is Tridib who provides the narrator with worlds to travel in, but it is his own flight of imagination, which enables the narrator to travel to distant locales even though he lives in Calcutta. However, his grandmother protests against the narrator's obvious pride in seeing himself as similar to Tridib. Her inability to recognize Tridib's transforming influence on the narrator stems from her discomfort with how she perceives Tridib. A student of archaeology who takes an obvious delight in inventing stories and regaling people at street corners, a man who does no constructive work, is at variance with her strict notions of how time should be utilised productively. She views Tridib with suspicion as a young man who does 'nothing.'

The narrator's fascination for Ila is an important part of his growing up. His response is more than just a young boy's growing awareness of feminine sexuality. The language used with reference to Ila presents her as 'foreign.' Her dress thus becomes an indication of this subconscious response. When Ila is dressed in a white and red saree, the narrator is disappointed because she looks like 'any Bethune College girl [...]' (18). It is when she is wearing 'clothes the like of which I had never seen before, English clothes' (43) that she becomes a site of desire, to which the narrator is readily drawn. Even, in retrospect, the narrator is unable to evaluate and analyse his response to Ila and later on, to May. Likewise, the narrator appears critically unaware of the ethos of colonialism and it is this absence of critical self-knowledge that detracts from his standing as the 'hero' of the novel.

We know that Ila's story about Magda is her private fantasy, a transference of her experience of racial discrimination and the valorization of Nick as a romantic hero. Even the description of Magda is telling because she is conceptualized in western referential terms as 'golden and blue eyed.' Ironically Magda/Ila is seen to excel in the very field that carries the mark of the coloniser, the imperialism of the English language. Yet Ila is never seen to resist or question instances of colonial power, except with reference to her being a part of the group protesting against racism. Her inability to accept the reality of Nick's character, results in her fictional construction of Nick as a hero. It is much later that the narrator, for whom Nick has been a mirror image, recognizes that his assumptions about Nick are at variance with the truth.

The narrator thus finds himself confronted with stories that conceal or suppress the truth. The interlocking narratives, the different stories and voices that speak through the materiality of the letter, photographs and newspaper accounts — are all open to the narrator's interpretation. No single character in the novel is presented with the omniscience of complete knowledge; and even the narrator's discourse is not privileged over the other narratives. The multiplicity of voices posits a partial truth or fragmentary information, which is later completed by another voice. For instance, the narrator discovers the discrepancy between Ila's projection of Nick as a chivalric hero who had protected her from a racist attack, and the fact that Nick had actually come back home earlier that day from school so as not to be noticed in her company. This he learns when May confirms to him that Nick had rushed back home from school that day. The narrator establishes connections and correspondences through these overlapping stories that assist him in reviewing his earlier responses. However, the narrator's credulous response to counter narratives prevents him from seeing the embodiment of values in these narratives. Take for instance, when during a conversation Ila asserts the supremacy of a Eurocentric historical experience, and at the same time disclaims the framework of historical events in the Third World countries, the narrator expresses his indignation at what she says but is unable to refute her rhetoric.

The elucidation of the text's meaning is dependent not merely on the narrator, who appears central to the narration, but on the varied experiences of the others — experiences that have been preserved, suppressed and finally recovered. Though the narrator grows up and acquires a certain measure of self-reflexivity, yet his position as an authoritative source of meaning and knowledge is not unquestionable. The multiple points of view, with none being privileged over the other, emphasize that there is no single unifying truth and hence no monolithic narrative.

The narrator while commenting on the ontological nature of reality realises that 'there are moments in the time that are not knowable' (68) as opposed to knowledge created by the 'weight of remembered detail' (67). It is up to the narrator to uncover the silences. After the Calcutta riots of 1964, the documentation appears marginal. It is from this peripheral position that the narrator embarks on one of his most significant journeys, namely, the journey that he undertakes to recover the hidden history of the riots. It is only later that he is able to perceive the link between his memory as a child, of the outbreak of a riot and the riot that claimed Tridib and others. Faced with the disappearance of the riots which seemed to have 'vanished, without leaving a trace in the histories and bookshelves' (230), the narrator begins to doubt the authenticity of his personal memory, which is denied agency and voice by public narratives. The recovery in the archives of this suppressed knowledge culminates in the discovery of the truth of Tridib's death, that he had died in a riot.

The chronology of events in *The Shadow Lines* commences in 1939, when Tridib was eight-thirteen years before the narrator was born, and it concludes with the revelation of Tridib's death sometime in 1979. It is also the most crucial event for the narrator as he had been struggling to come to terms with the knowledge and implications of Tridib's death.

Thus, while undertaking his journey into the past, the narrator discovers the absence of a stable and coherent relationship between the documented voice and the mnemonic self, *i.e.* between public chronicles and personal recollections. Tridib's death acquires import through the accidental discovery that there was a connection between 'my nightmare bus ride back from school and the events that befell Tridib and the others in Dhaka' (218). The separate stories of Robi and May help the narrator retrieve the hidden history of Tridib's death and the public chronicling of the event. The competing narratives enable the narrator to mediate between 'real' and 'fictional' histories, to discover the illusory nature of his earlier beliefs. The child narrator who had believed in the 'reality of nations and borders' has to relearn the meaning of the invisible 'shadow lines,' that demarcate geographical and cultural space.

The narrator who carries the responsibility of presenting and exploring the themes that connect people and events in *The Shadow Lines* is himself engaged in a journey of discovery and self-definition. The decentralised individual is reconstituted as he develops, by history, society and culture that are determining factors in the construction of identity. This identity remains open to change because within any social or historical moment different discourses exist simultaneously and contribute to the plurality of meaning. The narrator is hence defined and constructed through his narrative, where the act of narration becomes one of identity, of naming, and writing meaning into personal history.

Notes and References

1. Amitav Ghosh, *The Shadow Lines* (Delhi: OUP, 1995), 78. All references are to this edition and page numbers are given within parenthesis.
2. According to A.N. Kaul, the narrative of the novel begins in the year 1939 and it ends essentially in 1964 with the eruption of a cycle of violence in India and Pakistan. These are the two end-points of the novel. See his essay "A Reading of The Shadow Lines" in *The Shadow Lines*, educational edition (Delhi: OUP, 1995).

3

INTERROGATING THE NATION, GROWING GLOBAL IN *THE SHADOW LINES*

SOMESHWAR SATI

Amitav Ghosh's *The Shadow Lines* (1988) is best read as a novel that interrogates a political consciousness baptised in the crucible of national divides. This theme resonates with concerns and orientations linked with the emergence of a New World situation, brought about by a transformation within the capitalist world economy. The trans-nationalisation of the forces of production and the widening cosmopolitan scope of the market are rapidly pushing the world beyond familiar national dimensions. As capital flows across continent more freely than ever before and with a ferocious velocity hitherto never witnessed, the surface of the earth seems to be shrinking. A global village that claims to bypass even eclipse the national state is forging its way into prominence, as the nation seems to have become too small to contain within itself the global sweep of modern life. What happens across the seas over ten thousand miles away in New York is more important for an Indian living in New Delhi today than what happens about hundred miles away in Agra. The category of the nation as the structural basis of community formation seems to be losing its defining and determining hold.

The most significant effect of this New World situation is that it has resulted in a reorganisation of the earlier conceptualisation of social relationship particularly those in which the nation was taken for granted as the structural unit of political organisation. Ghosh's narrative which tears from one part of the globe to another with breathtaking speed collecting in the process within its global sweep artefact and experiences from a different civilisation and culture is a fictional rendering of such an international credo. It is a potent expression of a new civilisational ethos conditioned by the overwhelming dynamics of globalisation set into motion and propelled by the irresistible forces of international capitalism. It is only in the context of this New World situation that Ghosh's incisive critic of national borders gathers significance and relevance. This article seeks to document through a close reading of the text how Ghosh embarks on an endeavour to systematically deconstruct the category of the nation and the processes through which a sense of national identity is formed. But before moving on to the central concern of this article, it is necessary to provide a brief yet nuanced survey of how the category of nation has been treated in Indian fiction in English. What are the attitudes of the Indian novelists in English towards the question of national identity? Do these attitudes differ from one writer to another? How would one account for the differences in their attitudes? These and other related questions are what I shall now proceed to examine. Benedict Anderson in his influential work *Imagined Community*[1] poignantly argues that the community is imagined into existence *i.e.*, a sense of community whether of a tribe or a larger entity called nation must be first imagined for it to be real. One would find little difficulty in demonstrating that in this process narrative fiction including the modern genera of the novel plays a key role. The ability to create a sense of community is according to Meenakshi Mukherjee 'not only an attribute of the epic and the oral tale but one of the major powers of narrative fiction even today.'[2] In order to drive her point home she observes: 'All narratives are to be read in the context of a specific time and place but we must remember that while these narratives emerge out of a culture they also contribute towards the construction and definition of this culture. Stories and communities are thus bound together in a symbiotic relation. Stories can draw people together, make them perceive how their present flows from a common past [...].'[3]

The Indian novel in English from its conception in colonial India attempted to crystalise a sense of nationhood as a means to come to terms with colonial subjugation. Raja Rao's *Kanthapura* (1936) is a prime example of such a literary endeavour. In this fictional account of how a small and remote village of south India was caught in the whirlwind of the Gandhian movement for India's independence, Raja Rao generates a nationalistic discourse and constructs a unitary sense of nationalised identity necessitated by the priorities and strategies of the freedom struggle. Historically trapped in the need to project a homogenous community, Raja Rao pens the story of how the inhabitants of Kanthapura inspired by a local prototype of Gandhi willingly overlook their internal differences of caste, creed and religion and join hands against the British. At the heart of this story is thus an obvious 'us' against 'them' binorism — the exploited colonised against the exploiting coloniser.

But with the coming of independence such a homogenising narrative shaped by the twin impulses of Nationalism and Colonialism begins to fizzle out and by the time we reach Salman Rushdie's *Midnight's Children* (1981) the national ideal begins to be restructured and subverted. Rather than laying an insistence on a homogeneous identity, Rushdie offers a history of the nation not through a unilinear narrative, but in terms of disruption and discontinuity (in all its magnificient cruelty). He defines the nation not through the coming into being of some unified and singular national consciousness but in terms of the original '1001 marvelous promises of a luminous midnight.' Rushdie's novel has been diagnosed as a plural narrative that explodes the notion of the nation having a stable identity. It however does so without discarding the nation; it merely attempts to draw attention to the glorious multiplicity of this entity. Allen Sealy in his *Trotternama* (1988) and Mukul Keshavan in his *Looking through glass* (1995) follow in Rushdie's footstep. What they are attempting is to recuperate the silenced (submerged) history of those communities that lie on the margin of the homogeneous narrative of the Indian nation. In the case of Sealy the community in question is the Anglo-Indian section of the Indian population while the Muslims who refused to go to Pakistan after partition and preferred of their own account to stay in India are the narrative focus of Keshavan's novel. Both of them like Rushdie do not fall into the trap of a postmodern limbo, for they merely question the homogeneity of India by giving a plural voice to it.

In the case of Amitav Ghosh's *The Shadow Lines* what is posited as an ideal form of existence is 'a world beyond nation.' The coming into being of such a world would be highly desirable from the point of view of the forces of international capitalism for such a world would automatically imply the establishment of a global market free from the obstruction of national frontier that tends to impede the free flow of commodities across the communities. In fact the dynamics of globalisation is so overwhelming and the tendency of nations to submit themselves to the power of capital is so obvious and common place that Eric Hosbowm, the most eminent of the contemporary of the Anglophone sociologists, even goes to the extent of locating the nation on a declining curve of historical viability. He argues that the nation is no longer a potent vector of historical development. But the developments in Eastern Europe during the last decade of 20th century and the various identity movements plaguing the earth demonstrate the myopic nature of Hosbowm's claim. In Ghosh there appears to be an awareness of this limitation of Hosbowm's argument, for he realises the utopian dimension of the ideal of a world beyond nations. At the end of the novel Tridib who aspires to become a global citizen — a man without a country — meets his tragic end at the hands of a rioting mob in Dhaka. His vision seems to succumb to the brute forces of reality and it ultimately acquires a mythic rather than a realistic and plausible stature.

Despite being amply aware of the utopian dimension of a notion of the globe free from national divides *The Shadow Lines* interrogates the processes through which a sense of national identity is constructed. The construction of the sense of a national identity is the result of a dual dynamics — one which is homogenising and the other which is differentiating. In order to establish a sense of unity within the nation it is necessary to project the image of the entire community as unified, single and homogeneous. At the same time it is also imperative to differentiate this community from the other communities of the world. For example, if a sense of Indianness is to be created, all Indians are projected as brothers and sisters — members of a single unified family sharing a common past and moving towards a shared future having similar goals and aspirations. On the other hand these are different from those of other countries. To be an Indian means not to be a Pakistani, a French, an American, a British or a German and so on. Amitav Ghosh seems to demonstrate an intuitive understanding of this dynamics of nationness and he strikes at its very roots showing that these are misleading constructs — illusions that people are fed on.

Is the nation a homogeneous entity? This is a fundamental question that *The Shadow Lines* raises. It also furnishes the reader with a univocal answer — a firm and emphatic 'No.' Writing about the reasons for writing this novel Amitav Ghosh had revealed in a leading American magazine that the ghastly events that followed the assassination of Mrs. Indira Gandhi (1984) had deeply pained him. He was unable to understand how a community that was essentially Indian — the Sikhs could be made the victims of such an inhuman massacre by their own non-Sikh countrymen.[4] This incident had convinced him that there were deep fissures within the body polity of the Indian nation and it was this incident that inspired him to write *The Shadow Lines.* Though the riots that erupted in the aftermath of Mrs. Gandhi's assassination are not mentioned in the novel, there are a number of incidents that the novel narrates that shatter the notion of India as a homogeneous community. In 1964 the Hazratbal shrine in Srinagar had been defiled. Consequently communal riots had sparked off throughout the country. The unnamed narrator of *The Shadow Lines* was a school going boy then. But he could remember the incident quite vividly. Two communities, that is, the Hindus and the Muslims that had lived in relative harmony now were suspicious of each other. Rumours that one community had poisoned the water supply to exterminate the other community were fresh and circulating. The atmosphere was filled not only with suspicion but also with fear and hatred. Before the riots the narrator's best friend was a boy from the Muslim community called Montu (Mansur). But the panic and communal hatred that had gripped the entire nation had transformed this best friend into a feared enemy. Instances of internal divides within the supposedly homogeneous body polity of the nation punctuate the narrative of the novel with a frequent regularity that forces the reader to ponder about the unified nature of the country he lives in.

Not only is the nation portrayed as being an internally fractured entity, Ghosh also takes great pain to demonstrate that the public chronicle of the nation is at odds with the private stories of the individual. In the riots of 1964 the narrator's uncle Tridib had become a helpless victim to the maddening frenzy of communal hatred. This was a key moment in the story of the narrator's life. But when fifteen years later in 1979 the narrator attempts to recover the traces of this event in the archives of the Nehru Memorial Library, New Delhi he fails to find a mention of Tridib's death in the newspapers. It seemed as if his private story had no place in the records of the nation's memory. It seemed to have dropped out of memory into the 'crater of a volcano of silence.' It seems as if Ghosh is making a telling point — the story of the individual is swallowed by the history of the nation and in an age of agnostic individualism this tendency to erase the individual should be not only carefully guarded against but also fearlessly exposed and severely censored.

Ghosh's novel traces the growth and evolution of its unnamed narrator's consciousness from his childhood belief that national borders have 'a corporeal substance [...] that across the border there exists another reality,' to the mature realization in adulthood that this belief was a 'mirage.' The novel documents in minute details the deceptive nature of national borders that are constructed to project an image of difference across political divides. The narrator's grandmother, whose psyche was conditioned during the days of India's freedom struggle, firmly believes in the ability of national borders to differentiate her own community from the other communities. The narrator treats this living embodiment of fossilized nationalism with mocking affection. Tha'mma's nationalistic beliefs seem to be undermined as the novel unfolds. In 1964 as she plans her visit to Dhaka she wonders whether she would be able to see the borders between India and East Pakistan from the plane. Her grandson mocks at this thought and asks if the border was a long black line with a green on one side and scarlet on the other side as shown in the school atlas. To this question she replies, 'Of course not. But surely there's something-trenches perhaps, or soldiers or guns pointing at each other, or even just barren strip of land. Don't they call it no-man's land?' The grandmother's expectation of the visibility of the borders between India and East Pakistan may sound to be absurd but her concepts can be sympathetically understood as she had experienced the traumatic events of the partition. As the novel unfolds, the grandmother is forced to realise that the two sides of border were merely the mirror images of each other. They were not different in any sense. This realisation forces her to interrogate the very purpose of the nationalist cause and the reasons of war between the nations.

> 'But if there aren't any trenches or anything, how are people to know? I mean, where's the difference then? And if there's no difference, both sides will be the same; it will be just like it used to be before, when we used to catch a train in Dhaka and get off in Calcutta the next day without anybody stopping us. What was it all for then — Partition and all the killing and everything — if there isn't something in between?'

The logic of the partition appears to be arbitrary. The lines that divide India from East Pakistan are as illogical as the lines of the circle the narrator draws on the map with the help of his compass and pencil. These lines are merely the whims of politicians and nothing else as they cannot enforce cultural difference nor can they separate the two communities living across the border. Something or the other will always connect India to East Pakistan and Calcutta to Dhaka. No wonder the grandmother's old uncle refuses to leave Dhaka and migrate to India. This apparently senile old man seems to come forward as the sanest voice in the novel:

> Once you start moving you never stop. That's what I told my sons when they took the trains. I said: I don't believe

> in this India-Shindia. It's all very well, you're going away now, but suppose when you get there they decide to draw another line somewhere? What will you do then? Where will you move to? No one will ever have you anywhere. As for me, I was born here, and I'll die here.

The absurdity of the partition is a governing concern of this novel and Ghosh's narrative reiterates this theme over and over again. The story of the partition of the grandmother's ancestral house in Dhaka is a metaphorical and comic rendering of this theme. When Tha'mma was still a young child this house had been partitioned with the dividing lines going through doorways and the lavatory bisecting an old commode. Even the old nameplate had been partitioned into two. This rather farcical act calls into question the logic of the political division of the Nation. The partition of the country is therefore projected in the novel as an act of meaningless violence. Suvir Kaul rightly points out that in *The Shadow Lines* there is 'a growing sense that the logic of the nation state is necessarily at odds with various forms of subcontinental communality — that to be Indian is to be perversely and perhaps unsuccessfully define oneself against one's mirror image from across the border.'[5]

Ghosh further illustrates this theme by demonstrating that identical realities exist across territorial division, which were originally meant to mark out differences. When still a child both the grandmother and her sister visualised the otherside of the partitioned house as being upside down — an inverted image of their part of the house. But when the two returned to Dhaka to rescue their uncle they are presently surprised to find out that on the other side of the line there existed an identical reality. Category of difference and otherness is thus presented as a deceptive construct, as a fabrication of the human mind, as an illusion without any grounding realities. In the novel national frontiers are described as 'looking-glass borders' that create an image of otherness only to see itself reflected.

Central to the conception of the novel is the attempt to deconstruct the not quite dialectical logic of identity (internal homogeneity within the nation) and difference that defines the parameter and essence of national identity. Born in Dhaka and forced to migrate to Calcutta as a consequence of the bloodshed of the partition, Tha'mma feels that her sense of political identity — that being an Indian citizen — is at odds with her nostalgic longing for her roots that lies outside the political and geographical boundaries of India in Dhaka. It is this psychic confusion that is comically rendered in her inability to adequately describe her trip to Dhaka. Though she is going to Dhaka, she says that she is coming to Dhaka. This is because she views her journey to Dhaka as a homecoming. But Tridib's death at the hands of the rioting mob in Dhaka changes her attitude towards the place of her birth. Her nostalgic longing for her city of origin now gives way to a sense of hatred. 'Kill everyone of them' is what she says listening to the news about the Indo-Pakistan War on the radio. She even goes to the extent of giving donation to the War Fund. If the individual attitude toward the land can change so easily over a period of time, then how can the category of Nation be treated as the determining and defining structure of community formation? The endless queue of individuals seeking immigration to a new country for a better future in today's world really seems to undermine the influence that the nation has over its inhabitants. In this age of diaspora the nation is not a permanent but merely a transient category of belonging.

What is most remarkable is that other structure of community formation like religion also exercises a gripping hold over individual even across a national divide. The desecration of the Hazratbal shrine in Srinagar sparks off communal frenzy not only in Calcutta, but also beyond the geographical or political boundaries of India in Dhaka. An event that takes place in another country leads to a significant reprisal in one's own. Religion in this novel exercises a hold that defies national boundaries and is able to evoke a sense of loyalty and belonging that supersedes the one generated by a sense of Nationness.

The narrator is forced to ponder on these issues and he is ultimately made to realise the shortcoming of a political organisation of the world structured on the basis of national divides. If Ghosh is interrogating the nation as the structural basis of international relation, then what is the alternative that he is providing? In *The Shadow Lines* he attempts to create an image of global inclusiveness in which various cultures intermingle with one another to create a single unified global picture. The rain forest near Rai Bazaar is imported from Brazil and Congo. The global sweep of Ghosh's narrative is remarkable and it is not even matched by the encyclopedic knowledge of Tridib, or by the incessant travel of the globetrotting Ila. In this way it can be seen that *The Shadow Lines* has moved a long way from the totallising narrative of homogenised community as discernible in Raja Rao's *Kanthapura*. This change in a novelist's attitude towards the nation is but natural, for Ghosh lives not in days of India's freedom struggle: he is a citizen of a rapidly shrinking world; the subjectivity that he constructs in the novel is no doubt an elitist cosmopolitan Indian subjectivity conditioned by the imperative of his globetrotting class and we therefore should guard ourselves against the hegemonic tendencies of international capitalism that seeks to feed its own interest by disembedding the individual from the culture to which he belongs.

Notes and References

1. Benedict Anderson, *Imagined Community*, first edn. London, 1983, revised and extended edn. London, 1991.
2. Meenakshi Mukherjee, "Narrating a Nation", *New Horizon*.
3. *Ibid*.
4. Amitav Ghosh, *New Yorker*, August 15, 1997.
5. Suvir Kaul, "Separation Anxiety: Growing up Inter/National in *The Shadow Lines*" in Ghosh's *The Shadow Lines*, educational edn. (New Delhi: OUP, 1995), 280.

4

NATION AS IDENTITY IN *THE SHADOW LINES*

ALKA KUMAR

The narrative in *The Shadow Lines* takes us across the international border, continents and cultures, child time and adult time, past and present with such ease that one is simply intrigued. Sometimes, it traverses some of these realms simultaneously so that the complexity of the text is further enhanced. In the novel, there are some epiphanic moments or 'highpoints' both at the personal and political level, which suddenly illuminate such chunks of virtual time and life, thereby enriching the reading experience. Many of the important characters in the novel, the narrator and his grandmother, for instance, are locked in specific historical moments so that for them the passage of time becomes irrelevant. For example, for the old lady, her real home exists only in memory and she is unable to recognise Dhaka when she finally sees it, 'Where is Dhaka?' is her constant refrain. For the narrator too, (whose name we are never told), all places, including Dhaka, are alive in the present just as they exist in the past, through descriptions given by others: 'She had talked to me so often about that house and that lane I could see them myself, though only in patches, for her memory had shone upon them with the uninterrupted brilliance of a lighthouse beam.'[1]

Further, the text continuously subverts notions of truth — notions that are rooted in cultural, sociological, and historical realities while it exposes the arbitrariness of many kinds of lines, borders both personal and political. Strangely, the lines in the novel that divide people, places and realities are both not only arbitrary and shadow-like but also fixed and difficult to cross. Although the personal and political are intertwined in this novel, the personal story really recedes into the background, and it is the public face of the text that assumes primacy. In this complex fictional pattern, 'nation' presents itself as a crucial strand on the reader's sensibilities.

II

The paper sets out to contextualise 'nation,' through a close reading of this novel. But before I do that some general observations may be in order. Though we would like to treat the concept with some degree of stability, the conceptualisation of terms like nation-making, nationalism, nationality and their bearing on identity seem to be in flux rather than fixed, they are processes rather than finished products. This is obvious, as cultural or sociological paradigms are dynamic and unstable, they change, shift and rearrange themselves as a result of multiple factors like politics, religion, language. This is particularly true in the case of India where diversities and multiplicities abound so that the Nation with the big 'N' continually faces threat from all those smaller segments that strive for space. In the face of such development, against the backdrop of a series of divergent factors mentioned above that continuously change the social milieu, it becomes increasingly difficult to think of the 'nation' in fixed ways. The critique of the nation then, of necessity, must move along the working through process of revisions and redefinitions.

However, it is helpful to look at the issue from a cultural perspective, for the novel clearly shows that cultural formations are the sites within which one's nationality or individual identity may be constructed. Surely, the narrator, Tridib and the grandmother — despite their differences in age, location, ideology and varying perspectives on reality, share an innate Indianness, even a conceptual formulation of nationalism, which Ila, the Indian located in the West cannot envisage, and so cannot be a part of. Here what Benedict Anderson has to say about the nation is quite illuminating. It [the nation] is an imagined political community [...]. It is *imagined* because the members of even the smallest nation will never know most of their fellow members, meet them or even hear of them, yet in the minds of each lives the image of their communion.'[2] This makes it possible for emotional affinities to transcend some disruptive dissonances, thereby making space for a sense of nationness and nationalism. The narrator's grandmother, for instance, is one such character who conforms to this thinking and for whom the nation is a clear marker of identity. She is a votary of the nation in a sense in which none of the other characters are. In fact, she represents a legitimate view of the nation against which the viewpoints of others like those of Tridib, Ila and the narrator, may be perceived. Although she lives in the frozen past, the reality of nationhood is largely stable in her case. A fervent and militant nationalist, she worries about her old uncle dying in a country not his own, almost abandoned and alone in old age. 'It doesn't matter whether we recognize each other or not. We are the same flesh, the same blood, the same bone and now at last, after all these years, perhaps we'll be able to make amends for all that bitterness and hatred,' she tells her son (129). It is clear that she cares for the ties of blood and nationhood, and is prepared to let go the bitter memories of family feuds. It is interesting to note that the terrorists fascinated her, and she wanted to act like them for her freedom. In response to the narrator's query, if given a chance would she have killed the English magistrate, she says: 'I would have been frightened, [...]. But I would have prayed for strength, and God willing, yes, I would have killed him. It was for our freedom: I would have done anything to be free' (39).

Her quest for freedom is, obviously, a quest for attaining nationhood; and she is prepared to pay any price for it — a position which sets her apart from Ila, for whom freedom, as Tha'mma puts it, is nothing but the right to do what she pleases' in the permissive society of a country like England (89). But Tha'mma thinks that Ila does not understand the true spirit of England, and, so, does not have the right to be staying there. 'Everyone who lives there has earned his right to be there with blood: with their brothers' blood and their fathers' blood and their sons' blood. They know they're a nation because they've drawn their borders with blood' (78). Her militant nationalism comes out clearly when she explains the creed of Englishmen and relates it to the Indian context, thus: 'War is their religion. That's what it takes to make a country. Once that happens people forget they were born this or that, Muslim or Hindu, Bengali or Punjabi: They become a family born of the same pool of blood. That is what *you* have to achieve for India, don't you see?' (78). And, again, her nationalist fervor gets articulated when she gives away her cherished necklace, the first gift that she had received from her husband after her marriage, for the war fund in 1965. She justifies her action to her grandson, saying: 'I gave it away [...] I gave it to the fund for the war. I had to, don't you see? For your sake; for your freedom. We have to kill them before they kill us; we have to wipe them out.' And she continues, 'this is the only chance [...]. The only one. We're fighting them properly at last, with tanks and guns and bombs' (237). Having been through the trauma of partition, if not physically, at least mentally, and having lost her sister's son, Tridib, to a race riot in Dhaka and being its eyewitness, she sees the war with Pakistan as her last chance at self-assertion and revenge. The experience is so much unsettling that while listening to the war news on the radio, she lets her fist drive into its glass front, thereby injuring her hand seriously. But she soon regains her calm and says, 'I must get to the hospital [...] I mustn't waste all this blood. I can donate it to the war fund' (237). (Incidentally, this delineation of Tha'mma does not go well with her account before her death, when she is critically ill and irascible and strongly believes that Ila has cast a vicious influence upon her grandson. It is in this delirious state that she posts a short letter to the Dean of his college alleging that the latter visited whores in Delhi; her act nearly led to his expulsion.)

III

Tha'mma's sense of nation receives a severe jolt when she undertakes a rescue mission to Dhaka to bring back her Jethamoshai to India. Before her departure she wonders whether she would be able to see the border between India and East Pakistan from the window of the plane, to which her son sarcastically replies that did she think that the border would actually be a long black line with green on one side and scarlet on the other as in a school atlas! True, her response to the question of the border is naïve, but her expectation to find trenches or soldiers or guns pointing at each other or even no-man's land there, makes sense. But when she is told that she should expect clouds, and at the most some green fields, she is simply amazed, and her natural and forthright response is:

> But if there aren't any trenches or anything, how are people to know? I mean, where's the difference then? And if there's no difference both sides will be the same; it'll be just like it used to be before, when we used to catch a train in Dhaka and get off in Calcutta the next day without anybody stopping us. What was it all for then — partition and all the killing and everything — if there isn't something in between? (151)

It is easy to see why her simplistic, yet logical mind is unable to understand that the border is like a mirror, a looking-glass border, wherein one looks beyond to find self-reflections which mirror conflicts and riots for the sake of preserving a self — an exercise which seems arbitrary and meaningless.

Tha'mma feels utterly bewildered when she is further told that 'the border isn't on the frontier: it's right inside the airport. You'll see. You'll cross it when you have to fill in all those disembarkation cards and things.' And to her chagrin, she realizes that 'her place of birth had come to be so messily at odds with her nationality' (152). She is pained to know that she is much more a foreigner in her place of birth than May, as the latter does not need a visa to come to Dhaka. As for her Dhaka, it had long since disappeared into the past and she can visit and revisit it only in memory! Her poor consolation is that the memory cannot be divided. And what about the nation to which she belongs? It seems it has failed her, as it is aptly summed up by Tridib:

> [...] she was *not* a fascist, she was only a modern middle-class woman- [...]. All she wanted was a middle-class life in which, like the middle classes the world over, she would thrive believing in the unity of nationhood and territory, of self-respect and national power: that was all she wanted —

a modern middle-class life, a small thing that history has denied her in its fullness and for which she could never forgive it (78).

IV

As for the younger generation in the novel, they have inherited a nation, which is stricken with dissension and disunity. It can flare up at the slightest provocation. And this is exactly what happened when the narrator was a school-going child. There were riots in Calcutta. He and his schoolmates had suddenly felt disoriented in their own land, as the city had turned against them; and they were stupefied with fear. While reflecting upon this experience as an adult he says: 'It is a fear that comes of the knowledge that normalcy is utterly contingent, that the spaces that surround one, the streets that one inhabits, can become, suddenly and without warning, as hostile as a flash flood.' It is the entire subcontinent that experiences it, and it is this which differentiates it from the rest of the world — not language, not food, not music. 'It is the special quality of loneliness,' he tells us 'that grows out of the war between oneself and one's image in the mirror' (204). The image is, obviously of a deadly, ghastly reality that one tries in vain to grapple with. It is in the context of this traumatic experience that he learns a new meaning of 'distance.' He was given to understand as a child that space meant extension, but through his immediate experience, he learns that spaces can get interrelated through mutual discord or mutual concern, irrespective of distance. The theft of the relic at Hazratbal Mosque can be used as an illustration to clarify this idea. It concerned Hindus and Muslims alike. The targets of the rioters were not people, neither Hindus nor Muslims nor Sikhs but property identified with the government and the police; 'the theft of the relic had brought together the people of Kashmir as never before' (225). And yet there was the distant town of Khulna in East Pakistan where a demonstration in protest against the theft of the relic had turned violent, triggering violence in the neighboring towns and Dhaka. Subsequently, even Calcutta had erupted. As for Dhaka and Calcutta, they were more closely related to each other than ever before, so much so that the narrator 'had only to look into the mirror to be in Dhaka.' These areas were 'locked into an irreversible symmetry' through patterns of mutual discord and mutual concern of the people, on both sides of the border. It is in this sense that the line that was to set them 'free,' functioned like their 'looking-glass border' (223).

Likewise, Robi suffers the consequences of the nation in disarray, though in a much more poignant way. His elder brother, Tridib, had got killed in a riot in Dhaka, and he happened to be a mute witness to this gory incident. The most poignant section of the text is the account of Tridib's death, given fifteen years after the event for the first time by his brother Robi. Robi has been revisited by the same nightmare for long years and he tells it in a powerful and uneasy mix of dream and unreality. 'If only that dream would go away, I would be like other people; I would be free. I would have given anything to be free of that memory' (246). A chance remark by a Bangladeshi waiter in a cheap restaurant in London had opened up floodgates of anguished memories in Robi's mind. Subsequently they stand together — Robi, the narrator and Ila. 'We stood a long time like that, on the steps of that derelict church in Clapham, three children of a free state, together clinging' (247). This heart-rending cry of pain and helplessness should render meaningless, practically, all carefully constructed theories of the nation. The heart of darkness, the centre of the mob towards which Tridib fearlessly walks swallows not just Tridib but all sense of sanity and discretion, which makes human beings human. In the context of the painful death of his brother, Robi muses on the word 'free,' and finds it to be a 'mirage.' 'You know, if you look at the pictures on the front pages of the newspapers at home now, all those pictures of dead people — in Assam, the North-east, Punjab, Sri Lanka, Tripura — people shot by terrorists and separatists and the army and the police, you'll find somewhere behind it all the single word; everyone's doing it to be free.' As one who was entrusted with the job of running a district, he would have given orders for the killing of the terrorists if they were operating there — that was the price they should be willing to pay for preserving their unity and freedom, he told his officers. And when he went home, he found an anonymous letter, waiting for him. It said: 'We're going to get you, nothing personal, we have to kill you for our freedom. It would be like reading my own speech transcribed on a mirror. And then I think to myself why don't they draw thousands of little lines through the whole subcontinent and give every little place a new name? What would it change? It is a mirage; the whole thing is a mirage. How can anyone divide a memory?' (246-47). Freedom, then is a 'mirage.' If freedom were possible through killings, then Tridib's death would have set him free. But the fact is that a chance remark by a waiter in a restaurant sets his hand shaking like a leaf, fifteen years after the gruesome act, thousands of miles away in another continent. Even the division and subdivision of the continent cannot change the dismal situation.

The various sections of *The Shadow Lines* reiterate that personal freedom is curiously connected with political realities that are often divisive and disruptive; and, so, no freedom is unequivocal. Freedom for one set of people is attained at the cost of others and thus notions of freedom are both vague and shadowy, no truth is ever objective and no freedom unconditional. Notions of liberty are like shadow lines, sometimes shadowy and mirage-like, but often, real and rigidly drawn. The borders or the shadow lines are not always possible to perceive from the window of a plane but they are impossible to transgress without causing violence and bloodshed.

Take communalism, the other face of nationalism. The narrator recalls an incident in which the ugly face of communalism is clearly manifest: the silence and crafty mob lies in wait at street corners in Calcutta as the school bus carrying children speeds through the city, while rumours of the city's water supply being poisoned are doing rounds and evoke fear in the young children. 'That particular fear has a texture you can neither forget nor describe. It is like the fear of the victims of an earthquake, of people who have lost faith in the stillness of the earth' (204). The public chronicle is silent on this and the narrator searches desperately in the archives of Teen Murti to recover a past he remembers so vividly-indeed as immediate as his experience of sight, sound and smell, though he has travelled a long chronological distance from it. It is important for him to find public evidence of that childhood riot because his very identity is associated with it. Eventually, he is able to retrieve the lost moment through sustained effort and research. The gaps in history are suggestive of deliberate political initiatives; the latter were aimed at burying this incident in the volcano of silence. In such a situation, he feels utterly helpless, as he does not have words to express this silence. '[...] I know nothing of this silence except that it lies outside the reach of my intelligence, beyond words — that is why this silence must win, must inevitably defeat me, because it is not a presence at all, it is simply a gap, a hole, an emptiness in which there are no words' and no meanings (218).

V

The Shadow Lines is a novel where invented stories and lived reality coexist, the one as valid as the other, historical truth mingling easily with constructions. Such constructions may be 'stories,' which are embodiments of some versions of truth. Tridib tells the narrator that, 'Everyone lives in a story [...] because stories are all there to live in, it was just a question of which one you chose' (182). Ila, for instance, has chosen to be a part of the western nationalist master narrative, which makes her pronounce arrogantly that events of consequence have happened in Europe — events like the war and fascism; and that nothing really significant happens in areas like Nigeria, India and Malaysia. 'Well of course there are famines and riots and disasters [...]. But those are local things after all — not like revolutions or antifascist wars, nothing that sets a political example to the world, nothing that's really remembered' (104).

It is curious that the more Ila tries to belong to the western master narrative, the less she gets anywhere near it. Her experience of racial discrimination, which she projects on to Magda, her golden-haired doll; and Nick's neglect of her while she is studying at the same school where he does, and Nick's subsequent irresponsible treatment of her when they are married — all this severely jolts Ila's sense of belonging to the white community.

Though the narrator admires Ila's newly cut, curly hair as she marches to Brixton to 'confront a gang of jack-booted racists armed with bicycle chains,' (105) and her political friends talk of her as 'our own upper-class Asian Marxist' (97), he can see through those fine clothes and manicured hands and perceive the phoney in her. She has created a make-believe world around her. For instance, she paints Nick Price in attractive hues, investing him with qualities, which he never had. Strangely, she describes his infidelity as 'a bit of variety, his way of travelling.' The sophisticated Ila is indeed trapped within the web of her own needs and circumstances, pleading as she does, 'Don't you see I wouldn't leave him if he moved a whole bloody massage parlor from Bangkok into the house [...] I love him so much I could never leave him' (189). Is she the same westernized Ila, who had been outraged when Robi did not let her dance with a lecherous stranger, saying, 'You can do what you like in England but here there are certain things you cannot do. That is our culture, that's how we live,' and she had rushed out in anger, shouting. 'Do you see now why I've chosen to live in London? You see it's only because I want to be free' (88).

VI

The contradictions inherent in the term 'nation' are projected through the complex form of this novel. Although the nation is crucial to the conceptualization, scope and structure of *The Shadow Lines*, somewhere along the way it becomes an elusive and shadowy entity, as the principal protagonists in the drama are unable to make sense of its resonant contradictions. The grandmother who had passionately clung on to her space in the historical narrative, and who understands the forces of history — seeing them as catalysts of social change, is dead; and the younger persons in the novel are unwilling to take on the mantle at this stage. They want to be individuals rather than be aggressive citizens, with unconditional allegiance to the nation-state. Ila, Robi and the narrator — different versions of the post-colonial Indian, try to grapple with the reality in their own diverse way. Although they would like to believe that the boundaries between nations are like shadow lines, they find that precisely these shadow lines precipitate divisiveness and violence.

The form of the novel may be linked to a complex jigsaw puzzle with its pieces seemingly strewn about with haphazard randomness but it is really a carefully crafted structure. Both the narrator and the reader discover through this artistic form that the world is not a simple place that can be seen in an atlas. Though the solid lines that divide the nations may not be clearly visible, they are in fact an inexorable fact, as they lead to political aggression and violent bloodshed.

The Shadow Lines interrogates complex themes like political conflict, national identity, and cultural dislocation — through the use of memory, nostalgia, multiple subjectivities and overlapping stories. As for the historical contradictions that must of necessity mark the biography of the nation, they are projected through the highly nuanced and multi-layered metaphor of the shadow lines.

Notes and References

1. Amitav Ghosh, *The Shadow Lines* (New Delhi: OUP, 1988), 194. All subsequent references to the text follow this edition.
2. Benedict Anderson, *Imagined Communities: Reflections on the Origin and Spread of Nationalism* (London: The Thetford Press, 1983), 15.

5

The Shadow Lines Between Freedom and Violence

ALPANA NEOGY

Amitav Ghosh in *The Shadow Lines* has woven fact and fiction in a complex, absorbing narrative that mirrors lives across nations and spans almost half a century of recent Indian history. The reader looks at love and loyalty and examines the questions of fidelity and accountability, of tradition and modernity, of freedom and its evanescent quality.

As the British Empire collapsed and lines were drawn up dividing the Indian subcontinent, thousands were exiled. The changes brought about in three generations of a Bengali family dispersed across three countries as a result of historical changes in the land is the focus of this novel: it brings out the confusion and the trauma of the East Bengali *shikkhita madhyabitta* (the educated middle class) uprooted and lost after the dismembering of Bengal in 1947.

Meenakshi Mukherjee while reviewing Ghosh's latest novel *The Glass Palace* writes:

> Each of Amitav Ghosh's books, (except *Countdown*), invariably focuses on themes in history and connections across geography that have seldom been explored before, and does so with imagination supported by archival research, his narrative inventiveness matched by his luminous prose.[1]

In an article in *The Times of India*[2] written soon after the publication of the novel, *The Shadow Lines*, Ghosh had described the recent events in the country — the terrorist attacks, the caste riots, the shootings in Kashmir — as 'lurid hallucinations.' Most Indians and foreigners would consider these happenings as 'an endemic disease, a plague peculiar to the subcontinent.' But at the bottom all the uprisings revolve around a single issue: 'identity.' Ghosh believes that the issue of identity lies at the heart of democracy. Perhaps this 'disease' and the 'issue of identity' could be traced to the story of 1947, which according to Ritu Menon and Kamla Bhasin is:

> a gendered narrative of displacement and dispossession, of large-scale and widespread communal violence, and of the realignment of family, community and national identities as people were forced to accommodate the dramatically altered reality that now prevailed.[3]

Ghosh's novel incorporates all these traumas. Tha'mma, the narrator's grandmother, born and brought up in Dhaka, has to accept the grim reality that after 1947, Dhaka is no longer her home. She might have well asked, 'Who am I? Am I an Indian merely because I am a Hindu and live in Calcutta?' Given a choice, she would rather have stayed on in Dhaka. In Calcutta, where she settles down after the sudden death of her husband, she lives in the less-affluent locality of Bhowanipore. Dhaka would remain a 'home' only in her memory, a 'home' that she could not go to.

Ghosh explores the concept and meaning of freedom and identity, themes very crucial to the modern man. Political freedom was a momentous event that happened in 1947 when India became independent. Equality and freedom were granted to all the citizens of this country, irrespective of caste, creed or sex. By liberating themselves of the shackles of the British Empire, people thought, that they had achieved something very precious, which the Empire had denied them — the freedom of the individual.

Once this freedom was legally granted to them, it became evident that while it was easy to enact a law, it was very difficult to actually experience this freedom because of the complex and contradictory forces inherent in the Indian society. These forces are difficult to restrain or contain in the existing circumstances and they have introduced the divisive tendencies that tear the country apart. But what is freedom for one may be enslavement for another. The political freedom of 1947 may mean nothing to her/him who sees herself/himself now under another yoke, where earlier it had been a foreign one. One is almost forced to ask: can one really be free, personally, socially or politically?

The women characters in the novel — Tha'mma, Ila and May — from different cultures and generations, provide an apt study of this dilemma. Each has an incomplete understanding of the true nature of freedom. It is the narrator's point of view that is paramount. He interacts with each one of them and we get to know of their limited vision and their idiosyncrasies and foibles by watching them through his eyes. In the process, the theme of freedom is explored, developed and assessed.

Freedom means different things to the different characters, depending on the stage they occupy in the backdrop of recent Indian history. Tha'mma had been a young girl in Dhaka when the freedom struggle had reached its peak. Later she had witnessed the birth of two new nations, experienced the pain associated with the partition of the land, and participated in the new order and the new political system that evolved out of that experience.

To Ila, two generations later, the spirit of nationalism that had inspired Tha'mma, is a thing of the past. She is a post-partition child. She is unable to conform or adapt to the society that has developed in independent India and escapes to another society with a different set of values, a different social system. For each one of them, namely, Tha'mma and Ila, the concept of freedom has been moulded by their own individual experience and the different worlds that they inhabit.

As a student in Dhaka, Tha'mma had been exposed to the fierce revolutionary nationalist spirit that was sweeping through Bengal. She, too, would have liked to be a part of the freedom movement, to run errands for the terrorists, participate in demonstrations, to spread propaganda, and to hide and transport weapons, even make explosives — but was unable to do any of these because she was a 'woman'[4] (39). The annals of Bengal resonate with the courage and valour of many women[5] who had actively participated in the revolutionary movement in the 1930's. Listening about such deeds of heroism had shaped Tha'mma's entire personality. One has to be ready to die for one's country, ready even to kill, she tells her grandson almost thirty years later when he tries to make her believe that Ila had chosen to stay on in England because she wanted to be 'free' (88). Tha'mma never permits herself any over-indulgence, and works hard at her job. She feels that the political freedom obtained after long years of foreign rule required dedication of each citizen.

However, the freedom won in 1947 did not create that perfect order that Tha'mma had hoped for. In fact, the political freedom won by the nation had created grounds for animosity and hatred by drawing up superfluous lines, demarcating nations and boundaries. Curiously, she was an Indian national, but her place of birth was Dhaka. Her distress and disillusionment is evident when she has to fill up the disembarkation card before landing at Dhaka airport and she is not 'able to quite understand how her place of birth had come to be so messily at odds with her nationality' (152).

Her disenchantment is complete when she realizes that her sacrifice has been in vain:

> If there aren't any trenches or anything, how are people to know? I mean, where's the difference then? And if there's no difference both sides will be the same, it will be just like it used to be before [...]. What was it all for then — partition and all the killing and everything — if there isn't something in between? (151)

After Tridib's death, Tha'mma's idealism fades fast, as she witnesses the anarchic tendencies gaining control over the land. She reverts to a militant form of nationalism (Ila calls her 'a war mongering fascist') and she donates her jewellery to the Defence Fund. Now it is 'us' and 'them' — 'them' being all those who live in her former homeland now. The citizens were required to make sacrifices in order to preserve political freedom; it had to be defended from forces inimical to it. One must be ready even to kill to preserve this freedom.

Ila is an enigmatic character. She tries to be free and feels that Indian milieu is alien to her. Unfortunately, so is the other world that she has adopted as her own, where she believes she can be free. She tries her best to be accepted by the people of her adopted land, but her experience tells her that she will never be completely accepted by them. As a child she had attended various schools in different countries but in the group photograph of her class she figures as standing apart, not quite one of the group. However, she tries to convince the narrator that she was popular and accepted by her group. She is a victim of racism in the International school in England and suffers, physically and emotionally, as her classmates reject her. Naturally, she feels isolated, alone and miserable.

Ila wants to live in the present and experience the world through the senses. When she visits India, she insists that Robi and the narrator go with her to a bar for a drink. They reluctantly accompany her. But when Robi does not let her dance with a stranger, she is bitter and expresses her extreme disgust at the conservative nature of Indian society. Neither in India nor abroad does Ila show her awareness of the *bhadralok* lifestyle of modern Bengal, which is essentially a mix of 'modernity' and 'tradition' — the outward mannerisms of western speech and dress coexisting in complete harmony with orthodox basic concerns of family life and morality.

As an adult, Ila gives the impression of being a drifter, not quite sure about what she wants. Before her marriage, she lives with a group of youngsters who specialize in organizing pickets. They were very 'practical' (97) — for hours they argue about which kind of pen was better for drawing posters or they discuss how to go about making arrangements for lunch or tea. There were no political debates and it did not take the narrator long to observe that Ila was regarded as a kind of guest, almost a decoration. But Ila thought that she was politically committed. This superficial behavior she had displayed even as a child when she could associate Cairo only with the location of the 'Ladies' at the airport. No wonder, if Tridib said of her that even though she had lived in so many places all over the world, she had not really travelled.

Ila is unwilling to accept India as her home, as she has never really lived there and cannot identify herself with its culture. She also knows that her adopted country is not keen to accept her. She is an alien, an outsider and the desire for acceptance produces tension in her. Eventually, in her effort to establish her roots in the West, she marries Nick, an Englishman. He is disloyal to her soon after, yet much against her wish, she decides to shrug off his waywardness and stay in England and continue to be his wife.

Ila's disillusionment brings into focus the strengths and limitations of the two cultures. Ila finds Indian culture too restrictive, too conservative. But in India, generally speaking, institutions like marriage are considered stable. Ila rejects everything Indian, but eventually she finds herself 'clinging' to her uncle Robi and the narrator — the members of her family from India who have shared a common loss, the death of Tridib.

Ghosh does not project a society as superior to another society. What he does highlight, however, is the problem of freedom for the modern man. Ila's fight is against the traditions and restraints of a traditional society. She feels she would gain freedom and identity if she combats such forms of power. She fails to realize that the old forms of restraint are being replaced by new form of restraint, which warp one's personality. The sanctity of the man-woman relationship in a marriage is essential to the old order. In the pursuit of a new kind of freedom — one that would enable her to realize her true self, Ila is confronted with a different set of problems: the absence of fidelity and trust in her marriage.

As for Tridib's sense of freedom, we may mention that he wanted to meet May, who had come all the way from England, as a stranger, far from friends and relatives, in a place 'without a past, without history, free, really free, two people coming together with the utter freedom of strangers' (144). For a relationship to develop between two people, they must go beyond the limitations of the individual self, he believed.

Tridib tells the narrator 'one could never know anything except through desire, real desire, which was not the same thing as greed or lust; a pure, painful and primitive desire' (29). Undoubtedly, May too believes in this. Tridib was eight and May was a little baby when Tridib went to England. When they meet as adults for the first time in India, she is nineteen and he is twenty-seven. Before that they had corresponded with each other for a few years. When May finally visits India, Tridib is, for all practical purposes, a stranger to her. Yet, when they first meet at the railway station, they behave as if they have been close for years and in love.

Tridib had talked of going 'to a place where there was no border between oneself and one's image in the mirror' (29). This is a transcendental view, which closes the gap between imagination and reality. Only such a man reaches forth to others.

It is tragic that Tridib could realize his dream only in death. He tries to save a helpless old man from being attacked by a frenzied mob. He must have known in that movement that he was not going to come back alive. But it was in that moment when the border between 'oneself and one's image in the mirror' had ceased to exist for him. It was his final redemption.

Tridib had lived believing in an ideal world and remained within the confines of his room at Ballygunge Place or in ruins. He wanted to carry the limits of his mind 'to other times and other places [...]' (144) away from the crowd of friends, relatives and strangers — a world that was divided by rifts of all kinds. As such a world could not be avoided, he had to die the death of a martyr.

For May, her Indian experience haunts her for the rest of her life. 'Do you think I killed him?' (251), she asks the narrator. She finally gets a glimpse of the 'final redemptive mystery.' 'He gave himself up; it was a sacrifice' (251-52) and is at peace with herself. Till the time she understands the nature of his 'sacrifice' she is a tortured being who spends almost seventeen years of her adult life trying to understand *why* Tridib had died. She knows that if she had gone out to save Jethamoshai, the crowd would have melted away on seeing her, she being a young

English girl. At that crucial moment, it was she who had goaded Tridib to go and help. She had no other motive except to save the life of the old man and the rickshaw-puller. She did not realize that she was virtually sending Tridib towards his death. It is this guilt which haunts her. So traumatized is she that she is scared to be alone. The moment she enters her room in England lights switch on by themselves and the television automatically starts functioning. May feels 'free' when she gets an insight into the mystery of Tridib's death.

Ghosh probes the various facets of violence and how it masquerades as freedom. Violence runs as an undercurrent throughout the novel. It is explored at both the personal and the social level, as Ghosh investigates the complex connection between freedom and violence in our lives. Can one really be free? Does one have to kill to get freedom or to preserve it? How does violence enter our lives? Can there be violence, on the psychological level, even when there is no physical abuse, in a relationship between a man and a woman? These questions need to be answered.

Through Ila, Ghosh explores two kinds of violence. In peacetime England, an English girl attacks Ila after school hours. No one from her school comes to her rescue, and Nick rushes home early that day to avoid being seen in her company. Ila's knowledge of the English language is superior to that of the native schoolgirl's English. 'Well, Denise, perhaps you ought to take English lessons from *her*, even though it's your own language, not hers' (74), the teacher had remarked, when Denise was unable to write a simple sentence correctly. There are undertones of envy, racial hatred and the fear of the ascendancy of the 'other' in the attack that follows.

It is curious that when Ila's grandmother Mayadebi was in England during the Second World War, she had received warmth and friendship from everyone in war-torn London. There was 'a kind of exhilaration in the air,' a bond even between strangers, and people went out of their way to be 'friendlier' and 'nicer' and actually to be 'civil' (66) to each other. Mayadebi is impressed by this kindness and civility and says, 'I couldn't have chosen any better time to come to England [...] I've been able to watch England coming alive' (66). The enemy could be identified — it was Germany. Perhaps the fear of the *London Blitz* made the colour of one's skin of no consequence. When the fear and the danger of the war disappeared, the bestial nature of man surfaced once again. Ila, in peacetime England, realizes that her dark skin makes her vulnerable to racial attack.

There is another kind of violence that is not physical but psychological, normally seen in a relationship that has gone sour. This violence is not visible, it is subtle and soul-destroying and leaves behind it emotional and mental scars. Nick acquires sundry girl friends for the sake of 'variety' (188) after his marriage to Ila. Nick has no job, as no job is good enough for him. The couple lives in an apartment bought by Ila's father and he lives off her salary. Perhaps the best way Nick could establish his power over Ila is by being unfaithful to her. He knows she loves him and will never leave him even if he allows girls from a 'massage parlour from Bangkok' in their house (189). She hits back in the only way that she knows — by taunting him for living off her father's wealth. To humiliate him, she sarcastically says, in front of others that Nick meant to get into a partnership in a warehousing business. The narrator reports:

> She gave him a long look, her face going hard in a way I had never before noticed in her. Of course, she said, it takes hard work to make a success of a thing like that, and Nick, well [...] Nick's face crumpled, and he looked down at the carpet, hanging his head (189).

This marital violence, purely on the emotional level, is a sad reflection on the marriages of Indian Diaspora. The cultural pulls and the stringent economic demands of the present-day world reduce many marriages into strained relationships.

While exploring the genesis of violence on the social level, Ghosh reveals that sometimes, the seeds of discord are sown, unconsciously, in the minds of the children by the parents themselves. In early January 1964, when the narrator as a young boy catches the bus to school, he notices that there were only a few boys, all sitting huddled together at the back of the bus. In a 'tearful, sing-song sound' (which the narrator can 'still remember' as an adult), a boy tells him that his mother did not let him drink any water that morning because she had 'heard that they had poured poison into Tala tank, that the whole of Calcutta's water supply was poisoned' (199). There was no need to ask any questions. All the children knew who 'they' were. 'It was a reality that existed only in the saying, so when you heard it said, it did not matter whether you believed it or not [...] it only mattered that it had been said at all' (200).

The narrator is then accused of being a friend of the 'enemy.' His friend Montu is a Muslim. He saves his skin by lying. 'I haven't met Montu for months' (200) and he is once again included as being 'one of us.' A hollow relief follows denial and betrayal. 'I was very glad he hadn't come,' (200) says the narrator, spared as he is of any further embarrassment. As lines are drawn up to divide the society on purely religious lines, it is but natural that distrust, dissension and violence should vitiate the environment. There is no realization on the part of the narrator that he had betrayed his friend, no feeling of guilt, only relief that he belonged to the majority community. Just as, perhaps, Nick had felt when he ran home from school knowing that Ila would be attacked by a fellow English girl, he did not want to get embroiled in the quarrel, or even get noticed in her company.

Ghosh believes that the atmosphere of violence created by religious fundamentalism in India is chilling and fearful. When the 'enemy' is identified not as an outsider but as one living within one's own country, then the country can only be seen as going downhill.

We see such violence and chaos through the eyes of the uncomprehending, innocent children. Religious riots suddenly break out in Calcutta in free India. In their classroom, the children find it difficult to concentrate upon their lessons. Voices could be heard outside the window, quite different from the orderly roar of a demonstration.

> A shout followed by another and another, in a jaggedly random succession, and then, suddenly, silence, and just when they seemed to have died away, there they were, one voice, followed by a dozen, and then again a moment of silence (201).

The lines communicate the intense fear, the absolute terror. As the children hear the 'uniquely frightening [...] not elemental, not powerful [...] rather, a torn, ragged (sound)' outside, a child asks, 'Wonder who's batting?' (202) India was playing a Test match with England at Madras on that day. To the child, the cricket match at Madras and all the excitement associated with it was the sane world, the world he would rather belong to than the disordered world outside his classroom.

The children are caught in the middle of a communal violence on their way home from school. Ghosh does not describe the scene outside the school like a voyeur (the shops were shut, the streets were empty, the policemen were patrolling the streets) but to bring home the utter senselessness, the sheer insanity of mob fury. A group of boys on Park Street start racing after the bus. The children duck under their seats as stones are pelted against the windows. The bus picks up speed and leaves the attackers behind. 'When we got up and looked back, some of them were laughing, with their arms around each other's shoulders' (203).

The children are stupefied with fear as the world becomes disarranged before them. They realize that normalcy is 'utterly contingent' and that the street that one resides in may suddenly without any warning become dangerous and hostile any moment. As Ghosh states:

> It is this that sets apart the thousand million people who inhabit the subcontinent from the rest of the world — not language, not food, not music — it is the special quality of loneliness that grows out of the fear of the war between oneself and one's image in the mirror (204).

Ghosh makes his final statement on violence while recounting the events leading up to the killing of Tridib, Jethamoshai and Khalil, the rickshaw-puller. The following song of John Lennon written in 1975 that stirred a generation might have inspired Amitav Ghosh, when he created the character of Tridib.

> *Imagine there's no countries*
> *It isn't hard to do*
> *Nothing to kill or die for*

And no religion too.
Imagine all the people
Living life in peace [...]
Imagine no possessions
I wonder if you can
No need for greed or hunger
A brotherhood of man
Imagine all the people
Sharing all the world [...]

Tridib, too, had dreamt of 'a better place, a place without borders and countries' (186). He was happiest in neutral, impersonal places — coffee houses, street corners — as though he did not seem to want to get too close to the people he associated with. A few weeks before his most tragic death at the hands of a mob in Dhaka, May sees an injured dog by the roadside and threatens to jump out of the moving car to come to its aid. 'Let it be, May,' Tridib pleaded. 'There's nothing we can do.' But May is shocked at his passivity. 'Can't you help a bit? she said. All you're good for is words. Can't you ever *do* anything?' (173). He assists in putting to death an already dying dog, to relieve it of its pain.

This scene is replicated as a mirror image in the last scene at Jindabahar Lane. When the dog had been put to death Tridib had told May that she should not hesitate to do the same for him if he were dying. When his time to die actually arrived, May, unintentionally, contributes to his death. There are too many ironies here — the ladies had gone to bring Jethamoshai 'home' from an alien country when, as far as he is concerned, he is already at home. He is looked after by a Muslim rickshaw-puller, who really cares for him and loves him and looks after him. Their tender, endearing relationship is symbolic of the possibility of Hindu-Muslim amity in spite of the political divide. In his younger days, Jethamoshai would not have tolerated the shadow of a Muslim anywhere near him. Now he trusts no one, but Khalil.

The rescue mission turns tragic as Khalil, Jethamoshai and Tridib are killed by a frenzied mob. The shadow of this tragedy casts a gloom on all the characters in the novel for the rest of their lives. Robi, who was always keen to know what 'trouble' means, now finds himself troubled. He experiences a nightmare periodically. And May remains haunted by her earlier utterance: 'Can't you ever *do* anything?'

Tridib had gone on the trip to Dhaka merely because he wanted to be with May. May's visit to India was planned, not her trip to Dhaka. The rescue mission had gone to Jindabahar Lane after a chance acquaintance of Tha'mma had informed her that her uncle was alive and living in Dhaka. Again, it is a sheer chance that her brother-in-law, the Shaheb, is posted to Dhaka as a Councillor.

Further, there is no connection between Tridib, May and Tha'mma getting together in Calcutta to set off for Dhaka in early January 1964 and the incident of the theft of the Prophet's hair at the Hazratbal mosque in Srinagar. Yet Ghosh shows how these unconnected incidents across space and time get linked in the most haunting way.

The tragedy of Tridib is the central focus of the novel. His presence and his absence haunt the reader from the first page till the end when the mystery of his death gets unfolded. The absence of Tridib (and the violent manner of his death) is like an unexpressed sorrow, a silent pain, and a suppressed sob. When, finally, Ghosh talks about the killing of Tridib, violence is foregrounded, and we see the helplessness of the individual in the face of collective frenzy.

The novel shows how futile it is to draw lines and to expect people to stay within neatly drawn religious boundaries; and it shows that there is a thin line between life and death, unless we value life and care. The novel raises many political and ethical questions but over and above, there is hope. The tenderness and concern that the narrator feels for Tridib, Ila and his grandmother; the strength of the narrator's mother and her loving and caring attitude, the bonding and the affection between the Prices and the Datta-Chaudhris — these vignettes of hope and love endure throughout the novel.

Notes and References

1. Meenakshi Mukherjee, "Of Love, War and Empire," *The Hindu*, October 1, 2000.
2. Amitav Ghosh, "India's Search for Identity," *Times of India*, Sunday, December 30, 1990: 11.
3. Ritu Menon and Kamla Bhasin, "Recovery, Rupture, Resistance: Indian State and Abduction of Women During Partition," in *Economic and Political Weekly*, 28, no. 17 (April 24, 1993): ws2.
4. Amitav Ghosh, *The Shadow Lines* (OUP, 1998).
5. For example, Santi and Suniti, two schoolgirls from Comilla, shot Magistrate Stevens to death in December 1931. In February 1932, Bina Das attempted to shoot the Governor of Bengal at the Calcutta University Convocation. In September 1932, Pritilata Waddedar, a Chittagong schoolteacher led fifteen men in a raid on the Chittagong Club. After injuring at least ten persons and killing one elderly European woman, Pritilata swallowed poison and died near the club.

6

Time and Space in *The Shadow Lines*

ARVIND CHOWDHARY

Time and space are two essential elements of Amitav Ghosh's *The Shadow Lines*. In this essay, I shall try to investigate the nature of these elements; how they are created, and to what purpose.

I

As Ghosh's novel is located in a subjective consciousness, he rightly strikes a balance between time experienced subjectively and mechanical or scientific time. (Natural time, expressed in the form of the passing of seasons, the organic rhythms of growth and decay, etc. is conspicuously absent in his novel). It is a right kind of combination which allows Ghosh to locate his novel in a historical and geographical reality, and at the same time feel and understand with Auden that

> All our intuitions mock
> The formal logic of the clock.[1]

In other words, it lets him become aware of the richness of subjective experience, and enables him to weave and interweave a piece of 'virtual life' or 'virtual experience,'[2] which is liberated from time by memory and imagination.

II

E.M. Forster, while talking of the importance of the mechanical or clock-time, says that it is possible to deny time in

I am thankful to Dr. Ranjan K. Ghosh for initiating me into the topic of time and space, and to Dr. Udaya Kumar for critically evaluating the finished article.

our lives, 'but it is never possible for a novelist to deny time inside the fabric of his novel: he must cling, however lightly to the thread of his story, he must touch the interminable tapeworm, otherwise he becomes unintelligible [...].'[3] As a matter of fact, allegiance to 'life in time' or chronometrical time is inescapable, as the basis of all the novels is a story, and 'a story is a narrative of events arranged in time sequence.'[4] Taken in this light, Ghosh in *The Shadow Lines* clings tenaciously to his story. It has a narrative which spans from 1939 to 1979, or even beyond. If we go strictly in terms of the clock-time, it begins in 1925. 'My father was born in Mandalay, in 1925. My grandmother used to take him back to Dhaka every year for a couple of months to stay with her parents' (124). But as a memory novel this is how it begins: 'In 1939, thirteen years before I was born, my father's aunt, Mayadebi, went to England with her husband and her son, Tridib.' It was a historically significant moment when the Second World War ravaged England. The novel, naturally, relates Tridib's boyhood experiences in wartime London. This may well be considered as the chronological beginning point of the novel. But it is a mistake to think that the novel 'ends essentially in 1964 with the eruption of a cycle of violence in India and Pakistan,'[5] when Tridib, too, was killed. The narrative ends when May has an insight into her tragic situation, in the form of an epiphany:

> For years I was arrogant enough to think I owed him his life. But I know now I didn't kill him; I couldn't have, if I'd wanted. He gave himself up; it was a sacrifice. I know I can't understand it, I know I mustn't try, for any real sacrifice is a mystery [...].

There is enough textual evidence to support the fact that May experienced her epiphany in September, October 1979, which can be taken as the other end-point of the novel's[6] action.

III

But it does not mean that all the important and not-so-important happenings and events of the intervening period between the two end-points have been recorded in the novel.

For such a record of times, we have to turn to history books and chronicles, where facts of all kinds are presented in a chronological order. Ghosh selects and organises only such material from history as serves his artistic purpose: which is to create a post-partition traumatic experience, in terms of the death of the narrator's mentor, Tridib, in a race riot — with life in England serving as its background, and life in India and East Pakistan, mainly, serving as its centrestage and foreground, simultaneously. It is this very painful and tragic experience which colours and affects the personal and social lives of the characters — notably, of May, Robi, the narrator and the grandmother. And those who are not immediately affected by his death, say, Ila, serve as a foil to that extraordinary character. Even the times, which Tridib spent in England and India, get interwoven into the fabric of the novel. They enter the novel as the recollections of the narrator and the other characters, of the close conversations they had with Tridib and the photographs he had shown them of England's finest hour.

This 'experiential life' is what Susanne Langer calls the 'virtual life,' which is 'the primary illusion'[7] of all literary art. It may be created out of personal or collective memory (as is the case in Ghosh's novel), or out of imagination, but what is important about such life is, that it is presented 'in the mode typified by memory,'[8] the mode of completed experience or of the past. That should explain why the normal tense of literary narration is the past tense,[9] says Langer; and so it is of Ghosh's novel for the most part. But Ghosh also uses the present tense to create certain experiences, which seem to emerge with a completely unchronological freshness, as if they happened 'now.' Take for instance, Robi's vivid and detailed account of his dream regarding his brother's killing by a rioting mob, as told to the narrator and Ila. Though Robi has been experiencing the dream almost periodically, it has not lost the immediacy of an intense experience, and is rightly narrated in the present tense. As against this, May's short but vivid account of Tridib's death appears in the past tense. Both the instances demonstrate literary uses of tense[10] to create a completely experienced reality.

The 'virtual life' is composed of such emotionally significant events. It is 'always a self-contained form, a unit of experience, in which every element is organically related to every other.'[11] Though memory is a great organiser of consciousness, and as Whitehead says, it is something 'formed and fixed,' yet it lacks the 'unity' of the 'virtual past' or 'virtual memory,' which is created through the fabric of a literary piece. The past which literature engenders is 'experiential through and through,' whereas, there are 'non-experiential' factors in our experience of actual past.[12] The whole point and purpose of this little discussion is to indicate that, whereas our apprehensions of time and space and the forces that we encounter and contend with, are vague and fragmentary, the 'life' that is created in a literary piece is much more evaluated and perceivable.

The details in Ghosh's novel are organically inter-related, so that they get inextricably blended with the rest of the novel. In the light of this, I may, now, briefly, comment upon the beginning and the ending of the novel. When Tridib went to England in 1939, accompanied by his parents, it was a significant event in the sense that we are not allowed to forget it in the novel. England then was witnessing its finest hour. Even though it was war-affected, 'people were becoming friendlier,' Mayadebi noticed. It is a created element because its atmosphere, *i.e.*, 'England coming alive' (66) is contrasted with the 'euphoria' that had died down as they painfully realised that the Chinese army had driven the Indian army back (220). Similarly, it can be established through analysis, that the ending — which is 'the intense moment of personal experience' in which ordinary time is transcended, is inevitable, as it is closely related to other details in the novel. Such cohesiveness of events one can find in all successful fiction — certainly not in actual life, even in personal history or actual memory.[13]

Let me now come to 'the sense of time,' which the novel creates as 'the secondary illusion.' This unique literary phenomenon has been pointed out by Clive Bell in the context of Proust's famous novel, '*A la Recherche du Temps Perdu.*' Commenting upon the form of his novel, Bell says: 'Proust tries our patience so long as we expect history to more forward: that not being the direction in which it is intended to move [...]. It is in states, not action that he deals. The movement is that of an expanding flower or insect [...]. Proust does not get forward, we complain. Why should he? Is there no other development in the universe?'[14]

Though comparisons are odious, and we cannot and should not place Ghosh in the same category as Proust, still this criticism of Proust's novel can be extended to Ghosh's novel as well, without much reservation. Ghosh's narrative deals in states, primarily, and not action; it does not move forward much. We may say that, essentially, it moves in and around the past.

Returning to Proust, Susanne Langer comments upon this aspect of his literary merit thus. She says, 'Proust's notable trait is his feeling for time; time is not something he mentions, but something he creates for one's direct perception. It is a secondary illusion in his writings as space is in music [...].'[15]

Ghosh's *'The Shadow Lines,'* largely, measures up to this criticism. His characters exist in time, and in time they grow and develop; and the situations also unfold themselves in time. I may illustrate this with an example from the novel. Nick, for instance, grows and develops in the narrator's imagination over a period of time, in the past. All that the narrator's father could tell him was that Nick wanted to be like his grandfather Tresawsen. Subsequently, on the basis of what Tridib told him about Tresawsen, the narrator could conjecture that Nick, like his grandfather, wanted to travel around the world, 'to live in faraway places halfway round the globe, to walk through the streets of La Paz and Cairo.' Since the narrator himself wanted to travel around the world, he went on to think that he had found in Nick 'the kindred spirit' he had not been able to find among his friends (52). Thereafter, he learnt from Ila that Nick was bigger and better and in some ways more desirable'; and he believed Ila when she said: 'Nick looks sweet when his hair falls over his eyes; everyone says so' (50).

The narrator continued to cherish this image of Nick for three years before May shocked him with the true account of her brother: True, Nick's straw-coloured hair fell over his eyes, but he did not want to travel like his grandfather; he simply planned to become a chartered accountant; and that Nick was not considerate or helpful to Ila when they studied in the same school in London. Rather, 'he was ashamed to be seen by his friends, walking home with an Indian' (76). In brief, what the narrator learnt from May was that Nick was not at all like them. And when the narrator met him seventeen years later, he noticed that 'most of his breadth lay in the thickness of his overcoat and that his head reached no higher up Robi's shoulder than did mine; and that 'he looked older than he thought.' It makes sense when the narrator told Nick: 'I'm not meeting you for the first time; I've grown up with you' (55).

IV

That brings us to the question of time-shift in Ghosh's novel. It is curious that the narrator undertakes a back and forth mental journey in time, and quickly reaches the other end of the time-span of the novel — touching upon few significant events of the period — in the course of the first ten pages of the novel. We may complain that Ghosh takes a frequent recourse to time-shift, or that the management of time in his novel is apparently wanton and arbitrary. But time-shift is a very useful technique which allows Ghosh 'to make connections of causality and irony between widely separated events.'[16] By way of illustration, we may mention two remote but closely connected events in the novel, namely, 'the made-up story' told by Tridib to his acquaintances at the street-corner *addas*, and the other incident being the narrator taking a special note of a particular picture of May, a copy of which she was privileged to send to Tridib. Now, in the light of the later incident, the 'fictitious' story sounds essentially true — Tridib loved May; they had exchanged photographs; and were he not killed in a race riot he could have had English connections through his marriage with May.

According to David Lodge, 'Time-shift is a very common effect in modern fiction, but usually it is naturalized, as the operation of memory, either in the representation of a character's stream-of-consciousness [...] or more formally, as the memoir or reminiscence of a character narrator [...].'[17] In *The Shadow Lines*, memory manifests itself, essentially, in the form of a memoir or reminiscence — based on the narrator's own recollection of events, and his reporting of the other character's memories, though there are few representations of the narrator's or the other character's stream-of-consciousness as well in the novel. Take for instance, his reporting of an incident narrated by his grandmother, which related to her sister, Mayadebi. Mayadebi, we are told, had worked herself into a terrible panic because her son had chosen to fight a bully at the school. But that was how Mayadebi behaved even when they were students, she had told the narrator; and by sheer association of memory, the grandmother went on to recall a boy who had been with her in college in Dhaka: 'The shy bearded boy' who, it was discovered, had been a member of one of the secret terrorist societies since he was fourteen. He was, subsequently, arrested, tried and later deported to the infamous Cellular Gaol in the Andaman Islands. (Now, this is clearly an instance of a stream-of-consciousness in the novel, representing the grandmother's state of mind at a particular point of time, as reported by the narrator). After 'straying' into the memory lane for a while, the grandmother told the narrator, that after that incident whenever she and Mayadebi happened to walk past the *gali* in which the boy lived, and she would point out to it and tell the story, Maya would feel frightened every time. It is interesting to note that the narrative recoils from the idea of Maya being a fearful, timid person to involve itself again with the boy from the terrorist society — this time, in the form of a reverie: 'If only she had known, if only she had been working with him, she would have warned him somehow, she would have saved him [...]' (39).

V

Miriam Allott points out that when modern novelists resort to innovatory devices such as the abandonment of chronological sequence and the stream-of-consciousness method, their objective is to throw into relief those moments of heightened consciousness, called 'epiphanies,' 'which seem to take place in a dimension outside the time registered by the clock on the wall.'[18] Ghosh's *The Shadow Lines* has two such timeless moments. One is, when the narrator perceives that the places called Dhaka and Calcutta 'were more closely bound to each other after they had drawn their lines,' so much so that 'each city was the inverted image of the other, locked into an irreversible symmetry by the line that was to set us free — our looking-glass border' (233). It is understood that these cities, lying in different nations, got 'bound' to each other through acts of violence, and through few humane acts of saving innocent lives. The other epiphany occurs at the end of the novel when the tyranny of time loses its hold upon May, and she is able to 'see' that Tridib 'gave himself up' or that he met a sacrificial death — a moment which she shares with the narrator. He too is glad to have a 'glimpse' into 'the redemptive mystery.' No satisfactory answers can be found for such sacrifices through intellection, but they redeem us. Such rare moments, truly, comprise 'life by values,' transcending 'life by the clock'; and they surely extend the boundaries of our emotional experience.

Critics and literary artists tell us that epiphanies emerge in the modern novels in response to 'the discordant age' in which we are living, and are inspired by the sense of 'the inseparableness of us from the past.'[19] One major discordance that is felt through the novel is violence masquerading as political freedom. Tridib was a victim of such violence. It took less than a moment for Tridib to be killed by the rioting mob. But like the 'sacred time' or cyclical time, the moment returns, though not so periodically. It was a moment, which was directly experienced by May, Robi, the grandmother and the others. All these characters re-experience it at different points of time. And it is imaginatively lived and experienced by the character-narrator, through the other character's painful reminiscences, and through his own determined effort to find meaning into it, and not let the significant moment 'vanish without trace.' It moves them, overwhelms them, and acts upon them. Take for instance, how adversely Robi is affected by it in a London restaurant:

> If freedom were possible, surely Tridib's death would have set me free. And yet, all it takes to set my hand shaking like a leaf, fifteen years later, thousands of miles away, at the other end of another continent, is a chance remark by a waiter in a restaurant (247).

VI

The shape and direction of the narrative of *The Shadow Lines* is largely determined by the memory of a traumatic experience of the past-partition era. The moment has the power to expand, and present itself as a rich experience to the consciousness. Ghosh recreates it, proportionately, by controlling the 'musical' or reading time[20] of the violent episode. The discrepancy between the 'contentual' and the reading time is quite obvious. In terms of time, it is less than a moment, but it has been dealt with in quite a few pages, and there are scores of pages devoted to its victim Tridib, and the times in which he lived. As against this, the narrative relating to the grandmother's married life of twelve years is foreshortened to just one page. We may say that as a literary artist, Ghosh 'gives the image and sense of certain things while keeping them subordinate to his plan, keeping them in relation to matters immediate and apparent, to give all the sense, in a word, without all the substance [...].'[21]

VII

Returning to the clock-time, I shall briefly, examine here how Ghosh pays his allegiance to 'The Father Time' in *The Shadow Lines*. His novel specifically mentions particular dates for the major events in his characters' lives: 'the narrator's father was born in Mandalay, in 1925; in 1935, the narrator's grandfather caught a chill while supervising the construction of culvert somewhere in the Arakan Hills and died of pneumonia; in 1939, the narrator's father's aunt Mayadebi proceeded to England, accompanied by her husband and her son Tridib; Tridib's ninth birthday fell on the 25th of September, 1940; in 1947, came partition, and Dhaka became the capital of East Pakistan; in 1959, when Tridib was twenty-seven and May nineteen. They had begun a long correspondence; 1962 was an exciting year for the narrator and his family, as his father became General Manager of his firm; on 27 December, 1963, two hundred and sixty-three years after it had been brought to Kashmir, the Mu-i-Mubarak disappeared from its place in the Hazratbal mosque; by the end of January 1964 the riots had faded away from the pages of the newspapers; one day in the year 1965, more than one and a half years after her trip to Dhaka, the grandmother gave away the chain her husband had given her, to the war fund; the narrator went to England on a year's research grant from September 1978-September 1979 to collect material from the India Office Library ; one afternoon in 1979, soon after the narrator began work on his Ph.D., he went to attend a lecture in the Teen Murti House Library, where the speaker 'jogged' his and his friend's memories of India's war with China in 1962, and a discussion on the significance of that war, imperceptibly and suddenly, brought to his mind the no-less significant riots of 1964.

The above-listed mechanical time and the events in it clearly indicate that Ghosh is not afraid of a chasm in his created piece of 'history.' It needs to be mentioned that these important dates, of personal and national history, ultimately, point to the vagaries of mind or 'experiential' reality. It is interesting to note that the events after 1964 are seldom specifically dated, but are recalled in terms of years. To take just one example, the narrator met May in London for the 2nd time *after seventeen years.* As for the ending of the novel, 'the intense moment of personal experience,' as it has already been pointed out, ordinary time is transcended.

Ghosh's vigilant care for chronological accuracy is evident in establishing the relative ages of his characters, in giving essential information about successive generations in two families (one British and the other Indian) and in some cases even telling us the days and years of their birth, marriage and death.

Succession, flux, change — are aspects of time; and as time does not have a spatial form, the novelist has to take recourse to indicating them through the description of a place. Sometimes a mere mention of a place, in relation to its past location, can indicate change of times. Thus, Gole Park was once considered to be outside Calcutta; it was a far-flung area; but, as the city has expanded, the area is no more regarded as such. The change is made much more apparent through the *description* of the place itself: Nathu Chaube's paan-shop at Gole Park, as a landmark, is still there, though Nathu Chaube has returned to Benares. But the area around the shop has changed. In the early sixties there were few cars in that area, and the narrator and his friends could play football on the streets, making way occasionally for bus number 9. But, presently, the area is so congested that one has to push through the throng of people, shoppers and traffic to make one's way.

VIII

As we know, time does not always flow uniformly: in excitement it seems to flow faster, in boredom it does not seem to flow at all. Ghosh has created such moments of experiential time in *The Shadow Lines*. For instance, 'The rehearsal seemed to go on for ever' for May at the Orchestra, when all that she wanted to do was to think about Tridib and his invitation for her to visit India. Another example is, when the narrator desperately wanting to communicate to May that he was coming for the dinner, 'hurled' himself down the stairs, 'burst' into the kitchen, and virtually 'snatched' the telephone out of somebody. His actions indicate that the time was running fast for him. But, then, the time seemed to have stopped suddenly, for he experienced as if 'an age seem to pass before I heard May's voice' (249). But the perfect example is, when the narrator's mother, in order to provide care and comfort to her exhausted husband at the end of a hectic day, modulates the volumes and harmonies of their house to a whisper, reminding us of a silent moment in a musical composition (127).

It is not merely that the characters experience time, they also talk about it. Thus, for the grandmother, 'time is not for wasting, it is for work,' and it grows 'mouldy' if it is not used. As Tridib does not use it properly, it 'stinks'[22] (4). But the narrator values the time spent with Tridib, as he had given him 'worlds to travel in' and 'eyes to see them with,' though Ila could not understand 'what those hours in Tridib's room had meant to him' (20). How could she when for her what mattered was the present?

> For Ila the current was the real: it was as though she lived in a present which was an air lock in a canal, shut away

> from the tide waters of the past and the future by steel floodgates (30).

As Ila chose to see as little as was necessary to carry on with the business of living; also because she did not 'invent' what she saw, the reality passed her by. Tridib, on the other hand, could experience the reality as concretely in his imagination as Ila did through her senses, more so if anything, since to him 'experiences were permanently available in memories' (30). Guided by Tridib's wisdom, namely, that 'we could not see without inventing what we saw' (31), the narrator could reconstruct imaginatively the Solent Road, as it was ravaged by the Second World War — an experience that was lost to posterity; also he could recreate the old Dhaka on the basis of the fond recollection of the times his grandmother had spent there, and what Robi had told him about the place. And inspired by the example of his mentor, Tridib, who could partake of all times and all places, the narrator could construct a moment, outside the realm of time and space:

> Those empty corners filled up with remembered forms, with the ghosts who had been handed down to me by time: the ghost of Snipe in that far corner, near his medicine chest, worrying about his dentures; the ghost of the eight-year-old Ila, sitting with me under that vast table in Raibajar. They were all around me, we were together at last, not ghosts at all: the ghostliness was merely the absence of time and distance, for that all that a ghost is, a presence displaced in time (181).

Such a conception of a moment, or better still 'mental space,' is *not* 'a far-reaching play of imagination,'[23] but is close to human reality, and bespeaks of the depth of experience. It complements the fictional time and space of the two stories that are inextricably blended into the structure of the novel.[24]

IX

That brings me to the point where I can talk of the treatment of space in *The Shadow Lines*. There are no 'neutral, impersonal places' as such in Amitav Ghosh's novel. Even coffeehouses, bars and street-corner *addas* assume a definite character. There are the places 'where people come, talk and go away without expecting to know each other any further' (9). Such places have their 'uses.' For instance, Tridib uses 'that conversation-loving stretch of road between Gariahat and Gole Park' to distract himself (8).

But 'places' are used in subtler ways in Ghosh's novel. For instance, they are used to reveal the personality or psyche of the characters. To illustrate, the eerie emptiness in May's life is reflected by the way she arranges her room: the light and sound of a television-set — which is kept on all the time, fill up the room, but it also indicates that there is something seriously amiss in her life; so do the cushions casually thrown on the floor (16). Surely, it did not look like a room where visitors were often expected. Tridib's room is equally uninviting, but it reflects intellectual taste: 'an oddly monastic room — a naked light bulb, stacks of books, piled up like newspapers, on the floor, a couple of mats and pillions strewn around [...]' (174). However, Mrs. Price's large and spacious room looks rich and 'crowded' with furniture and things.

That places are no neutral, objective entities, but are meant to be experienced, is stated succinctly by Tridib thus: 'a place does not merely exist,' but 'it has to be invented in one's imagination' (21). For Ila, a place merely 'exists,' and is no more than a utility — as is brought out by the narrator's apt observation regarding himself and Ila in this regard: whereas, the narrator longed to visit Cairo, to 'see' the world's pointed arch in the mosque of Ibn Tulun and 'touch' the stones of Great Pyramid of Cheops, the Ladies were 'the fixed points in the shifting landscapes' of Ila's childhood. To her Cairo was no more than 'a place to piss in' and the underground 'a means of shifting venue'! (20-21). No wonder, if Tridib thought Ila to be in some ways a very limited person: 'although she had lived in many places, she had not travelled at all' (21). Likewise, the narrator opined that 'the places went past Ila in an illusory whirl of movement like those studio screens in old films which flash past the windows of speeding cars' (23). Interestingly, Ila had 'invented' some cities on the world map for the narrator in a restricted, unimaginative way, 'not like those fairylands Tridib made up for you' (24).

But Tridib however, being an archaeologist would not be interested in fairylands. However, he wanted that people exercised their 'imagination with precision' (24) when it came to viewing places and things. Even Ila, under fear and apprehension, was forced to experience what it means to see a snake:

> [...] looking at the snake's head, she saw it more clearly than she'd ever seen anything before, with the telescopic clarity of absolute concentration. She could see its tiny eyes, the flaring nostrils at the end of the sharply pointed head, the tongue, no longer flickering drawn into the soft pink mouth in readiness, the fangs erect now, and dripping (27).

But, under normal circumstances, if Ila were to see the tail of a cat, she would think that she had seen it all, and shoo it away.

Using 'imagination with precision' did not merely mean looking at an object with full concentration, but, essentially, exploring its unrealised possibilities. Tridib had driven home this point to the young narrator thus:

> Did you notice that Ila's house had a sloping roof'? — Thereby he wanted him to imagine, 'what it would be like to live under a sloping roof — no place to fly kites, nowhere to hide when one wanted to sulk, nowhere to shout across to one's friends (29).

It is ironic that Ila, who looked for the world of 'here and now,' found herself a very little space in it, as is evidenced by the photographs she possessed of her school days. They revealed that she was either unaccountably absent in the pictures, or was inconspicuous in them (22).

And it was unfortunate that not being rooted in Indian culture, she could not understand the concept of a *veranda* — a place which connected one to the outside world. As against hers, Tridib's concept of space was vast and comprehensive. He once told the narrator that one could never know anything except through 'a pure, painful and primitive desire,' which meant that one strove beyond 'the limits of one's mind to other times and other places, and even, if one was lucky, to a place where there was no border between oneself and one's image in the mirror' (29). It was a kind of transcendental space, which partook of all times and all places — to which one could orient oneself, provided one desired keenly.

Ghosh also deals with mental spaces — which reflect the reality of our so-called real world. For instance, in the child Ila's conception, a house is incomplete if it does not have a 'baby' in it (71). However, 'a crazily tilted chest of drawers' would do for an office (72). But the adult mind looks at the world differently, as is borne out by the narrator's conception of it — the world, he realises to his chagrin, is too materialistic and pragmatic to accommodate the painful reality of his grandmother's death: 'She had always been too passionate a person to find a real place in my tidy late-bourgeois world, the world that I had inherited in which examinations were more important than death' (92). A similar mental space finds its expression through a vivid, descriptive account of the bleak, ghetto-like surroundings of his relative's dwelling, as seen from its long *veranda*-like corridor (23).

This perfect picture of penury and squalor 'invented by the narrator in his imagination, with its 'little clumps of shanties,' surrounded by sludge-choked pools, at the edges of which women washed utensils and scrubbed their children, and with figures dotted all over the slopes of a mound, picking up bits of rubble off it — was a 'landscape' which was palpably felt everywhere in their house. It was 'that landscape that lent the note of hysteria to my mother's voice when she drilled me for my examinations; it was to those slopes she pointed when she told me that if I didn't study hard I would end up there [...]' (133-34).

But Ghosh does not merely dabble in mental states; he associates places with actions of all kinds. Take for instance, Nick's pronouncement upon the life in Kuwait. 'There is nothing to do there,' he says, 'except drink and watch video films.' But, as May, rightly, points out to him, 'grandfather Tresawsen would have made a little more of Kuwait than you did' (58).

Ghosh is at his best for creating places, which are affected by violence, or even are remotely connected with it. Thus, a

3. E.M. Forster, *Aspects Of The Novel*, ed. Oliver Stallybrass (London: Penguin Books, 1990), First Published by Edward Arnold, 1927.
4. *Aspects of the Novel*, 44.
5. A.N. Kaul, "A Reading of *The Shadow Lines*" in Amitav Ghosh's, *The Shadow Lines*, Educational Edition (Delhi: OUP, 1988), 301.
6. It was the last day of the narrator's stay in England (247). He went to pay a visit to May in the evening before coming back to Delhi. (The narrator, we may recall, had gone to England on a year's research grant from September 1978 - September 1979 to collect material for his thesis from the India Office Library). This was his third visit to May during his stay in London.

   It may be noted that the narrator began work on his Ph.D. at the Teen Murti Library in late 1979 (219). It was sometime after this when he was able to establish a connection between the violent incidents in Dhaka with the Calcutta riots of 1964 and learn 'the meaning of distance' (218-33). It implies that this incident happened after the time of the actual end of the novel. This point of time, that is, late 1979 or even early 1980, is the chronological end-point of the novel.

'Primary' does not mean here first established, but *always* established. See Langer, *op. cit.*, 84.

Ibid. 264.

The normal tense of literary narration is the past tense. For a further discussion on this, see *Ibid.* 264.

bid. 266-68 for a detailed account of literary uses of the present nse.

id. 262.

id. 265.

d. 264-65.

l. 300.

l.

id Lodge, *The Art Of Fiction*, (Penguin Books) 75.

d Lodge, *op. cit.*, 77.

m Allott, *Novelists On The Novel*, 185.

185.

as Mann uses the terms 'musical' or reading time, and ntual' time, in the context of a novel. For a discussion of his ee Harvey, *op. cit.*, 107-8.

particular *gali* in Dhaka — where a boy who was a member of a secret terrorist society lived, frightens Mayadebi every time she passes beside it, and she holds on to her elder sister's hand and hurries past that *gali*. And then there is a space outside a school in Calcutta, which gets changed suddenly from its peaceful, environ to 'the authentic sound of chaos' as the rioters come rushing there baying for innocent lives. In the wake of the imminent violence, the streets get totally transformed. The school children realise on their way back home that

> [...] something on those streets had changed in the couple of hours since we had last driven through them: we saw that street twice everyday, but now it seemed unfamiliar. The pavements, usually thronged with vendors and passers-by, were easily empty now — except for squads of patrolling policemen. All the shops were shut even the *pan*-stalls at the corners: none of us had ever seen those shut before (202).

In one such street a rickshaw stood inclined at an angle, eloquent of an intent, which they could not fathom. Was it meant to keep Muslims in and Hindus out? Surely, they felt disoriented in such space. Such a traumatic experience, when recalled, could force one to think that 'the spaces that surround one, the streets that one inhabits can become suddenly and without warning, as hostile as a desert in a flash flood' (204).

Ghosh equally well treats a place, which is affected by domestic discords. It is that part of the 'huge, lop-sided, step-pyramid' like house where the narrator's grandmother lived, as a child along with her parent's sister, uncle, aunt and her three cousins. When the quarrels in the family persisted, it had to be divided to pathetic limits:

> [...] The two brothers, insisting on their rights with a lawyer-like precision, demanded that the division be exact down to the minutest detail. When the wall was eventually built, they found that it had ploughed right through a couple of door-ways so that one could get through them any more; it had also gone through a lavatory bisecting an old commode. The brothers even portioned their father's old nameplate.

> It was divided down the middle by a thin white line, and their names were inscribed on the two halves — of necessity in letters so tiny that nobody could read them (123).

Such family 'distances' do not ensure peace for the inhabitants of the house, rather they fill it up with 'eerie silence' and painful memories, so that even a well-meaning person like the narrator's grandmother would not like to visit it once she got married.

But rifts and distances, at the social and national levels, do not beget even uneasy solutions through the partition of the bigger nation-state, as violence does not get driven to the borders. The places called Dhaka and Calcutta, in the two independent states, do not drift apart and become the 'other' reality but flare up at the slightest pretext. The pattern of violence relates these places to each other as never before, so much so that each city was 'the inverted image of the other.' The narrator undertakes a voyage into this land, which exists 'outside space, an expanse without distances; a land of looking-glass events.' He is simply amazed to find that the border did not 'separate' these places, rather locked them into 'an irreversible symmetry,' as identical scenes of violence were witnessed on both sides, with few humane incidents of saving lives — that indicated a kind of 'indivisible sanity that binds people to each other independently of their governments.' The line acts like 'a looking-glass border' (233). The narrator's concept of distance, in terms of separateness, receives a severe jolt in the process. It was this irony that killed the protagonist of the novel, Tridib, and prompted the narrator to undertake this journey into the virtual space, and to learn a bewildering new meaning of distance. It is in the context of such space that the Middle English story narrated by Snipe to Tridib assumes importance — the sad story 'about a man without a country, who fell in love with a woman across — the seas.' The story could happen in any part of Europe, as Europe then was 'a place without borders and countries.' It is not as if the continent did not have distinct cultures, but then the entire land could partake of the essential reality. Tristan-and-Iseult story could happen everywhere. It will be erroneous to assume that Europe then had homogenous uniform space, but a space, which was not

divided and sub-divided by man-made borders and line
to this ideal space that the protagonist of the novel,
wanted to return in his personal life. He wanted to r
beloved, May, as a stranger, in a ruin. Rather, 'he want
to meet as the completest of strangers — strangers a
seas' in a ruin — which was a nearly-ideal place, 'with
without a history' — a place away from their rel
friends, and virtually transcending the profane time

As we know, Amitav Ghosh's novel weaves and
a 'spatial form,' through a pattern of interconn
such as nationalism, political freedom, personal
(This form can be perceived by 'reading over' or b
'spatial readings' of the novel.) Thus understo
associated with these motifs, get cohesively o
fabric of the novel, such that the places in En
kind of perspective to the places in Dhaka an

X

One interesting question, which we ask
protagonist of a novel, is the process of cha
decay) which he undergoes during the c
Surely, the character-narrator of Ghosh's
comes of age after his painstaking *a la*
perdu,[25] through memory and imaginati
himself with the world in which his me
died a sacrificial death in a riot, he mak
consciousness of the times and its mean
The traditional concepts of time an
terms of distances and divisions or b
the course of this journey into the p

Notes and References

1. W.H. Auden, *New Year Letter*, Lin
Faber, 1941). Cited by W.J. Harv
(London: Chatto and Windus, 196
2. For the concepts of 'virtual life' o
life,' see Susanne K. Langer, Cha
(London: Routledge and Kegan
212-13 and 291.

7.
8.
9.
10. I
11. Ib
12. Ib
13. Ibi
14. Ibi
15. Ibid
16. Dav
17. Dav
18. Miri
19. *Ibid.*
20. Thom
'conte
view,

21. Henry James' remarks in the *Preface to Roderic Hudson* (1876), included in the section on *Structural Problems* in Miriam Allott, *op. cit.*, 253.
22. Ironically, when grandmother retired, she had 'time — great livid gouts of it'; and it was stinking, 118.
23. A.N. Kaul, *op. cit.*, 304.
24. It refers to the love story of Tristan-and-Iseult and Magda/Ila episodes.
25. It translates as 'remembrance of things past' in English.

7

Tha' mma My Grandmother: Imaging The Elderly in Amitav Ghosh's *The Shadow Lines*

RUPALI SIRCAR

The theme of ageing is reflected in literature more often in two distinct ways: stories of the ageing other — parents, grandparents and elders in the community; and those of the ageing self — the female protagonist or the narrator or the writer as the subject. In the first instance, the speaker or the narrator is young or middle aged but has some compelling reason for observing elders or listening to their stories. In the second, ageing is something that is happening to the writer, the protagonist or the narrator. In portraying the ageing other, writers have demonstrated how by custom and convention the aged is often deprived of power and placed at the margin of society. Writers have also treated ageing characters as points of significant reference to their young protagonists. The young are seen to make journeys in search of their elders to see who they were, and who they are themselves. Such a search for formal identity, by reaching into the past of the elders has a special meaning for those writers whose cultural traditions may differ from the mainstream, such as African-American, Asian-American and Latina or for writers like Amitav Ghosh whose worlds of identity are demarcated for historical reasons by shadow lines. Thus the strategy of portraying elders helps to negotiate the treacherous currents of a pluralistic society. The figure of the grandmother, for instance, draws on a strong cultural tradition of reverence for elders. The aged also play an inspirational or redemptive role by rescuing the young protagonist from indecision or desperation, as we see in the bonding relationship between Tha'mma and the narrator of *The Shadow Lines*.

Silver-haired with a long nose 'my grandmother Tha'mma,' short for *thakuma* in Bangla, seems to dominate the pages of the novel by her very presence — moving between generations — represented by her grandparents, her parents, her's and her sibling Mayadebi's family, her son and daughter-in-law and her own grandson, whose myriad questions asked and unasked hang loose in her head for a very long time. This is a story of a family, of a people, of nations, of individuals with complex shadow-lined psyches. The narrative delineates the relationship between the child narrator and the grandmother who is always referred to as 'my grandmother.' She is an image of authority and control when we first meet her in the novel.

The child narrator images himself on Tridib, his father's cousin who Tha'mma does not approve of. 'He's a loafer and a wastrel,' she says. She refutes her grandson's assertion that he resembled Tridib.

> [...] my grandmother was quick to contradict me. She shook her head firmly, looking up from her school books and said: No, he looked completely different — not at all like you.[1]

The image quickly metamorphoses into a determining agent, a medium and a looking-glass through which the reader will witness the historical, the political, and the familial. Yet as in life so in literature the individual lives of the elderly are lost in a jungle of scholarly critical treatises. The elderly in *The Shadow Lines* are seen as icons and relics of a past, which is no longer relevant except as an ironical commentary on the present. They are mirages or shadows that appear and disappear, lengthen and shorten as time passes back and forth in this novel. They are 'set apart' in the same way as the 'thousand million people who inhabit the subcontinent from the rest of the world — by a special quality of loneliness that grows out of the fear of war between oneself and one's image in the mirror' (204). Their experiences are discounted through sentimentalizing gestures and their struggle is forgotten in the buzz of youthful voices. Grandmother Tha'mma is imaged as a decrepit nationalist hanging pathetically to nation and nationality:

> I could see that she was going to end up in a hopelessness — she'd not been able to quite understand how her place of birth had come to be so messily at odds with her nationality (152).

Her ageing is detailed in terms of disintegrating imagery, making her an unreliable chronicler. Her stubborn, 'No, this is not Dhaka' places her in a sepia-tinted twilight zone in which the elderly are allowed to live a somnambulistic life. In contrast, it is the daydreaming, sexually fantasizing Tridib who exerts a real influence on the narrator. It is like Tridib that he wants to be and it is in Tridib's stories that he longs to live. Grandmother's instincts tell her that Tridib is a 'loafer' and can cast a vicious influence upon her grandson. She has a similar bias towards the Shaheb whom she considers a drunkard, and she disapproves of Ila because she thinks that her liberal attitude is that of a prostitute's. She has hardly any sympathy for relatives who have fallen on bad days, simply because no one ever helped her in her days of struggle.

The other elderly characters in the novel, like grandmother, represent something other than themselves. Jethamoshai, the grandmother's parents and her aunts, Mayadebi and even Mrs. Price do not influence anybody or anything. Biologically trapped in ageing bodies, they are seen as spectators and their participation in the events is either ignored or made invisible. They are a finished force whose bodies are debilitating. There were raids all the time in the colleges and the university when the narrator's grandmother was a student. 'We'd grown up with it,' she says. Looking at the figure of his grandmother perched on an edge like 'a fragile porcelain bird as she recounted stories of those days of struggle for freedom,' he tries to fit her into that extraordinary history, with astonishment writ large on his face. The story of the quiet, non-descript young man who is imprisoned for subversive activities is reminiscent of Nadine Gordimer's, *My Son's Story*,[2] where the young fragile wife of a revolutionary is discovered by the police to be a terrorist/

freedom fighter, to the utter disbelief of her own husband. Tha'mma too would have acted like a revolutionary, if given a chance. Would she not have felt frightened while killing the magistrate, her grandson asks her. 'Yes. But I would have killed him. It was for our freedom: I would have done anything to be free' (39). The point, which the story is highlighting is, that she doesn't get her opportunity to kill the magistrate. The fact is that no one who lived in those times could remain a mere spectator.

Tha'mma is a woman like countless others who experienced displacement and dispossession, struggle and fear and witnessed violence in those horrific days, following the independence and the partition of the motherland. But now that she is sixty years old, she has ceased to be a person, she is a non-entity.

The grandmother whose name we do not know is treated like a child, the same way as the white colonial masters treated their black subjects — like the misguided children of a lesser god. Her expression: 'That's not what I meant' lacks the earlier confidence. As she is old and powerless now, her family members are kind to her but they do not take her seriously. She is considered a whimsical old person who must be kept in good humour and sometimes scolded like an errant child. Returning late from a walk in the park, she is scolded by her impatient son. He considers it unsafe for her to be out in the dark. Even the grandson feels compelled to warn her when she is travelling by the aeroplane, she must not roll down the windowpanes, or do a similar foolish thing. He, too, like his father, forgets that his Tha'mma has a Bachelor's degree in History and that till very recently she had been the Headmistress of a large girls' school; and that she had taught many children and read many books and travelled across national boundaries and lived through many monsoons.

> [...] Didn't he know she retorted that she hadn't been born yesterday?

Unfortunately, it is to this 'yesterday' that we see her lapsing into. A common image of an ageing woman. We are told that she accompanied her grandson when he went out to play cricket. There in the park she would often meet other elderly people and they all talked about the past. Her son asks her what she and her friends talked about, in the same way as she herself might have asked an erring schoolgirl about her ways. Prompt comes the answer: 'the past is what we talk about.' The elderly live in the past because they value the good old days when they were young. They are unable to live in the present because they are no longer young now and considered old and useless. The family is relieved that the old woman goes out and has found company. 'She had become easier to cope with now that she was going out of the house regularly and meeting people of her own age group' (27).

Sadly, the elderly people internalize such images. 'They are all dead, the people in 'the past' and I have nowhere to invent stories about and nowhere to escape to,' is how Tha'mma expresses her anguish.

In the house in Dhaka, four elderly persons, namely, Tha'mma's uncle and aunt, and her parents could not be made to 'forget the past.' The walls of the house contained decades of hostility and they liked the wall now, it had become a part of them. The past also held the 'best parts of their lives.' But for Tha'mma that was already over and the present held out no hope, no energy. The child narrator is acutely conscious of the passage of time and its effect on his grandmother, especially during the post-retirement period. 'In our old flat my grandmother had always been careful to maintain a titular control of running our household. Now she didn't seem to care' (120). A strange withdrawn creature sat staring out of the window — 'a shrunken fragile little figure, gazing out across the lake' (120). The words evoke pity and a sense of deep loss. The 'distracted' creature was a ghost from the past, and the child narrator feels frustrated at the disconnection with his Tha'mma.

It is at her retirement day farewell party that we get a glimpse of Tha'mma's public life. She had successfully completed twenty-seven years of teaching and had been the headmistress of her school for a decade. She had endeared herself to the staff and the students by her dedication and innovative methods of teaching. The local government authorities acknowledged her contribution to education and society. They sent her bouquets on the day of her retirement. She was excited about it all. We are told that her grandson did not know how to cope with the discovery that 'my right hand had been infringed by a whole school' (115) — an expression which brings out his right to love his grandmother exclusively. But very soon we see her acting like a senile dodo, ending up mixing names and saying atrociously inappropriate things and even making a girl cry, inadvertently. Already she has been relegated to the realm of senility — associated with ageing. Overnight, she turns into a nagging mother-in-law picking faults with her daughter-in-law's housework. Her paranoia expresses itself in an anxiety of losing her hair and turning bald. We see a ludicrous figure, sitting with enormous turban made out of a saree, staring statue like out of the window. A fearful apparition. Montu, her grandson's classmate, is mortally terrified. Embarrassment and fear of social ridicule make the narrator pose a hysterical question, 'What's happened to her head?'

'Plenty,' is what is implied; the laughter which accompanies the explanation is sufficient to establish the image of an old woman bereft of any productive work and slowly disintegrating. It is the 'head' that is affected. 'Soon her mind would wander off.' Withdrawn and forgetful, Tha'mma does not participate in any event in the household now. No longer, we are emphatically told, does she take interest in her son's promotion. 'My grandmother, who had always been quick to tell our relatives about every small sign of success in my father's career seemed hardly to notice this unforeseen spectacular advancement' (119). We are not told or given a hint as to why this active, confident and capable woman has all of a sudden turned into a jellyfish. 'My grandmother's placental presence was slowly withdrawing from the rest of the house and concentrating itself within the four walls of her room.' This mole-like life is the inevitable result of ageing!

But the grandmother is not a spent force. There are moments even at this stage of her life when she behaves like the earlier sprightly, youthful person that she was. 'Her eyes had lost none of their glitter nor her walk its old rhythm or energy' (119) but also the damning, 'there's something stirring in her head.

Hibernating in her own mind, 'my grandmother,' whose 'attention strayed,' who 'gazed out of the window,' who 'sat in a trance' had practically nothing to do. In a horrified yet censuring whisper we are told: 'I know what she had in her hands, Time — great livid gouts of it, I could smell it stinking' (118). Tha'mma's 'tyranny' is any day preferred to this slow decaying stink! Ironically, it is the grandmother herself who had hated the stink of wasted time. Unnerved by this putrefying, stagnating entity — which was once a living, breathing person with rhythm and energy, the desperate narrator uses 'ruses' and 'ploys' like 'spilling ink on my textbooks to keep her attention from straying.'

The child's relationship with the grandmother is a secret recognition of a mutual dependency and marginalisation. Nobody wants the grandmother, just as nobody wants a naughty cantankerous child. For that matter, old people and children are segregated from actual adult life. It was a 'relief' when she began to go to the park — it was easier to 'cope' with her — she must go away to Dhaka for a while — only then will the others get some 'rest.'

She is not allowed to do any housework. There is practically nothing for her to do. No books to read, no letters to write to, no friends to share one's thoughts with. The only activity that she could think of was to visit her old place of work and indulge in vicious staff-room gossip. Quite out of character for the former headmistress of a school! And then one day the new headmistress of the school phoned her son informing him that his mother was not welcome to the school. It is difficult for the reader to reconcile these pathetic images with the earlier empowering ones. We are not told why at sixty, Tha'mma is unable to take care of her life. She has been in charge of her life for such a long time. Tha'mma has gone through almost all of life's experiences — marriage, motherhood, euphoria of independence, the brutality of India's partition, displacement, widowhood, poverty, professional achievements and public accolade and the satisfaction of seeing one's grandson grow up.

The image of the elderly as portrayed in *The Shadow Lines* discounts their courage, their struggles and the sense of commitment that they had felt when they were young and continued to feel even as they grew old. They were the products of their times, and they had lived through those painful, unimaginable times with grit and determination. They, essentially, continued to preserve these attributes, even in old age. If dispossession of homeland did not fracture their lives, how could retirement or physical weakness affect their spirit?

The much-lauded symbolic relationship between the grandmother and the grandchild, on closer scrutiny, reveals a relationship, which is need-based. At first, it is the control and authority wielded by the older person due to economic status, experience and productivity which allows the child, himself a powerless dependent creature, to find refuge from the tyranny of direct parental authority. With the passage of time the roles enacted within the household change and there is a subtle erosion of the authority of the elderly Tha'mma, now that she does not have economic and physical status.

These changes affect the relationship of the elderly with the world outside as well as with the members of their family. This is clearly evident in *The Shadow Lines*, in the context of the elderly Tha'mma.

Her family does not even recognize the grandmother's anxiety associated with her visit to Dhaka at the invitation of the Shaheb and Mayadebi. 'I don't know if I should go [...]. I don't know, I feel scared. Do you think it will be wise after all these years? It won't be like home any more.' Wishfully thinking a relief from the old lady if she is not around, a condescending chorus of voices cajoles and coaxes her to go to Dhaka; she is offered a basket of tempting possibilities if she goes there.

'The cham-cham and all the other sweets will be the same, mother said encouragingly. And so will all the fish. And there will be lovely Dhakai sarees to buy [...] and imagine, my father said, you will get to fly in an aeroplane for the first time' (149). The voices are familial and their intimacy tempts her. Her real objective for her wanting to visit Dhaka is to bring back Jethamoshai. But it is ignored as a childish desire of an old person. She is 'stung' when her son suggests she better go, 'as it will be a good holiday for her.' '[...] It won't be for a holiday [...] if I go it will be for the sake of Jethamoshai.' She is focused about the objective of her visit. It is not going to be a nostalgia-inspired trip. She considers it her duty to bring the poor old man back. Tha'mma's unconscious empathy with the old man is an attempt to establish a kind of comradeship with the elderly person. 'Poor old man — to die in another country abandoned and alone in your old age.' It is only the voice of her sibling, Mayadebi, on a long distance call, which finally dispels her doubts and anxieties and fills her with a vigour and determination. Thereafter the rejuvenated Tha'mma sees herself as a young person on a mission to rescue an old man. This is the secret of her newfound vigour.

The narrator's overpowering concern for the grandmother, which seeps into the capillaries of the narrative ends up trivializing her genuine concern for her uncle. 'Her eyes got misty at the thought of rescuing her uncle from his enemies and bringing him back where he belongs, to her *invented country*' (Italics mine) (137). Although Jethamoshai later declares that he does not believe in 'India Shindia,' the truth of the matter is that his disbelieving will not make it disappear. The partition of the subcontinent was a reality, and not a piece of fiction. It is obvious that growing old has not affected Tha'mma's mind. She is not keen to prolong or nurture old family feuds, least of all hostility towards Jethamoshai, but that is because it was all between their parents, and she and Mayadebi had nothing to do with it. The moment she hears he is alive, she is determined to somehow get him across. 'There's only one worth-while thing left for me to do in my life,' she announces. 'And that is to bring the old man home [...].' The self-knowledge that she is the only one to care for her old uncle propels her into action. Her passivity forgotten, she gears herself to leave for Dhaka. The earlier 'I don't care' is replaced with 'since I am the only one who cares.' 'I don't care' was both an act of defiance as well as of surrender and defeat.

'Later that evening she announced that she wanted me to spend the night in her room [...]. I was hoping she would ask me.' The connection with the child is renewed. A deep sense of empathy and need is forged. In contrast, at the airport her family expresses a sigh of relief. The oppressive presence of the elderly is closely observed and recorded by the narrator. 'My mother allowed herself at last to breathe a long deep sigh of relief—till then she had not really believed that my grandmother had really gone [...].'

Once free of the perpetrators of her passivity, Tha'mma is imaged in her youthfulness — 'giggling like a school girl,' she is transformed like the aeroplane, its 'gracelessness was gone; the power of the engines had given [...] the lean, muscular tautness of the neck of a heron in full flight [...] riding the sky.'

'Where is Dhaka? I don't see Dhaka' is not, as we would like to believe, a crazed query by an old woman who has lost her bearings. The question is pregnant with a heightened expectation of a traveller returning to a once beloved place. It is in a manner of speaking an acknowledgment that the intervening decades would have changed the skyline. It is also the recognition that a city where you have lived out your growing-up days is a 'person' and not just a place. It is a relationship forged over happy days. These are natural responses — they do not stem out of hysteria or amnesia, although years later the narrator attempts to imbue it with just that. Tha'mma is not a Rushdien midnight's child. There is no schizophrenia with which her psyche is stricken, no shadow lines, which divide her mind. It is the adolescent narrator who has yet to come to terms with himself and has been living in other people's second hand, even third hand stories. Nor is her life lived out in the archival womb of libraries. She had seen a great deal of trouble and it had tempered and seasoned her and made her fearless. The image of the old woman whose mind had 'cracked' is replaced by a caring person, one who is resolved to do her duty towards her old uncle. That this is temporary in nature — an aberration triggered off by an obsessive foolish nature of the 'duty,' the mission impossible, which she has undertaken, is equally true. The house, which has now a workshop with its pools of 'grease and discarded tyres,' has sent her daydreaming about the old house. But she shakes herself out of this soporific feeling and pulls herself out of the morass of daydreams. She had taught her grandson that 'she hates nostalgia.' He tells us that 'my grandmother, she has spent years telling me that nostalgia is a weakness, a waste of time, that it is everyone's duty to forget the past and look ahead and get on with building the future.' The expectations and perceptions we have of the elderly are stereotyped. They are reinforced through images in literature and cinema. And so are they reinforced through The Shadow Lines. I can see her wandering into that yard [...] gazing up at the balconies [...] knocking her knees against a set of twisted handlebars [...] looking at the grease-blackened face of Saifuddin and inquiring from which section of the house this, her relative she can't remember has appeared [...]? Saifuddin and Mayadebi gently hold her, as she seems to totter. Mayadebi does not need this kind of support. She is younger! She has not yet slipped into the twilight zone. And again, 'my grandmother didn't care any more.' It was not the house she remembered.

This perpetual, deliberate severing of relationships with places and people and things is a defense mechanism, attributed to the elderly and is also reflected in the portrayal of Mrs. Moore[3] — an aged woman who comes to India to be with her son. She is unable to understand India and her ageing self is blamed for her inability to cope with a new situation — in this case, the colonial divide. She severs all her relationships, only hearing a strange distorted echo 'ouboum' inside her head. But we are allowed, occasionally, a glimpse of Tha'mma's resilience — her 'prodigious will,' as her sense of 'duty brings her back to the present.'

These negative images persist in literature tutoring our attitudes and responses to the elderly. 'Do you think he will agree to go?' You must persuade him to do this. 'It's for his own good' gives us the impression as if we are talking about a stubborn child. In actuality, it is a reference to Shri Goshtobihari Bose, also known as Ukil-babu, a lawyer by profession. Most importantly, Tha'mma's Jethamoshai, 'who until very recently had been drafting wills and affidavits and even going to the High Court once in a while' (190). He is ninety years old. He was now 'completely bedridden,' we are told, and 'his mind is wandering a lot.'

When we first come across him in the old house in Dhaka,

he is looking out of the window vacantly, reminiscent of the grandmother gazing vacantly out of the window of her Calcutta home soon after her retirement. Robi who later recounted the story of the old man shrinks back with revulsion. 'He had never seen such an old man — shrunken, tiny with spit hanging out in threads from the corners of his mouth. He was so old he was childlike' (212). A reduction to imbecilic infanthood is the net import of the whole episode. Stuck irrevocably in the past, the words pour out of his mouth in a spate of petulant, incoherence.

'His sagging mouth had fallen open and his tongue spilled out from the gaps between his teeth' (212). With 'eyes which looked like punctured egg yolks' and 'his arms like matchstick,' Jethamoshai is altogether a repulsive and fearful image of ageing. The ludicrous salute to the king Emperor endorses what the novel has meticulously attempted to portray — for the elderly Time always refers to the past. His recognition of the King's dust and cobweb-laden picture and snatches of the Anthem, which he sings, is ample proof of his clear memory. To the grandmother's gentle 'You don't understand [...]' the 'very old man' responds firmly; 'I understand very well [...] I know everything. I understand everything,' and it is true. Only thing is that the truth comes out of that 'gaping mouth with bare black gums.' He recalls clearly that he was 'born here' and he is determined to 'die here.' When told that he must move he asks pertinently, 'Move where? His wisdom speaks when he says that 'once you start moving you never stop.' The statement is borne out by the fact of history in India and elsewhere, it is prophetic.

Saifuddin who had moved from somewhere else negates the elderly man's reasoning. 'He's not responsible for what he is saying it's the same as being mad.' It is only Khalil who everybody says is 'simple minded' like a child himself and, in whom May sees a wonderful 'quality of mind,' who recognizes this very old man's worth. He extends him a love, which keeps him alive. Both Tha'mma and Khalil have a legitimate claim on him. 'He's like a grandfather to my children now [...] what will they do without him?' After his father's death Jethamoshai had tried unsuccessfully to step into his stern shoes. He was 'undeniably eccentric' and the children did not take him seriously. He rapped them hard on their knuckles when they failed to recite their alphabets and when they screamed he kicked them in the shins. Later he would make amends and give them toffees. He was as topsy-turvy as his 'upside down house.' He was an odd man, we are told. He was cadaverous-looking even when he was young, with bright piercing eyes set deep in the hollows of his gaunt face. He had 'odd notions.' He ate his food standing up because he believed that cows did just that and had a wonderful digestive system. His asking Khalil to get toilet paper in case May wanted to 'shit' might have caused embarrassment and laughter, but it is indicative of his awareness of what divides people. The visit to Jethamoshai's house is punctuated with such pathetic expressions as the 'poor old man,' 'that old man' was so orthodox he wouldn't let a Muslim's shadow pass within ten feet of his food, 'look at him now paying the price of his sins' etc. And he does pay on that fateful day, when lured by Tha'mma and Khalil, he moves out naively believing that he was going to the Courts.

While recounting those horrific details May says, 'your grandmother screamed at me [...] she said [...] I'd get everyone killed. I didn't listen, I wasn't going to listen to a stupid cowardly *old woman* (italics mine) but she knew what was going to happen, that's when the old man's head had been hacked off.' Shri Goshtobihari Bose, Ukil Babu had finally paid for the sin of believing that there are only shadow lines dividing the nations. It is regrettable that the death of this very old man is treated as a public rather than a personal loss.

Such conventional images of the ageing person extend to other elderly characters in the novel as well. Grandmother's father was a stern unsmiling man 'with perpetually etched frowns.' People spoke in whispers when he was around. And he rapped the knuckles of little children with the handle of his umbrella.

In England, Mrs. Price opens the door and seems 'to have grown even smaller and frailer.' She listens to the conversation but it is 'evident that she is already tired.' The narrator is able to gauge her physical debility, her sense of exhaustion and he can see that 'she was wondering how she was going through another half hour' (180). She is so typically the old, gentle, kindly, homely, English lady — baking cakes, shopping for groceries, with her motherly concerns. Shrunken and tired and stooped with age, short-sighted with slightly worried frown, she wears 'a severe military green skirt.' She suffers from a sense of guilt for not having done enough for her brother when he had an accident. A translucent skin reveals 'an intricate circuitry of veins filigreed on her skin' (59). Like her, Tha'mma too has 'polished silver hair and a tracery of veins on her cheek.'

Lionel Tresawsen, as we know, is the father of Mrs. Price and the grandfather of May and Nick. The narrator traces at length his growth from youth to middle age and to 'almost old' age. His has lived a life of travel and hard work — setting off from a village called Mabe in Southern Cornwall, he came to India and then went back to England to a small Buckinghamshire village. In his youth he was a prolific patent maker, in middle age he tries to set up a homeopathic hospital in a village near Calcutta, and when he is 'almost old,' he slips into neurosis, attending séances and planchette sessions and calling his favourite spirits. He had a square face, 'white hair' and a walrus moustache.

Cushioned in a comfortable 'free' world, the narrator displays immaturity in his understanding of events in history. His spectator's knowledge of the 'courage' displayed by his peers during Naxalism-related disturbances in Calcutta does not match the courage of the grandmother. 'And I am not going to be scared off by a little trouble,' she says.

She doesn't subscribe to that particular fear, which he says 'has a texture you can neither forget nor describe [...] the special quality of loneliness that grows out of the fear of the war between oneself and one's image in the mirror.' If there is going to be trouble she feels that is all the more reason to get her uncle out while there is still time. 'I've come all the way to Dhaka for his sake [...].'

Her grandson's question 'would you have also killed?' is redundant. She would have killed for their freedom. In mirroring himself in Tridib's image — the narrator takes on the essential loneliness of the character he has chosen to be [...]. He is imprisoned in that mirror image and is unable to do a reality check of the lives of Tha'mma, Jethamoshai and Mrs. Price — the truly 'old' people. No one can ever live somebody else's life, and grandmother does live her own. For instance, if the grandmother says 'this is not Dhaka,' then it is not the city she has known, and her statement is valid and sane.

The experiences of the elderly are somewhat devalued, while the narrator is himself able to walk about London on the basis of just hearsay, remembering places as if he had walked those streets before — mapping out the stories which Tridib told him, does not in anyway make it a real experience. By, eventually, freeing herself of the nostalgia, relating to the old ancestral house in Dhaka and the city in which she grew up, Tha'mma endorses what she has accepted long ago — that the country that she had come to was another country and the house she happen to visit was no longer theirs. The narrator, on the other hand, wants the borders to be shadow-like — his anxiety is an unsubstantiated anxiety, and his sense of displacement is unreal.

Different experiences in the novel — the fond recall, the anxiety because of division of experience, the interrogation of political and historical events — all this filters through the narrator's consciousness, as he grows from childhood through adolescence to adulthood. The elderly in the novel, on the other hand, wax and wane depending upon the narrator's whimsy — a narrator who has chosen to live somebody else's life and one who traverses places experienced by this other person.

He mirrors his inability to face the truth of Tridib's brutal death because it is his own self that has been annihilated. That is why there is a painful compulsion to image the disintegration of those who have lived through those times. His survival seems to depend on that. Finally, the facile solution lies in the ageing arms of May who has rid herself of the guilt of Tridib's death and it is there that the narrator finally finds refuge.

But what of Tha'mma, my grandmother? In 1965, a year and a half after the tragic episode in Dhaka, where she witnessed the killing of Tridib and the ninety-year old Jethamoshai, we find her on her knees hugging the radio, its sound blaring loudly.

Why is she locked up in her room? 'Who's to know but god.' She hasn't eaten all day, who cares? Her grandson does, as he goes pounding up the stairs. At once he notices the precious gold chain missing from her fragile neck. She wore the necklace 'because he had given it to me — your grandfather.' She had defied social norms and expectations of what a widow could or should wear.

And now she had given it away to the war fund. She had to, 'For your sake. For your freedom.' At last she was screeching hysterically. 'We are fighting them properly at last with guns, tanks and bombs. It was for his freedom and for his sake, we have to kill them before they kill us; we have to wipe them out.' 'Her hair hanging in wet ropes over her face, her eyes were glazed, her spectacles had fallen off. I was frightened by the sight of her [...]. I wished I hadn't shut the door behind my back.'

The eyes are glazed and unfocussed. The loud blaring of the radio drowns her screaming statement. Driving her fist into the radio, she shatters it, her flesh gouged out, her hands bleed — 'blood dripped down the side of her sari dyeing it a gentle batik-like crimson.' But no sooner she says: 'I am perfectly calm now. I mustn't waste this blood. I can donate it to the war fund' (237).

Watching his grandmother stain herself in blood the narrator screams holding his head, his eyes closed. He screams we are told from the 'pit of his stomach.' It is not the blood, which disturbs him. It is his fear and apprehension that he has lost Tha'mma, his grandmother forever. What happened to Tha'mma? 'They took her away to a nice hospital [...] doctors and nurses will look after her, and she will be calm and happy.'

For the ageing observer witnessing death becomes experiential. Emily Dickinson, for instance, challenges the conventional wisdom that religion comforts the bereaved. 'I Heard a Fly Buzz — When I Died' (c. 1862) describes the final stages of death, while in the 'Last Night That He Lived' (c. 1866) the subject's death shatters the speaker's equipoise. Tha'mma too has witnessed the death of her ninety-year old Jethamoshai and that of her young nephew Tridib in a bloody mob attack in

Dhaka. She feels responsible for their death and is deeply affected by the tragedy.

The death of the old is sometimes treated as a public rather than a personal loss. Jethamoshai's death is one such instance. Like the sacrificial goat, he is both — a victim and a redeemer. More than Tridib it is he who is a representative of the history and politics of the sub-continent — his ninety long years striding the colonial and the postcolonial worlds. He is both a witness and a participant.

Tha'mma fails in the last worth-while mission she had set for herself — that of bringing her old uncle to the haven of her invented country. She fails despite steeling and convincing herself that one must do one's duty, despite storing aeons of memory and deep wells of warmth and affection within her. In the sanitized confines of the hospital, shut away from the sounds of screeching airplanes dropping napalm and the roar of tanks crushing enemy, 'my grandmother' is now enconsed in a drug-induced somnambulistic world where the shadows draw schizophrenic lines between sanity and insanity.

'She's never been the same you know since they killed Tridib over there.' 'It's this war with Pakistan.' The death of the ninety-year-old man doesn't merit a mention. 'Don't worry about Tha'mma,' the narrator is consoled. She is old!

Notes and References

1. Amitav Ghosh, *The Shadow Lines* (New Delhi: OUP, Fifth impression 1998), 3.
2. Nadine Gordimer, *My Son's Story* (London: Penguin Books Ltd., 1991).
3. E.M. Forster, *A Passage to India.*

   I have benefited from the following works: Robert N. Butler, "Psychiatry and the Elderly: An Overview", *The American Journal of Psychiatry* 132 (September 1975); Kathleen Woodward, Simone de Beauviour: "Aging and its Discontents" in *The Private Self: Theory and Practice of Women's Autobiographical Writings*, ed. Shavi Benstock (1988); Evelyn Rosenthal, ed., *Women, Aging and Ageism* (1990); Ann M. Wyatt-Brown and Janice Rossen, eds., *Aging and Gender in Literature: Studies in Creativity* (1993).

8

IMAGERY IN *THE SHADOW LINES*

RITA JOSHI

Amitav Ghosh's novel, *The Shadow Lines,* focuses on the trauma of individual lives caught in a changing world where new nations are formed and old identities have to be arbitrarily replaced by new notions of national identity, causing cultural and physical displacements from old contexts into new ones. In the contemporary era, the problem gets aggravated as further displacements take place with travel and immigration, bringing about their own kinds of alienation and heartbreak.

The protagonist of the novel, Tridib and his English girl friend visit Dhaka. Tridib is killed by a mob during a Muslim riot there. It is this traumatic experience which severely affects the lives of almost all the major characters in the novel. Ghosh employs certain key images to highlight his major concerns in the context of this core experience of the novel. Maps, mirrors, spectacles, stairs and photographs, etc. recur in the novel emphasizing notions of nation, identity, and illusion and for highlighting such ideas as the search for reality and the role of memory in confronting the present.

In her essay, "Maps and Mirrors," Meenakshi Mukherjee states: 'If maps are an attempt to chart the earth's surface precisely, mirrors deal with illusory space.' She further states that there is a resultant 'shifting reaches of meaning' in the idea of 'the simultaneity of precision and illusion.'[1] Another way of interpreting the drawing of maps is to see them as an artificial and arbitrary postcolonial exercise to impose divisions between people — through travel and memory of previous times; and looking into mirrors can be understood as an attempt by individuals to confront their real identities.

Maps and boundaries are mentioned in the novel frequently — the London A-Z;[2] the boundaries between India and Pakistan: 'this is the modern world. The border isn't on the frontier: it's right inside the airport' (151); the Bartholomew Atlas belonging to the child Tridib in London which finds its way in Delhi, itself crossing the boundaries it describes. Further, this is how the narrator challenges the notion of nationalism set up by maps:

> [...] There had really been a time, not so long ago, when people, sensible people, of good intention, had thought that all maps were the same, that there was a special enchantment in lives [...] they were not to be blamed for believing that there was something admirable in moving violence to the borders [...] they had drawn their borders, believing in that pattern, in the enchantment of lives [...] when they discovered that they had created not a separate, but a yet-undiscovered irony — the irony that killed Tridib: the simple fact that there had never been a moment in the four-thousand-year old history of that map, when the places we know as Dhaka and Calcutta were more closely bound to each other than after they had drawn their lines (233).

In 1964 the stealing of the relic of Prophet Mohammad's hair in Srinagar did not lead to riots in that city but there was a reaction in the distant Khulna in East Pakistan. In order to investigate this strange phenomenon, the narrator draws a circle on a map of Asia, with Khulna at the centre and Srinagar on the circumference. He finds it to be 'an amazing circle' (231), touching among other places, areas in Sri Lanka, Thailand and China. The narrator discovers, for instance, that Chiang Mai in Thailand is much closer to Calcutta than Delhi is; that Chengdu in China is closer to Calcutta than Srinagar is. And yet, nothing happened in the foreign areas adjacent to Indian cities, because of the negative developments in the latter. But, alas! Maps are not made keeping sentiments and geographical proximities in mind.

Tridib highlights the significance of the mirror theme in the novel thus: he tells the narrator that if one strives and is also lucky, one can travel 'to a place where there was no border between oneself and one's image in the mirror' (29). Thinking of herself as a baby in a gas mask during the War, May tries to see her old contrasting self: 'May was looking into the mirror, laughing silently' (166). Later, May tries to hide her true response to Tridib's death from the narrator: 'She turned away so that I couldn't see her eyes, even in the mirror' (204). Going back in time to newspaper descriptions of the events of 1964, the narrator tells us: 'I began my strangest journey; a voyage into a land outside space, an expanse without distance, a land of *looking-glass* events' (224).

Photographs—in which the past survives as a visual, living presence, keeping alive memory, recur in the novel. Tridib's world, certainly, comes alive for the narrator through the former's collection of photographs. A key example is an old photograph wherein Tresawsen, Dan, Mike and Franscesca walk down happily, and a week later, they are killed in a bomb attack or die subsequently. Though photographs can and do record some rare moments for the posterity, they cannot convey the inner lives of people:

> Nobody knows, nobody can ever know, not even in memory, because there are moments in time that are not knowable: nobody can ever know what it was like to be young and intelligent in the summer of 1939 in London or Berlin (68).

Staircases in the novel, like maps, mirrors and photographs, also signify division or contradiction — in this case, literally between the architectural levels; they can also be viewed metaphorically — that is, as the indicators of different levels of reality. Take for instance, when Ila draws a map of a house and its stairs. Since it is a flat representation, the literal mind of the narrator cannot accept it: 'there can't be a staircase because it's flat, and staircases go up, they aren't flat' (70). When the narrator visits the Prices, May opens a door 'tucked behind the staircase' (116) and a hidden world of books is discovered; in the room behind, the narrator's sexuality is awakened at the sight of a half-naked Ila. In the latter case, the staircase divides the public and the private spatially. In Dhaka, in the old house, 'the stairs are slippery with dirt' (172), reminding us that time has brought decay for many. Children run up and down these stairs but the upstairs is, primarily, for the very old.

In a letter, Tridib describes a scene in a bombed cinema hall, wherein a boy climbs the stairs to an undamaged gallery — signifying the still undamaged aspects of lives and the world after the War. Here, a man and a woman enter and make love on the aisle, not knowing that a boy is observing them. The staircase divides the world of the gallery *i.e.* the observer from the world of the performers — signifying active and passive principles in the unfolding of human lives.

The images of spectacles and cigarettes in the novel are linked with some thoughtful pursuit. Probably, Ghosh is influenced by Conrad here. In Conrad's novel. *Lord Jim,* Marlow is visualized sitting in the dark, telling his story to a group of listeners and occasionally lighting a cigarette to dispel the darkness. In Ghosh's novel, however the lighting of a cigarette and the emitting cigarette smoke are linked to moments of deep concentration. For instance, the narrator fondly recalls Tridib lighting a cigarette and then getting deeply absorbed in his reading: 'I had found him, as always, lying on a mat in his room at the top of the house, reading, with a cigarette smouldering in the ashtray beside him' (10). Again, the narrator asks Ila if she remembers Tridib sitting in his room, 'Cigarette smoke spiraling out of his fingers' and Tridib telling them about 'the behavioral differences between the Elapidae and Viperidae families of snakes, or the design of the temples at Konark, or the origins of the catamaran' (19). However, in the scene pertaining to the stolen view of the sexual act in the cinema hall, a woman just attracts the attention of a man by lighting a cigarette. Tridib's gleaming spectacles are frequently mentioned in the novel and are a part of his introspective, probing personality, as are cigarettes and cigarette smoke.

An unusual feature of Tridib's personality is his Gastric: 'the truth was that his digestion was a mess [...] every once in a while a rumble in his bowels would catch him unawares on the streets and he would have to run to the nearest clean lavatory. This condition was known to us as Tridib's Gastric' (4). Gastric can be obliquely related to Tridib's startling, innovative ideas.

Similarly, there is an image, which is related to Ila, exclusively. Magda is Ila's doll and her 'make-believe' baby. She is Ila's other and her alter-ego. She has blonde hair and blue eyes, suggesting Ila's desire to be an English girl. Surprisingly, though Madga is English in appearance, she is treated as a subaltern Asian as she is beaten by Denise, her classmate. Eventually, she is rescued by Nick Price. But, after recounting the incident to the narrator, Ila bursts into tears. Subsequently, the narrator learns from May Price the cause of Ila's anguish: 'that wasn't quite what happened [...] Nick didn't stop to help Ila. He ran all the way back [...] Nick didn't want to be seen with Ila. Ila didn't have any friends in school you see' (76).

Magda acts as a metaphor for Ila's various experiences. Through the aforesaid story, Ila tries to project her own crisis of identity as a despised Asian, on to Madga. It will be correct to say that Ila rewrites her own story when she makes Madga undergo experiences similar to hers, but with a different ending.

That she is being neglected by others and feels alienated, becomes further evident when she draws an imaginary room in an imaginary house for her doll in the sand. The imaginary lines, of course, remind us of the imaginary lines of maps, but, essentially, they are drawn by Ila to create a world for herself — a world where she is secure. However, it is a make-believe world — and with a doll as a relative, it simply highlights her isolation, her alienation from others in the actual world.

Another episode worth mentioning in the context of imagery is the one narrated by Ila, which describes their home in Colombo. A *thala-goya,* a type of large lizard, is mistaken by servants for a crocodile. Ila's mother, a westernised lady, nicknamed Queen Victoria, is not frightened by it and adopts it and keeps it in her back garden. The lizard evokes different reactions from the characters, revealing their cultural biases: the servant, Ram Dayal, says, 'why did I come to Lanka [...] I knew Ravana would come to get me' (24). 'Queen Victoria,' on the other hand, says: 'a heck of a huge great lizard [...] wandering about in my garden like a governor at a gymkhana' (25). However, she summons up her courage to prove her class: 'being as she was, the daughter of a man who had left his village in Barisal in rags and gone on to earn a knighthood in the Old Indian Civil Service, she retained her composure' (25). Later the lizard is kept in the garden — and is treated as a pet, indicating the cross-cultural leanings of the family.

This pet saves Ila's life. In this particular episode, a snake slithers near Ila, ready to strike her. The lizard notices the snake and makes a reactive movement. The snake is momentarily distracted. Ila manages to upset her chair and move out of danger; the snake strikes the fallen chair. The lizard then chases the snake away. The snake here represents a destructive principle, the lizard — a salvation principle. To elaborate, if we take the lizard as a cross-cultural symbol, it is implied that Ila's travels and cross-cultural encounters have a liberating, salvation aspect; the snake on the other hand, can be here taken to represent a cloying, destructive and narrow spirit of tradition.

There are three images that occur successively in the novel and have individual as well as composite implications. These are the cotton man, the Victoria memorial and the wounded dog encountered by May, Tridib and the narrator.

During her sojourn in Calcutta, May happens to go round the city in the company of the narrator and encounters a 'cotton man,' twanging on his harp. May takes him to be a musician. He represents to her an old, indigenous aspect of Indian culture, untouched by western colonization. Subsequently, May visits the Victoria memorial. She reacts sharply to the statue of Queen Victoria and turns her eyes away from the statue and the building. She says: 'Let's go, please, I can't bear it [...] it shouldn't be here [...]. It's an act of violence. It's obscene' (176). Here, May reacts against the colonial experience of India — the statue of the Queen Victoria presents a different, rather an ugly facet of Indian history, as against the one represented by the cotton man; the statue, obviously, is to be taken as a symbol of oppression and subjugation.

Later May agrees to see it the way Tridib sees it: 'This will do for our ruin' (170). By linking herself and Tridib to the

Memorial, which she has initially described as a symbol of violence, May is ironically suggesting the violent end of Tridib, when indeed their relationship will exist only in memory — as a 'ruin.'

Soon after this, May forces him to stop the car so that she could put an end to the agony of a seriously injured dog by slitting at its jugular vein with a penknife. May and Tridib participate in a violent, though well-meaning act, which foreshadows the death of Tridib in an act of bloody violence.

Towards the end of the novel, the rickshaw carrying the old man, is visualized as becoming a vast monster: It symbolizes the mob violence growing out of proportion, and overtaking the rickshaw puller and its rider, and any alien person who comes in its vicinity.

The Shadow Lines is a novel where the visual imagery is used not for producing any dramatic effects, but as a mode for projecting the essential concern of the novelist: which is, mainly, to give expression to the theme of illusion and reality. The images function almost like the characters in the novel — bearing their own contradictions and complexities, they carry out the novelist's purpose effectively.

Notes and References

1. Meenakshi Mukherjee, "Maps and Mirrors" in the edition of *The Shadow Lines* by Amitav Ghosh (New Delhi: OUP, 1988), 255.
2. Amitav Ghosh, *The Shadow Lines* (New Delhi: OUP, 1988), 58. Subsequent references are to this edition and the page numbers are included in the text.

9

'Going Away' and 'Coming Home': *The Shadow Lines* and the Travel Motif in Children's Fiction

NIVEDITA SEN

Ruskin Bond's children's story, 'The Great Train Journey,' the title of which suggests the celebration of a travel experience, is paradoxically not about the young hero travelling by train through quaint and exotic places at all.[1] By showing the schoolboy protagonist Suraj to be harbouring the illusion that he has run away from home till such time as he realizes, with a mixture of shock and disappointment, that he had been on a circular goods train which has traced its way back to the very station from which it started, the end of the story leaves Suraj perplexed about whether he 'went away' or 'came home.' The story is an example in which the distinction between coming and going is blurred to the extent that one does not know one from the other.

The two key phrases 'going away' and 'coming home,' used in the *The Shadow Lines* to separate the two parts of the novel, with an ostensible agenda of structuring it, describe the trajectory usually followed by fiction for children of the school going age-group. In these stories the child rebel/adventurer/traveller/dreamer makes a journey away from home, regales the reader with incredible experiences in unfamiliar situations and remote places, but ultimately returns to the protective fold and the *status quo* of his home. The intermediary experiences are usually an attempt to escape the stifling regimentation and sham morality of his/her home or school environment. What happens to Suraj usually happens to the other child protagonists, except that they voluntarily come back after a brush with the outside world, which makes them aware of its insecurities and hazards, as well as the relative comforts of the homes they have left behind.

In *The Shadow Lines*, however, the paradigm of 'going away' and 'coming home' is worked out at a much more complex level than in children's fiction, and that is what marks its departure from the genre of children's literature or travel and adventure stories. Using 'going away' and 'coming home' as basic props on which a narrative edifice of intertwining human relationships (and their accompanying exchange of ideas) during a critical period in history is constructed — is a strategy that makes it an adult novel. Such a strategy deconstructs the very assumptions of the travel motif in children's fiction and divides the story neatly into 'escaping from home' and 'coming back to reality.' In fact, the seeming polarization of the two words 'come' and 'go,' verbs that literally mean the opposite of each other, is one of the major 'shadow lines' that is sought to be demolished in the process of the unfolding of the narrator's experiences. It results in an ironic destabilization of the very principles on which the two-fold structure of the novel apparently rests.

In this essay, I am going to try and examine the use of the two catch phrases 'going away' and 'coming home' to see if they help to highlight some aspects of Bengali children's fiction, with the sole purpose of trying to find out some obvious and not so obvious differences that go on to make *The Shadow Lines* much more than a children's travel story, an adult novel.

I

The first question that we can ask with regard to the novel is about its genre. As a bildungsroman, the narrator's story from innocence to experience and from childhood to adulthood is articulated through both his real and his vicarious experiences, ranging from those heard from Tridib and Tha'mma to those actually lived with Ila, Nick and May. It is the kind of Bakhtinian 'novel of emergence' in which 'man's individual emergence is inseparably linked to historical emergence [...] on the border between two epochs.'[2] It is also an inverse variation of another kind of Bakhtinian 'novel of emergence' that 'traces a typically repeating path of man's emergence from youthful idealism and fantasies to mature sobriety and practicality.' It is towards the end of his fictional journey that the narrator wishfully reverts to a kind of childlike innocence in a romantic idealization of a world without 'shadow lines.' Bakhtin takes into account the complications that arise on the way due to varying degrees of skepticism and resignation, which the narrator of *The Shadow Lines* also feels at every phase of his growth. But in the wishing away of 'shadow lines' of various kinds in this process, and in attributing some value to the great 'sacrifice' performed by Tridib as a message of co-existence and harmony among human beings, the narrator displays his inability to accept the brute facts of 'growing up' or 'experience.' His behavior amply demonstrates that he would rather cling on to an unfeasible, utopian vision of a world, which is not irrationally, unjustly, and cruelly divided into fragments. The journey, therefore, is not just from innocence to experience, but also back to a sentient, sensible and sensitive 'innocence' that expresses itself fully only when the narrator has crossed childhood and adolescence, and is on the threshold of adulthood. The novel, therefore, also problematises an easy demarcation between 'innocence' and 'experience,' faith and cynicism, or rebellion and resignation, that is so central to the conventional bildungsroman.

The novel, at another level, is a take-off on Bengali travel literature. As Meenakshi Mukherjee says, 'real journeys within the country and imagined travels to far away places outside national boundaries have always fascinated the Bengali middle-class.'[3] However, despite the cartographic details in the novel and the names of outlandish places on the globe with their accompanying unusual experiences, much of the 'travel' of the narrator is not just about 'going away' to England. It also displays the ability to be vicariously transported to various times and places merely by listening spellbound to stories by Tridib and others, and virtually appropriating those experiences as his own.

The use of the recurring mirror image in the novel, bringing into focus two people who are similar, or explaining situations that reflect each other, is an artifice that aids the narrator to acquire the moratoria prerogative of being in other people's *shoes*, at many places and times simultaneously. The metaphor of the mirror is deployed throughout the novel to accentuate the likeness between two people, events or even nations that reflect each other by using what would, according to common sense, be considered inadequate criteria of comparison. The narrator, for example, always thinks of Nick as his mirror image, although Nick is fairer and taller than him, probably because he senses that they are both attracted to Ila.

'Going' and 'coming' can also be seen as mirror images, although the two are far from identical, for a mirror image portrays reality, but is also at the same time away from reality. 'Going away,' therefore, in this novel, is a take-off from reality, which imaginatively turns to Tridib, Robi, May or even Nick and Ila — despite their cold-blooded pragmatism. 'Going away' describes people and events in England, or simply allows the narrator to imaginatively recreate people, places and events; while 'coming home' turns to Tha'mma or May, or some kind of introspective reasoning, whether it is in Calcutta or London.

Travelling, therefore, is not just between two geographical locations or two points in history, but is the ability to shift from experience to experience, both in terms of time and space — imaginatively erasing the 'shadow lines' between two people's experiences in disparate geographical contexts and at discrete historical junctures, and at times trespassing into the formidable or forbidden domain of people who are slotted higher or lower in the hierarchy of class or race. While doing this, it sometimes becomes equally necessary to jump the border between real and imaginary experience, as borne out by the scene in which the narrator and Ila play 'house' and give away many of their real and gut emotions of love, hate, fear and persecution. In the process, the very confusion in the meanings of the words 'come' and 'go' that the narrator always teases his Tha'mma about, becomes for him an equivocation that he not only enjoys playing around with, but also has to negotiate and come to terms with in the course of his own experiences. Given his kind of temperament that finds it difficult to accept the lines between most man-made differences, it is he who understands and sympathises most with the mystification of the two words used by his Tha'mma.

In traditional Bengali households, there is something inauspicious about saying, 'I take your leave' or 'I will go now,' when one actually means to depart for any destination, because it could mean that he/she might never come back. When one is going away, therefore, one is expected to say *Aashi,* which literally means its opposite, that is 'I am just coming,' its nearest English equivalent as a farewell statement would be 'See you soon' or 'Until we meet again.'

The interchangeable meanings of 'come' and 'go' are attributed initially to Tha'mma because of a change in national identity, subsequent to the partition. Brought up on the ambivalent connotation of the words 'come' and 'go,' it is not surprising that Tha'mma clings on to and internalizes this prevarication to suit her needs. Having lost her home in the aftermath of the partition, she cannot complacently accept or adjust to the new 'home' in Calcutta, to which she must now 'come' rather than 'go.' She is equally outraged at having to 'go' to Dhaka, which is her real home, when she visits her sister. She feels far more at ease with herself to say that she will 'come' to Dhaka and 'go' to her home in Calcutta. As I have said already, the point is reiterated in the narrator's private jokes about 'coming' and 'going' with his Tha'mma.

The novel takes up as its ideological agenda the critique of such a nationalism that leaves one bewildered about whether one 'comes' or 'goes' to one's own home. And in doing so, it experiments with the narrative technique, doing away with a chronological sequence of events, also collapsing the categories of the 'past' and the 'present.' Both in its content and form, therefore, the novel is preoccupied with qualifying absolute ideas of space and time. In this sense, travel becomes a trope for passing through space or time into situations outside oneself and one's social place and national identity, ruthlessly dispensing with all kinds of 'shadow lines' in the process. Travel is also not linear, but cyclical, enriched by repetitions and meaningful resonances of details from other times and places.

II

The narrator 'goes away' or lets himself go with the help of his uncle Tridib, an archetypal figure of inspiration in children's fiction, who leads the child through a maze of insightful stories that cannot be judged by normal middle-class common sense. Such alternate mentors appeal to children much more than parents or teachers, and perhaps for that very reason, are usually presented with and tempered by a word of caution from fictional parents and teachers, or sometimes the author. Bengali children's fiction is replete with instances of the child protagonist's undiluted adulation for such eccentric and unconventional uncles or cousins, who, despite their *Bhadralok* backgrounds, do not follow the dictates of genteel decorum, discretion and discipline. Over and over again, the child protagonist associates and identifies more with such non-conformist uncles than with stuffy and self-righteous parents, limited by their *Bhadralok* preoccupation with rules and regulations, academic success and worldly wisdom, and by their anxiety as not to violate the norms of respectability and decency.

The novel follows the stereotypical trajectory of a lot of children's stories written in Bengali, which are about the child protagonist's refusal to adjust and be complacent within a system in which he/she sees himself/herself as trapped. In such stories, a sporadic and unsystematic though valid critique of the system emerges from a reading of the discontent expressed by the child character. Often, the child protagonist experiments with outlets and fantasies from the established order of his/her home and school, escaping with the help of an external human agency in the form of an uncle, a cousin, a domestic servant or a street acquaintance who is also a magician or a performer. Yet the modes of escape offered by these tempters who inspire the child to an alternate way of life contain within them something illusory or hazardous. Despite the child's refusal to be restricted within the parameters of established norms, there is a simultaneous and anomalous inability to break free of it. The adult perspective of most of these stories sees any kind of childhood rebellion as potentially dangerous, and therefore does not permit it beyond a certain limit. The most radical implications of the child's critique of the establishment, therefore, are ultimately contained and reassimilated within the middle-class worldview of such fiction. The oft-repeated configuration, therefore, is of the child getting into a scrape which not only opens out new possibilities for him/her, but also shows a dormant desire in him/her to challenge the assumptions of his/her family and society in order to be a part of the 'other,' and a cautiously presented fictional 'loop,' whereby the child has to ultimately return to the fold. The adventurer returns, the dreamer awakens, or the truant traces his way back to home or school.

Returning to *The Shadow Lines*, the relationship between the narrator and Tridib is a standard, fictional one between a growing boy and a larger-than-life person who opted out of the mainstream, yet whose intuitive, unsophisticated response to the world around attracts the narrator to him. It is this character that he hero-worships and tries to identify with and it makes the novel a complex variation of children's fiction. In children's fiction, such persons are represented as follows:

> The general out-group, the people to be avoided…the adults whose candy must not be accepted. In their anxiety to build a shield against harm into their children's minds and to bind their children to themselves and their own kind, parents project many fantasies of evil into these 'strangers.'[4]

In Bengali children's fiction, the servants Jhagru and Phagu in Lila Majumdar's short stories, and the street-side juggler Haarunda in Satyajit Ray's *Phatikchand* are just two examples among many of such peripheral characters that capture the imagination of the children. Such characters are, in spite of and perhaps because of their unconventional ways, role models for the child protagonists, even if they have no claim or say in the matters of the more privileged families to which the children belong. Among fictional uncles who entice the children away from the complacent insularity of their parents and homes, a typical case is that of the *Chotomaama* in Lila Majumdar's Gupi and Paanu stories. *Chotomaama*, who has dropped out of college but is supposedly building a rocket to go to the moon, holds the children's interest by his experiences and his experiments, because they are so far removed from the reality of the children's lives that they stir their imagination into a possible escape from the drudgery of home and school. A vicarious participation in *Chotomaama*'s offbeat ventures even allows Paanu, a disabled boy, to create an imaginary world in which he can transcend the limitations of his own physical handicap for some time. Sanjib Chattopadhyay's *Baromaama* also has in common with all such uncles, an expansive imagination, and the ability to make the fictional nephew an accomplice, willingly or otherwise, in all his weird enterprises, which opens out a world of fun bringing on disaster for him. The *Kaakababu* stories of Sunil Gangapadhyay, about the detective hero *Kaakababu* with his nephew Santu as assistant, and *the Feluda* stories of Satyajit Ray, with Feluda and Topshe working likewise as a team of a detective and a collaborator, introduce an uncle/cousin in yet another sub-genre within children's fiction. This genre is of mystery or adventure stories, in which the uncle/cousin similarly lures the child away to picturesque, exciting but perilous locales where they solve criminal cases together.

Like Tridib, they are also repositories of all kinds of knowledge, which fascinates and attracts the child towards them all the more. Being serials, the stories necessitate a return of the child character to the humdrum reality of his quotidian existence before the next adventure begins. But it is, by and large, also true of other stories in which the ubiquitous uncle plays a major role in opening up an unknown world and tempting the child protagonist to transgress his/her monotonous routine. In Satyajit Ray's *'Atithi'* (later filmed as *Aagantuk)*, the child's has a great rapport with an elderly great-uncle who is a dropout, a freak, a Bohemian and refreshingly different from his smug, professionally successful father and his conventional housewife mother. This demonstrates that the child protagonist, over and over again, is enthralled by the exploits of such eccentric uncles, and temporarily enjoys their friendship over the relationship they have with their run-of-the-mill parents.

Tridib, like many of his counterparts in children's stories, is a virtual dropout from the system. He lives on its periphery. Unlike his two brothers who are professionally successful and study abroad or get foreign postings in their jobs, he does not work for a living, and is not averse to spending his adult life in a shanty room on the terrace of his ancestral home. The alternative that he offers the narrator of a normal, middle-class, straitjacketed and 'decent' response to the world around him is on the basis of his rich accumulation of stories from real life as well as his knowledge of archaeology, geography and history. He opens out an imaginary space for the narrator that not only heightens his awareness of the world, but also gives him unusual though valid perceptions about things. Tridib, says the narrator, 'has given me worlds to travel in, and eyes to see them with' (20). The narrator first experiences the world through Tridib's eyes and then through first-hand experiences in and around the places and times in which Tridib lived. When he is in England, for instance, he reconstructs Tridib's encounters by going about the city like a live map, prioritising the places that were important to Tridib over other, lesser areas that were not in his scheme of things. The narrator undertakes imaginative and real forays into unknown places, spearheaded by the live Tridib and attributed to his memory when he is dead. It is these experiences and views, which constitute much of the 'travel' in the novel. They cannot be evaluated by the standards of normal intelligence or middle-class common sense that the narrator has been brought up on.

Since *The Shadow Lines* is not a children's novel, the prototype of the tempter-uncle is not absorbed back into the system to accommodate a 'happy ending,' that conveniently suppresses the questions raised in the course of the novel. In Lila Majumdar's *Gupi and Paanu Stories,* for instance, the *Chotomaama* is made to return to college to study for his B.A. degree before being allowed to engage in any more amateur sleuth-like enterprises, with Gupi and Paanu as accomplices. In Satyajit Ray's *'Atithi'* and *Phatikchand,* these stock characters are weeded out and made to go their way alone, to make smooth the return of the prodigal child to his own accepted milieu.

Although 'the tempter-uncle' in this novel actually dies, he not only leaves the narrator to cope with the world alone (a world that did not understand the former), but also continues to haunt and torment the memory and conscience of his nephew, and Robi and May with many unanswered questions. Ironically, therefore, it is in this adult novel that there is some 'future' for the dead uncle who had instigated and provoked the child to overstep the restricted milieu of his family and social class, giving him something much more valuable than asking him to pass examinations and be successful in worldly terms.

III

One such intellectual legacy inherited by the narrator from Tridib is his persistent questioning of everything around him, from trivial family assumptions to political decisions and philosophical ideas. Somewhere between the simultaneous experiences of 'going' and 'coming,' the narrator primarily interrogates the 'lines' that his world is made up of — the demarcations between so many areas of human experience and understanding, which he construes as illusions.[5] This perceptiveness helps him in negotiating a world full of artificial barriers between times and places, between people and their classes, and lines between innocence and experience and reality and imagination.

That the narrator would like to live in such a world where there are no man-made boundaries, no bloodshed and violence, is obvious. He is amazed to see that an incident in Srinagar, across the national border, should have stirred such a hornet's nest in distant Khulna, but the adjoining areas remained unaffected. Any atlas could inspire him to work out these equations for himself, but it is poignantly significant that an atlas, which he has inherited from Tridib, should do so.

In geo-political terms, the demarcation between India and Pakistan, leading to a reordering of the distinction between 'coming' and 'going,' is thin for the most affected victim of the partition in the novel, namely, Tha'mma. Tha'mma is a serious critic of nationalism, not unlike some contemporary historians, who have said that nationalism merely 'invents nations where they do not exist'[6] and that 'nations lose their origins in the myths of time and only fully realize their horizons in the mind's eye.'[7] Borders between nations are equally thin, in fact, non-existent for the narrator, as he belongs to the privileged socio-economic class, for whom the world is small as it has shrunk to a cross-cultural, cosmopolitan yet a complex heterogeneity, which can nevertheless be conceptualized as a single entity.

Taking the end of the novel into account, for instance, it is not easy to say which has become the narrator's real home — the truncated version of his family in Calcutta (India) which is now without its most motivated, opinionated, energetic member in the person of Tha'mma, with whom he shared a love-hate relationship, or May's home in London where he gets an insight into the significant event of Tridib's death and the desirable experience of his first adult, sexual relationship. Like his affluent and globetrotting relatives, he, too, becomes a citizen of the world, though perhaps at some human cost to himself and his identity. In the process, the contradiction in terms of the interchangeability of 'coming' and 'going' becomes more of an acceptable way of life for him than the jocular interludes with Tha'mma would suggest.

As I have said before, the lines of chronology, that distinguish a remembered past from an actual present are done away with, as the narrator narrates his tale. As a result, the form of the novel does not follow a linear time sequence, but keeps shifting between the past and the present resulting in 'an imaginative renewal of times, places, events and people past, through the recuperation of stories from the family archives.'[8] Reverberations of past things, which lend credence and meaning to present events, posit a cyclical notion of time. The patterns of repetition juxtapose the personal upheaval in the life of the narrator against the public turmoil that the country is going through.

The narrator also writes in a mode, which tries to overcome what human reason believes to be the watertight categories of two people's experiences. He is able to conquer the impenetrable spaces that lie between people to a certain extent by living through their experiences; his credibility as a narrator could come under question otherwise. The novel recounts the experiences of May, for instance, through a letter that Tridib wrote to her about the bombed out cinema hall, or through Robi's and May's account of the events leading to Tridib's death, which are all recovered through the narratorial voice. In the process of the narrator's flouting of these principles of division, the novel dwells on a potential collapsing of categories between a certain reality and an imaginative exploration of other realities that appear to be out of reach. The narrator's jumping of the borderline of reality to reach forth towards that which he experiences only through imagination, is one of the major 'shadow lines' that he attempts to transcend in the novel.

It is an equally exciting imaginative experience for the narrator to trascend the hierarchies of social class. Unlike his middle-class mother, who desperately wants to cling on to her niche in that class after the dislocation that she suffered during the partition, he does not seem to be content with his child's position within a middle-class family. He is far more interested in wishfully participating in the goings-on in the Mayadebi branch of the family, which did better than his family, both financially and socially. These relatives, like Ila and her mother, provide the narratives that transport him to places like Colombo and Cairo, although most of the extraordinary experiences in the novel are recovered through the street-corner stories of Tridib. The latter cannot presume to be the voice of the authenticity that is attributed to the success and prosperity of that class, and yet has the narrator and other younger boys mesmerized.

The narrator is equally curious about those relatives who could not make it like those boys, for instance, the Dhakuria branch of Jethamoshai's family. They do not seem to be overly conscious or troubled by differences of class suggested by the sordid ambience of their living quarters in Dhakuria. The pronounced economic and social disparity between the two families is prefigured in Tha'mma's sarcastic rejoinder to the maid who comes to show them the way to the place, and introduces herself as Mrinmoyee, for 'she was always savagely cutting with maidservants who had names which struck her as being pretentious for their station' (130). Although intolerant of the 'lines' between nations, Tha'mma is a self-righteous upholder of the 'lines' between classes.

The narrator realizes that it is the landscape to which Mrinmoyee introduces them that 'lent the note of hysteria to my mother's voice when she drilled me for my examinations' (134), and that all it would take, was a couple of failed examinations for him to get sucked into that landscape. Even as a school going boy, the narrator ironically realizes it to be 'that sludge which gave our genteel decorum its fine edge of frenzy' (134). However, in the course of this episode, it is the narrator's father, not his mother, who is afraid of losing his security by reestablishing a familial connection with relatives who live in a virtual slum and whose twenty-five-year old, good-for-nothing son could influence the decent upbringing of his own son at an impressionable age. For the narrator, however, it is as easy to politely look away as to subsume within the reality of his existence as imaginative yet full-blooded a partaking of the experience of the 'other' as his family would permit him. Although the narrator's privileging of the upper class experience in foreign locales as a way of life that opens out the world at large to him is what concerns most of the novel, his latently uninhibited response to relatives who are lower down in the social scale, prompted by his Tha'mma's excitement at meeting them after so long, and his mother's humane concern after actually being told about the problems they face, is suggested, but not developed in the course of the novel. The desire to jump the 'lines' between people, times, classes and nations is in consonance with the structure of the novel.

The two parts of the novel do not demonstrate a thesis and an antithesis, or a point and a counterpoint, but are the aspects of a whole that cannot be divided into two self-sufficient aspects of 'going away' and 'coming home.' They coalesce to make it an organized whole, a structure of experience somewhat similar to the formulaic structure that one finds in children's fiction.

IV

However, it is not a matter of arbitrary structuring that the scenes that question the 'lines' of hatred between nations fall in the second half of the novel. These scenes help the narrator to 'come home,' or perceive and recognize certain home truths about the world around him. A premonition for some kind of coming to terms with the reality around him happens in three episodes of the novel. The first is when his Tha'mma questions the rationale behind the meaningless bloodshed, violence and trauma caused by the partition of India and Pakistan, though it has not even succeeded in creating an actual border that is visible from a plane. 'What was it all for then — partition and all the killing and everything — if there isn't something in between?' (151-52), she asks. She also cannot understand 'how her place of birth could be at such odds with her nationality.' In the second instance, a relatively unimportant character in the novel, Jethamoshai challenges anybody who would engage him on the issue of the 'home.' He does not want to come to India, declaring that he cannot be expected to shift his home any time the borders between the two countries are drawn. There is a rhetorical flourish in his question 'suppose when you get there they decide to draw another line somewhere? What will you do then?' (215)

I have already discussed the third instance, which is one of the climactic scenes in which the narrator communicates with himself and interrogates the dividing 'lines' between countries. Beginning 'a nostalgic journey down the land of looking-glass events' (225), he is upset, even horrified to realize that equidistant parts from the centre on the globe have the capacity to arouse such vicious passions or leave a person cold, depending on what man-made boundaries lie between the centre and the different points on the circumference. Yet the irony of all this 'enchantment of lines' is that

> There had never been a moment in the four-thousand-year-old history of that map, when the places we know as Dhaka and Calcutta were more closely bound to each other than after they had drawn their lines [...] (233).

These scenes in the novel augment the narrator's awareness of the significant realities of the world around him, and are hence deeply felt experiential constituents of the novel, which makes it a bildungsroman. In travel literature, the adventurer/traveller always returns home, and in the kind of children's fiction that takes the child protagonist through a real or imaginary escapade out of his/her limited and limiting environment, the child usually returns home. *The Shadow Lines* is not a children's story; despite the title of the second part, it does not suggest a literal coming back to India and home. At the point the novel ends, 'coming home,' for the narrator, is literally just one 'airlines flight' away. But apart from the scenes of 'coming to terms' discussed above, its 'coming home' happens through the narrator's relationship with a woman, which would not have been the case if the novel were just a children's story. In the last interlude, he 'comes home' to roost in May's arms, and finds a one-night haven in her home just before he is due to return to India. In this 'coming home' scene, she reconstructs the facts of Tridib's death, letting the narrator know the truth and her interpretation of it. In the process, the two rediscover each other, in the context of Tridib's death. The coming together of the narrator and May is not just closeness between two people, but a solidarity of certain convictions they share with some other people in the novel too, who are no longer alive. Tha'mma, Jethamoshai and Tridib, all of them, in their own way, help the narrator to realize the futility of 'lines.' Subsequently, the Atlas scene, May's account of her naïve but uncompromising stand on communal violence, the scene of Tridib's death which was a 'mystery' that 'redeems' all earlier impressions of him as a 'wastrel' and 'loafer' — all these serve an educative purpose for the narrator.

Whether the bonding between May and the narrator, predicated on a sympathetic understanding of and identification with Tridib as a person, and peace and communal harmony as a cause, is fragile or not is something for the reader to decide. But it is precisely her idealistic position about certain things that makes her a sympathetic character, one who shares, in a very fundamental way, a kindred line of thinking with the narrator, tormented by the 'lines' between nations, communities and people, in the Atlas scene.

May is all what remains of the memory of Tridib, yet May is unlike Tridib — she is not a deviant, a freak or an idler. Her acts of social conscience do not show any fundamental differences with the establishment of which she is a part. She is sufficiently rooted in the values of the system, and is prepared to deviate from it somewhat, if required. She is altruistic and socially conscious — she collects money for charitable causes and sleeps on a mattress because she does not feel the need to sleep on a bed, with its superfluity of cushioned comfort. She feels strongly about certain social issues and quietly contributes to social cause. She is politically correct, as she always takes the side of the oppressed; even a wounded dog merits her attention. Unlike Ila, she does not wear her ideology on her sleeve. Nor does she brandish her 'unconventional' views about things, or dabble in radical politics, as Ila does.

The narrator lets himself 'go away' with the help of Tridib, and 'comes home' with the help of May, the two characters in the novel who are closest to him in their imaginative participation and social conscience about the world around them. Ironically, the narrator 'comes home' when he is in the arms of an Englishwoman in a country, that is far away from the same geographically and socially delimiting 'home' which had been offered to him both by his Tha'mma and his own mother. When the narrator finds himself seeking a haven in May's bed in the last scene, is he like the hero of children's story, *returning* to a conventionally good person's charge? Or is he choosing an option that is a deviation from the norm — a temporary solace from an Englishwoman, the girlfriend of his dead uncle, and much older than him? May's ambivalent position between a conventional mother-sister-girlfriend figure and an unconventional person to turn to for an ordinary, middle-class Bengali young man, makes it a complex and adult novel. Unlike in children's fiction, the narrator, who is at the threshold of adulthood, finds 'home' in woman arms, far away from his literal home. The coming together of May and the narrator is based on a promise that the Tridibs of the world will not be forgotten. The novel ends on an unarticulated hope of keeping alive the Tridibs of the world, who are obliterated from, or at best marginalized in the memories of 'respectable' people. This would not have been the case, if the novel were meant for children. But it was given to Ghosh to resurrect Tridib in an adult novel.

Notes and References

All references to the text are from Amitav Ghosh, *The Shadow Lines*. Delhi: OUP, 1998.

1. Ruskin Bond, 'The Great Train Journey' in *The Ruskin Bond Children's Omnibus* (New Delhi: Rupa & Co., 1998).
2. Mikhail M. Bakhtin, 'The Bildungsroman and its Significance in the History of Realism (Toward a Historical Typology of the novel)' in Caryl Emerson and Michael Holquist ed. *Speech Genres and Other Late Essays* trans. Vern W. McGee (Austin: University of Texas Press, 1992), 22-23. The other references in the same paragraph are also from Bakhtin's discussion of what he calls 'the novel of human emergence' that shows 'man in the process of becoming.'
3. Meenakshi Mukherjee, "Maps and Mirrors: Co-ordinates of Meaning in *The Shadow Lines*" (Delhi: OUP, 1998), 257.
4. Lee, Alfred McClung and Elizabeth Briant, *Marriage and The Family* (New York: Barnes and Noble, 1969), 111.
5. A.N. Kaul, "A Reading of *The Shadow Lines* in *The Shadow Lines*, Delhi: OUP, 1998, 299.
6. Ernest Gellner, *Thought and Change*. London, 1964, 169.
7. Homi Bhabha, *Nation and Narration* (New York: Routledge, 1990), 1.
8. Suvir Kaul, "Separation Anxiety: Growing up Inter/National in *The Shadow Lines*" in *The Shadow Lines* (Delhi: OUP, 1998), 269.

PART II

10

Nationalism and the Question of Freedom in *The Shadow Lines*: A Gender Perspective

MEENAKSHI MALHOTRA

In this paper I use the category of gender to look at the crucial questions of freedom, nationalism and globalism in *The Shadow Lines*. Though my paper, primarily, deals with Nationalism and freedom, globalism as a concept enters the discussion as Ghosh interrogates the nation from the perspective of globality.

In the recent times, which have witnessed the collapse of different political blocks and nation states, nationalism has been discredited and reduced to an outmoded 'grand narrative' of history. It is a legacy of the colonial political heritage that has continued to trouble us: a legacy that post-colonial writing constantly seeks to dismantle and erase. Ghosh, likewise, in *The Shadow Lines*, through his interrogation of borders and boundaries, questions the relevance and continued validity of the concept of 'nationhood.'

In the text, Ghosh offers different attitudes to and competing versions of freedom. Thus, while the narrator's grandmother's idea of freedom is tied up with freedom *from* the colonial power and attaining nationhood, Ila's concept of freedom is, basically, a struggle for personal identity or a quest for personal freedom in a post-colonial, post-modern context.

As against these versions of freedom, the narrator's idea of freedom, under the influence of his mentor Tridib, assumes an intellectual cast, so that he is able to perceive the shadow lines that intersect our lives — as individuals, as a community and as a nation. In the course of my essay, I want to develop these ideas of freedom and see how they help us in arriving at Ghosh's understanding of and attitude toward the complex question of nationalism.

I

In her essay, *Of Shadows Lines and Freedom,* Seema Bhaduri observes:

> Lives of the characters in this novel are determined largely, by their idea of freedom and this idea is shaped by the history of the times [...]. The major characters, here, move towards a global humanitarianism coming to grips with the realization that freedom can't be geo-politically defined or delimited.[1]

Though this criticism of the novel holds good for Tridib, the narrator and May, it is difficult to see how, with justification, it can be applied to Tha'mma, the unnamed narrator's grandmother and a major figure in *The Shadow Lines.* She thinks of freedom in terms of political freedom for the nation. Obviously, it means freedom *from* the colonial power: "I would have done anything to be free", even killed for it, she says.[2] Subscribing to a view of freedom forged in the crucible of violent anti-colonial struggle, she cannot see how Ila can seek her freedom by living in London, as she does not belong there. She believes that:

> Everyone who lives there has earned his right to be there with blood, with their brother's blood and their father's blood and their son's blood. They know they're a nation because they've drawn their borders with blood (77-78).

Borders to Tha'mma are absolute physical and tangible realities. As she plans to fly to Dhaka in 1964, she wonders whether she would be able to see the border between India and Bangladesh (erstwhile East Pakistan) from the plane. When her son laughs at this and says, did she really think "The border was a long black line with green on one side and scarlet on the other, like it was in a school atlas", she muses:

> But surely there's something [...] if there aren't trenches or anything, how are people to know? I mean, where's the difference then? What was it all for then — partition and all the killing and everything — if there isn't something in between? (151).

That Tha'mma's ideas are interrogated and undercut in the novel is quite obvious. What needs to be mentioned here is that her views on freedom and the nation, and her severe criticism of Ila's choices fit into the larger contemporary discourses of gender and nation. To be more precise, they are indicative of the uneasy relationship between overarching nationalisms and individual freedom(s) of its citizens, especially its women.

Tha'mma's brand of nationalism has been variously described as militant, primordial and ethnic by critics — terms which require some explanation and discussion. Theorists have characterized as ethnic or primordial, a nationalism that is based upon shared cultural traditions and a common inheritance from the past. They often consider it as backward-looking, and chauvinistic, on the one hand, and, civic and progressive, on the other, 'associated with a given territory, depending upon universalist political rights accorded within that territory, and forward looking.'[3] Though theorists have attempted to go beyond this dichotomy, it has, nevertheless, proved to be convenient for the analysis of kinds of nationalism.

In his article, "Are there Good and Bad Nationalisms", David Brown has pointed out the illiberal atavistic cast of ethno-cultural nationalism, and the progressive nature of 'civic' nationalism.[4] Now, in *The Home and The World* (1915), Tagore anticipates and projects the 'good' and 'bad' nationalisms into Nikhil and Sandip. Couching his criticism in the figure of the extremist Sandip, Tagore contrasts him with Nikhil the liberal humanist and 'civic' nationalist. This analogy I bring in to point out that both Tagore and Ghosh eschew cultural nationalism, the former from a realization of its divisive potential in a multi-cultural, multi-religious social context, the latter from the perspective of globality. Also, the surprising, common point in the texts is (considering that there is a period of over seventy years separating the two novels), a similar role being played by women *vis-à-vis* the question of nationalism.

The nation has been described as 'Janus-faced,' one looking forward, one looking backward. In the context of the texts under discussion, while women are identified with the nations' 'backward look,' that is, its putative origins and traditions, men represent its modern aspect. As Anne McClintock puts it:

> The temporal anomaly within nationalism [...] nostalgia for the past, and the sloughing off of the past — is typically resolved by figuring the contradiction as a natural division of gender. Women are represented as the atavistic and authentic body of national tradition [...]. Men, by contrast, represent the progressive agent of national modernity.[5]

It is so since the relation between women and the nation is envisaged in familial terms. The 'backward look' encompasses women as mothers of the nation. Since the 'maternal image is a powerful one: it allows a particular group to identify itself in terms of an organic unit: the family.'[6]

In Tagore's *The Home and The World,* this symbolic identification between the mother and the nation is realized in the character of Bimla. Sandip — a militant nationalist deifies her as the iconic 'Devi' and the symbol of the motherland, before the latter exploits her by embezzling her funds. In a similar vein, Tha'mma, brought up on the stories and actual experience of revolutionary terrorism, uses the words 'blood,' 'father,' 'brother,' 'killing' while talking about the nation. But the innocuous actions of this fiery nationalist contribute to personal tragedy. Further her severe censure of her grandson because of his attraction of Ila, and her indictment of Ila as a 'greedy little slut' (79) portray a limited and biased mindset. But, unlike Sandip, she is the victim of her own actions, as she is deeply affected by them. She is one of the 'traumatized' women in the novel. As Suvir Kaul states, that Ila in particular, but also Tha'mma and May 'are represented as carrying the greatest burden of historical dislocation.' And he continues by saying that, 'as we have learnt to expect from the place of women in colonial and post-colonial Indian society, the weight of sexual and cultural definition is borne unequally by men and women, with men as the putative agents of socio-cultural transition and women as its more or less traumatized subjects.'[7]

II

Feminist theorists on women and nationalism also point to the fact that women are made to bear the burden of cultural tradition, which also exerts pressure on them to be exemplars of virtue. This has been pointed out by Nira Yuval Davis in *Gender and Nation* (1997) thus:

> The burden of representation on women of the collectivity's identity and future destiny has also brought about the construction of women as the bearers of collectivity's honour.[8]

It is this burden of representation that Ila seeks to escape. In the nightclub scene where Robi enforces appropriate female behaviour on her, she tells the narrator that she has chosen to live in London to be 'free of your bloody culture and free of all of you' (88-89). However, Ila's notion of freedom is undercut by the narrator and Tha'mma, as well as by the consequences of Ila's own choices, later in the narrative. Ila's attempt to free herself from the cultural burden of Indian womanhood meets with failure, as, even while staying abroad, she is caught in other people's inventions. Thus, when the narrator half-jokingly imagines Nick's misdemeanors, she bursts out:

> Could I ever have imagined, she said, that I, Ila Datta Chaudhari, free woman and free spirit, would ever live in that state of squalor where incidents in one's life can be foretold by a bad television serial? (187)

Ila's situation is the result of a failed cosmopolitanism. She does not fit in either the restrictive upper class Bengali society, or in the easy and casual promiscuity of her society in London, though she is viewed by her group exotically as 'our own upper-class Asian Marxist' (97). None of her aspirations, namely, her fond hope of winning Nick's loyalty to herself and her attempted identification with European culture, get realized. Her supposed superior and privileged position as the inheritor of a tradition of radical struggle from Tresawsen and his friends, and her confident assumption of being a dominant actor, in the future, on the world's political scene, are undercut by the narrator (104-5). Her assertion that nothing really important happens in that part of the world to which the narrator belongs — except famines, riots and disasters, is a limited Eurocentric view.

Ila's own experience of racism belies her statements about her 'free' state. And when she condemns Tha'mma as a fascist, Ila, it is implied, views Europe as a group of free states, upholding an ideal 'civic' nationalism — a society where anyone can 'integrate into the common culture, regardless of race or colour.'[9] The fact that European nation states were originally constructed on the basis of race, religion and language escapes her.[10] This evasion of history deludes her and finally renders her unfree; ironically, if any thing, it leads her into a deep bondage, as is borne out by her experiences in London. It is unbelievable that 'free woman and free spirit' is willing to remain bound to Nick, in spite of his disloyalty towards her.

III

May Price is the only woman whose journey towards freedom is posited as real and also endorsed by the narrator, in sharp contrast to Ila's and Thamma's illusory freedom seeking ventures. Even though she is an English woman, she has the courage to look back on the Empire and speak. Take for instance, her criticism of that 'worthless bit of England' — a large table which Tridib's grandfather had bought on his first visit to London and got it shipped to Calcutta, where it lay unused in a room. She is filled with indignation when she sees it and expresses her strong disapproval of it saying: 'I wonder how many roofs that money would have bought for those huts we saw on our way here' (48). Again, she cannot stand the sight of the Victoria Memorial. 'It shouldn't be here, she blurted out. It's an act of violence. It is obscene' (170).

Her observations reveal a breadth of mind and a special ability to empathize with others — qualities that set her apart from the other women characters in the novel. But when she brings to bear these qualities on such a volatile situation as a riot, she appears to be behaving in a Quixotic manner. Her stepping out of the car to rescue the old man in a riotous situation, is a false step, which prompts Tridib to follow suit and it costs him his life. She holds herself responsible for his death: 'your grandmother [...] said, I'd get everyone killed. I didn't listen; I was a heroine' (250).

May traverses a guilt-ridden tortuous path for seventeen long years. In the meantime, she lives a self-abnegating, austere life and works for global relief agencies, like Amnesty and Oxfam. Eventually, she reaches the realization that she did not cause Tridib's death and that he died with full knowledge of the grave consequences of his action, he 'gave himself up, it was a sacrifice' (252). With this realization, which she gladly shares with the narrator, she is relatively free.

IV

For the grandmother's generation, as mentioned earlier, freedom remained tied to nationalism. Nationalism, however, has yielded a bloody harvest, and has hardly moved in a progressive direction.[11] The central theme of *The Shadow Lines*, therefore, is the need to go beyond nationalism if true freedom is to be sought. In the novel, the bearer of this internationalism is Tridib, and following him, the narrator of the novel himself.

Tridib, the second son of Mayadebi is a sensitive and intelligent eight-year old boy, who visits England during the outbreak of the Second World War. Tridib's varied experiences there initiate him to see imaginatively and not to be trapped, unthinkingly, into accepting other peoples' interpretations. Subsequently, it develops into a credo, a way of life, namely, 'using one's imagination with precision.' This is his legacy to the narrator : He wants him to look beyond competing master-narratives such as colonialism or nationalism. He makes him aware of the multifaceted nature of reality. It can be looked at from different perspectives; one has to 'invent' it in ones' imagination, so to speak. In order to drive home his viewpoint, Tridib asks the young narrator: 'Did you notice that Ila's house had a sloping roof?' (29) — a seemingly innocuous question that opens up new vistas to the child-narrator.

This apparently simple question is not merely meant to be

taken as a pointer to the different aspects of reality, but is suggestive of a view of reality which is superior to that of Ila's and her mother's. The latter, it is suggested, are too preoccupied with the banalities of day-to-day existence, and for them 'the world as it is' is a reality. Moreover, the question suggests that the spectatorial mode is decidedly the superior one. It is implied that the first person narrator, who speaks for the three generations of the extended family, and whose coming of age story encompasses the salient aspects of the life of the nation, is in a privileged position.

V

In her essay on 'Investigating Middle Class Subjectivity' in *The Shadow Lines*. Babli Gupta has pointed out the inevitable limitations, which result when 'a middle class transnational subjectivity' is made the exclusive agent for exploring themes as vast as the life of a nation and nationalism.[12] The Middle Class perspective, for all its advantages in representing the nation before an international audience, is an exclusionary one, as the working classes and the peasants, the oppressed and the poor, and women are left out. Though Tridib is socially mobile, he can hardly represent this wide spectrum. However, his death, which is a 'sacrifice' (252) achieves this, at a symbolic level.

Tridib's death is significant in that it shows him transcending race and class. He could have retreated to the protective cocoon of the car, but he decided to force his way into the mob, to rescue the old man and the others. Earlier, he had tried to rescue May by not letting her proceed towards the mob. But his end is replete with ironies : a spectator so far, Tridib is now an actor in his own tragedy; the pacifist who eschewed violence falls prey to it. For the grandmother, the moment of 'homecoming' turns out to be a moment of mourning.

Whether it happens in Ghosh's fictional world or in our world of diminished possibilities, one or more deaths hardly help in raising social conscience; at the most they affect the victim's immediate circle. The narrator is the one who is the most affected by the personal tragedy. He digs out the facts of a riot, which killed his mentor — facts, which were relegated to the past even by Tridib's own family members.

It is interesting to note that Tridib had expressed a longing to reach forth towards a transcendental kind of reality. He wanted to go beyond the limits of his mind to other times and other places — a kind of virtual place, where 'there was no border between oneself and one's image in the mirror' (29). By delineating Tridib in these terms Ghosh is advocating intellectual freedom.[13]

VI

Though this paper has attempted to deal with the problem of nationalism from the viewpoint of gender, it needs to be pointed out that Ghosh's treatment of nationalism is somewhat incomplete. For instance, it ignores the progressive and radical potential of nationalisms in newly emerging nations outside Europe and America. Ghosh divests even the best traditions of left politics (Tresawsen's 'proletarian internationalism') of any productive or lasting value. Ghosh's text can be finally taken as a timely warning about the dangers of ethnic nationalism and fundamentalism, sweeping India and the world even today.

Yet, for all his 'secular' perspective, *The Shadow Lines* embodies an implicit phallocentricity, which shows up in its conceptualization of women. The narrator openly denies Ila the privilege of inheriting Tresawsen's legacy of selfless action; that privilege is meant only for the visionary Tridib and the reflective unnamed narrator. The weight of the cultural baggage carried by the women in *The Shadow Lines*, excepting May — and that too, partly, denies them any capacity for selfless action. They are made the locus of the problematic aspects of militant nationalism.

Notes and References

1. Seema Bhaduri, "Of Shadows Lines and Freedom" in *The Shadow Lines: Critical Perspectives*, ed. Novy Kapadia (New Delhi: Asia Book Club, 2001), 223.
2. Amitav Ghosh, *The Shadow Lines* (New Delhi: OUP, 1995), 89. All references to the text are from this edition.
3. Tricia Cusack, "Janus and Gender: Women and the Nation's Backward Look", *Nations and Nationalism* 6(4), 2000: 542.

4. David Brown, "Are there Good and Bad Nationalisms," *Nations and Nationalism*, 1999, in Cusack, 543.
5. Anne McClintock (1993) in Tricia Cusack, *Janus and Gender*, 545-46.
6. Deniz Kandiyoti, "Women, Islam and the State" (1991) in Cusack, *Janus and Gender*, 546.
7. Suvir Kaul, "Separation Anxiety: Growing up Inter/National in *The Shadow Lines*" (New Delhi: OUP, 1995), 285.
8. Nira Davis Yuval, *Gender and Nation* (London: Sage, 1997), 45.
9. Kymlicka, (1995) in T. Cusack, *Janus and Gender*, 542-43.

10,11. It is worthwhile to refer to Aizaz Ahmad's summing up here that: 'Nationalism itself is not some unitary thing with some predetermined essence and value. There are hundreds of nationalisms in Asia and Africa today; some are progressive, others are not. Whether a nationalism will produce a progressive cultural practice depends, in Gramscian terms, upon the political character of the power bloc which takes hold of it and utilizes it, as a material force, in the process of constituting its own hegemony,' Ahmad, A. *In Theory: Classes, Nations and Literatures* (Verso, 1992; OUP, 1994). According to David Miller in *Nationalism Reframed* (Camb: C.U.P., 1996) nationalism is a constitutive part of our personal identity. While Anthony Smith and other writers make the point that nationalism and ethnicity should not be conflated, there is a tendency to associate Western nations with 'civic-territorial' and Eastern nations with 'ethnic-genealogical.' This dichotomy, however, breaks down when confronted with nationalist politics in actual situations. A generally acceptable definition is the notion of an 'imagined community' constituted by belief.

12. Babli Gupta, "Investigating Middle Class Subjectivity in *The Shadow Lines*" in *Many Indias, Many Literatures* ed. Shormishtha Panja (Delhi: Worldview, 1999).
13. It is worthwhile to look at Robi's desire for freedom from the haunting memory of a gruesome act. His experiences as an IAS officer reinforce his feeling that the notion of freedom is a 'mirage' (247).

11

Lines and Their Shadows: A Reading of Gender Roles in Amitav Ghosh's *The Shadow Lines*

ANGELIE MULTANI

This essay will attempt to draw attention to the ways in which gender is represented in the text *The Shadow Lines*. It will look at how both male and female roles are constructed in the text as well as how the reader is led to approach the text in certain ways which influence the meaning constructed. The reader is usually positioned as predominantly male; that is, in most texts, the reader is addressed in ways that assume that the reader is self-evidently male. This also leads us to certain ways of approaching the characters, whether male or female, with certain pre-conceived notions of gender and gender roles — that is to say, within certain mainstream definitions of gender attributes. This can be done through the introduction of various characters or through their descriptions, and also at the level of discourse. At this level, the analysis would examine the various situations that the characters are placed in and their reactions or responses to those situations.

One important aspect of reading gender roles in a text is to look at the ways in which characters are described. Usually elements which are described for the male characters are those which are evident when they are in face to face contact, while the ones for the female characters are those which have to be observed when the character is portrayed as an object to be seen.[1] The female character is thus immediately located outside the reader and is projected through a male perspective, in a sense leading the reader to react to the female character in a sexually conditioned way. When Tridib initially talks about May at Gole Park, the first question that is asked is 'and what's she like? [...] Sexy?'[2]

May is then described in purely physical terms, fragmented and broken up — her hair, jaw, shoulders, smile and her blue eyes. Ila is also constantly described in terms of how she appears to the narrator — the clothes she wears, her hair, breasts, the movement of her body. Thus, both May and Ila are set into sexual references by the text itself, positioned as characters who must be approached through their sexual identities unlike the male characters who are approached through a bonding based on similarities (Tridib and the narrator, the narrator and Nick).

I

While reading *The Shadow Lines*, the reader is introduced to four of the main characters within the first four pages of the text itself — Tridib, the grandmother, Ila and, of course, the narrator himself. There is no open or overt indication that the narrator is male — we, as readers, presume this for various reasons. In the first place, the author is male, and the narration is in the first person. This leads to a certain tendency to blur the distinction between the author and the narrator, so the reader tends to act on the presumption that the narrator is male. Secondly, the narrative itself points us in this direction. The narrator identifies himself with his uncle Tridib, on the very first page of the text: 'I have come to believe that I was eight too when Tridib first talked to me about the journey. [...] In the end, since I had nothing to go on, I had decided he looked like me' (3).

The main characters of *The Shadow Lines* are the narrator, Tridib, Ila and the grandmother. Nick and May are significant characters who play a far more important role than the 'secondary' characters, but are not part of the primary narrative in quite the same way as the four first mentioned. The 'secondary' characters are the 'others' — the narrator's parents, Ila's parents, Mayadebi and the Shaheb, Robi and Mrs. Price.

All the characters are introduced in relation to the main protagonist, the consciousness which forms the centre of the narrative. 'Thirteen years before I was born, my father's aunt, Mayadebi, went to England with her husband and her son, Tridib' (3). The grandmother is also 'my grandmother,' and Ila is introduced as only indirectly related by blood with the narrator. 'Of Tridib's two brothers, Jatin kaku, the elder, who was two years older than Tridib, was an economist with the UN. He was always away too, somewhere in Africa or Southeast Asia, with his wife and his daughter Ila, who was my age' (6).

From a gender perspective, it is important to note that most of the male characters are introduced as professionals — Jatin kaku is an economist, Tridib's father a diplomat and the narrator's father is a junior executive. The only exception to this is Tridib, who is outside the framework of the 'normative' male. However, Tridib is also certified with a profession, but it is one that is conventionally seen as 'less masculine' — he is an academic. Although there is one female character in these introductory paragraphs who does have a profession — the grandmother — but it is mentioned only in passing. The narrator's mother is a 'housekeeper,' Ila a child, Mayadebi and aunt/wife/mother/sister. There is no special statement about the job that the grandmother has — as there is about the other jobs — she simply has a 'traditional' female occupation.

The family of the narrator is drawn and upheld as a model, a standard of 'normalcy' — unlike the other families mentioned in the introduction; they are culturally rooted, specifically located in a cultural milieu. 'In our flat all of us worked hard at whatever we did: my grandmother at her schoolmistressing; I at my homework, my mother at her housekeeping, my father at his job as a junior executive in a company which dealt with vulcanized rubber' (4). It is important to note that the only 'job' which is described in some detail is the 'main job,' that of the father.[3] We are told not only that he has a job, but also what his status is, (unlike the grandmother), where he works, and what the firm deals in. The narrator's nuclear family is also located very firmly in a middle class work ethic — everybody works hard at his or her respective job.

All the male characters, except Tridib, are constantly conscious of hierarchy and status. The Shaheb, Mayadebi's husband is uncomfortable talking to his relatives until he can assign a hierarchical position to his nephew and fit him into his 'own promotion scheme.' 'So you see, my father explained to my mother when he came back from his trip to Africa; that day when we went to their house in Raibajar he had given me parity with a third secretary' (41). The narrator's father is acutely aware of how he and his parents had to struggle in order to earn their place in the middle class world. The constant presence of the 'other side' of middle class gentility is a fact that the whole family is aware of. However, when the grandmother discovers the old relatives, her uncle's daughter-in-law's family, somehow it is all right for the women to visit, but not for the narrator. 'Turning to me he said: Stay here with me. I don't want you to go up there' (131).

All the 'secondary' characters fulfil their traditional roles. The narrator's mother is a 'good cook,' an obvious contrast to the grandmother who can only make 'leathery squiggles' for omelettes. The father is a hard working successful man, who provides for his family and is looked after by his wife, who 'naturally' becomes the number one priority as soon as he comes home. The 'other' men and women also fulfil all their traditional roles; they are the pillars of society whom Tridib and the narrator try to understand, gifted as they are, with a 'special imagination'; while Ila and the grandmother are the figures which threaten that fabric. Mrs. Price, Mayadebi, and the mother keep their homes safe for their children, while the men provide for them and support them. For instance, Robi is a traditional male — he is strong, atheletic and rooted in his culture. He is protective of the women and stands up for the underdog and earns his great-aunt's approval. He too, like the narrator's grandmother does not understand or approve of Ila's desire for 'freedom.' For both the characters, a young woman's desire for freedom can only be understood as sexual transgression, which must be curbed by the family/society.

II

The desire for freedom from time/space that is manifested through the character of Tridib is, on the other hand, completely positive. Tridib is *one* of the most positive (if not the most positive) characters of the text. Throughtout the novel he is described as being a non-conventional male character — he is not physically strong, he is not a figure of action, he does not fit into any conventional category of a 'male hero.' The narrator, through his identification with Tridib established early on, also falls into the same unconventional category. As Rajeshwari Sunder Rajan points out in her essay. 'The Division of Experience in *The Shadow Lines*,' that the text 'reverses' the conventional gender characteristics of 'active-passive.' Traditionally, binary oppositions set up between male/female roles tend to associate the male with active, which is also positive. The female, conversely is usually viewed as passive, which is perceived as a negative quality. (Ila and the grandmother too are described in many ways as non-conventional females. This point will be taken up later in more detail in the next section.)

Both Tridib, and later the narrator, are outside the traditional male roles in terms of their character, obsessions as well as choice of profession. They are academics, researchers into the past, rooted in an oral history, taking delight in listening to and telling stories, which is a traditional female occupation. As Robin Lakoff states:

> Another group that has, ostensibly at least, taken itself out of the search for power and money is that of academic men. They are frequently viewed by other groups as analogous in some ways to women — they don't really work, they are supported in their frivolous pursuits by others, what they do doesn't really count in the real world, and so on.[4]

This condemnation is repeated by the grandmother *vis-à-vis* Tridib — 'He's a loafer and a wastrel, I would sometimes hear her saying to my parents; he doesn't do any proper work, lives off his father's money.' Although we are told that the grandmother had an 'inordinate respect' for academic work, Tridib doesn't earn any credit in her eyes — he is too 'irresponsible.'

Both the narrator and Tridib have a fascination for stories and for recreating the past. This quality more traditionally associated with women empowers both the narrator and Tridib, and its absence in Ila becomes a negative marker of her lack of imagination, confining her, paradoxically to the conventional 'inner' or 'private' space assigned to women, while Tridib and the narrator have unlimited access to outer 'public' spaces. The narrator frequently takes Ila and others into the past, through his narration, attempting to create a link with the present. Ila, on the other hand, is completely disinterested in history, more concerned with the immediate, the present. The narrator and Tridib are thus able, through their imagination to break free not only of space but also of time, free to travel through countries they have never seen and time in which they have never lived. Ila, however, is a limited person due to her lack of imagination. She is bound to the inner private space of her own world.

III

As discussed earlier, Ghosh evaluates the 'passivity,' to use Rajeshwari Sunder Rajan's term, of the males in a positive light, while the active imagination of the female characters is seen as negative. Ila uses her imagination to create a fantasy life for herself — a life where she is popular, dates the best looking and most desirable boys in school and most importantly, Nick who is her hero, who is not ashamed of her race/colour, and one who saves her from bullies who are jealous of her.

Even as an adult, Ila creates an illusion, (ultimately self-defeating) of being worldly wise and sexually active, to disguise her 'true' life, to create a self which is more in tune with the image that the narrator had of her. She says:

> I wish it *were* like that, she said with a tired little shake of her head. I wish I could say to myself — why I used to do that kind of thing too, it doesn't mean anything. But I never did, you know. You see, you've never understood, you've always been taken in by the way I used to talk, when we were in college. I only talked like that to shock you, and because you seemed to expect it of me, somehow. I never did any of those things; I'm about as chaste, in my own way, as any woman you'll ever meet (188).

Ila says that part of the reason why she created that illusory impression was because the narrator seemed to expect it of her. It is this expectation; the slotting into a particular category that robs Ila of the freedom to choose her own identity, how much so ever she wants to run away, to be 'free.' As the narrator points out, Ila can never be free, for they are 'within each other.' As a woman, Ila is more constrained than either the narrator or Robi, the other 'two children of a free state.'

Apart from the illusions she creates (or attempts to create, because we are told that the narrator always suspected that she was hiding something) *vis-à-vis* her private life, Ila's politics are similarly limited to the realms of wishful thinking. She participates in discussions about revolutions and popular movements, but is almost powerless.

When Ila and the narrator play 'Houses' under the table in the old family house at Raibazar, Ila cannot fathom the need for a veranda. The narrator, for his own part cannot imagine a house without a veranda — 'otherwise how will we know what's going on outside?' (70). If we look at the text as reversing the traditional attributes of male/female, but nevertheless eventually valorising the male, through the characters of Tridib and the narrator, it is also possible to read this incident as pointing out the male desire to communicate, to be 'open,' while Ila remains, as always, confined to the 'private.' In her essay "Maps and Mirrors" in *The Shadow Lines,*'[5] Meenakshi Mukherjee refers to Ila's inability to understand the need for verandas and terraces. Professor Mukherjee interprets this as 'underlining the essential difference between the cousins.' She says 'Terraces and verandas are traditionally female spaces in our culture and Ila's inability to comprehend their importance may at a realistic level be attributed to her upbringing in other countries while at a metaphoric level it highlights her total self-absoption.'[6] If one looks at the reversal of 'positive' attributes of gender as delineated in *The Shadow Lines,* the rejection of 'traditional female spaces' by Ila and the openness of the male narrator to the spaces outside is perfectly consonant with the overall gender ideology that the text displays.

Despite the reality of Ila's travels all over the world, she remains trapped in her own limitations — all the countries she has been to are identified by the location of 'the Ladies' in the airports. Ila remains bound, limited and enclosed while the narrator is able to perfectly re-trace steps that were taken years before in a country he has never visited.

Similarly, Tridib, is able to see everything in his mind's eye — a quality which the narrator envies and values: 'And still I knew that the sights Tridib saw in his imagination were infinitely more detailed, more precise than anything I would ever see [...]' (29). The grandmother, on the other hand, simply inverts everything that is not part of her reality — everything in her uncle's house was upside down. For all her passionate desire to be part of the freedom movement, she failed to recognize the student revolutionary who was in her class simply because he did not fit into the image she had of a revolutionary. 'She'd been expecting a huge man with burning eyes and a lion's mane of a beard, and there he was, all the while, sitting at the back of her class, sitting shyly by himself' (39).

The 'active' imagination of the grandmother actually does end in disastrous consequences. It is the grandmother who rules in the nuclear family of the narrator, and who is responsible for the renewal of contact with the past, that renewal which is not non-disruptive and comforting like Tridib's or the narator's, but which constructs the situation which destroys the old uncle as well as Tridib. In her desire to bring back her past, to re-join a branch of the family which had been torn asunder, (obviously, an impossible and non-desirable act) the grandmother's stubborn act ends up killing three men, all 'good,' 'passive' and 'benign.'

The grandmother has her own understanding of 'freedom' — she would be willing to die for freedom, to sacrifice everything for it. This understanding for a 'nationalist freedom' is another factor that sets her against Ila. The grandmother believes Ila has 'no right' to live in England, because it is the British who fought and died for their freedom and the privileges it brings, privileges which Ila has no right to enjoy. She condemns Ila's own desire for freedom as nothing but a desire for sexual freedom, one that automatically makes her a 'whore.'

However, the grandmother's desire to hold on to her own personal freedom, is misunderstood and becomes a cause for disharmony in the larger family. Largely, the grandmother also creates this disharmony herself; she herself has construed various slights as 'natural' outcomes of her conditioning. The narrator says,

> Usually when she spoke of them, it was to remind us that it was all very well for Uncle So and So to smile and grin at us whenever he saw us now, but we ought not to forget that he had been quick to turn the other way during her hard years. She chose to forget that it was she who, in the fierceness of her pride, had severed her connections with most of her relatives, and had refused to accept any help from them at all even from Mayadebi, her own sister (129).

This 'pride,' a desirable quality in men, is constructed as a negative one by the text; one, which is implicitly, criticized by the 'normative' woman — the mother and also by the narrative itself. Nick, the man who accepts 'help' from his wife's family is thus a 'weak' man, one to be pitied and who in some ways is almost justified in revenging himself through his infidelity to his wife, while the grandmother's refusal to accept help, even from her own sister is implicitly portrayed as a weak point in her character.

The roles played by the women characters are those of providing ways for the males to transcend or fall — May is 'responsible' for Tridib's death, also for Tridib's final redemption, sexually she is his 'love from across the seas,' his transcendence of borders, boundaries and history. May also allows the narrator a 'glimpse into the final sacrifice and redemption' of Tridib; and in the sexual union with May, May disappears but the narrator re-discovers Tridib and himself.

Ila who is in a position of power *vis-à-vis* the narrator is 'tamed' by Nick, through his infidelity. The hurt caused to Ila by Nick finally allows the narrator to overcome both Ila and Nick and in fact, as Suvir Kaul has remarked, he now includes Nick in his feeling of pathos for Ila, 'This unexpected act of homosocial fellowship derives from the narrator's continuing sense of Ila as a disturbing figure of female power, able to unsettle and even deny male desires or comfort.'[7]

The grandmother is also a threatening figure, as is Ila. As Rajeshwari Sunder Rajan points out, she, is jealous of the love the narrator feels for Ila and contemptuous of Ila's idea of personal freedom (which contrasts with her own idea of 'nationalist' freedom), almost destroys her grandson's career by writing a letter to the Principal of his college, accusing the grandson of visiting prostitutes. The point that the narrator, does, in fact, visit prostitutes, is glossed over as ironic, but the gendering of the malicious act of writing the letter as an act of spiteful jealously and 'madness' is inescapable.

It is interesting, and then how Ghosh manages to reverse some of the traditional characteristics attributed to 'male' and 'female' roles. The reversal is apparent even in the most obvious traditionally 'male' characteristics — for instance, Ila, a female is openly applauded as 'braver' than the narrator:

> [...] I had been with Ila once, when she had come out of the hairdresser's shop, her hair all new and curled, and marched straight off to Brixton with her little crew of friends. To confront a gang of jack-booted racists armed with bicycle chains. As for me, I knew I would not have dared (105).

Despite this reversal, in the final analysis, it is the non-conventional male attributes which are valorized while some of the most fundamentally negative 'feminine' characteristics — jealousy, spite, destructive activity are reinforced through the representations of Ila and the grandmother. It is only one important female character, that of May Price, who stands outside this negativity. This is discussed in the next section.

IV

The woman who seems to straddle both worlds — the positive and negative, is May. May is crucial in the text, for she is the one who links Tridib and the narrator, after separating them, metaphorically and literally. She was Tridib's love — his 'own true love,' from 'across-the-seas.' She was the one who had 'stolen Tridib' from him:

> I was jealous, achingly jealous as only a child can be, because it had always been my unique privilege to understand Tridib, and that day at the Victoria Memorial I knew I had lost that privilege; somehow May had stolen it from me (170).

It is also May herself who finally reunites Tridib and the narrator — Robi also tells the story of Tridib's death, but Robi's telling is uniquely presented from his own perspective — it is a dream. It is May who narrates the details — baldly, in a matter of fact way. It is May who gives the narrator the glimpse into the 'final redemptive mystery.'

May embodies the qualities of a saviour, nurturer and a protector — she is politically active in a positive way, contrasting with Ila and the grandmother, compassionate, understanding. She is a 'good daughter,' 'good sister' who stands up for her brother even while explaining an indefensible act of cowardice, when Nick ran away because he was ashamed to be seen walking with an Indian: 'You shouldn't think too badly of him, May said. She was pleading with me now. He was very young, and at that age children want everyone to be alike' (76).

May is the only character who is 'alive' throughout the text, who lives up to all the exceptions of the narrator. She remains a positive character for the narrator from their very first meeting, in his childhood, right until the end, when she initiates him into manhood and the 'final redemptive mystery' of Tridib's death. May is also one of the few characters who takes responsibility for her action — she believed for a long time that she had killed Tridib, but eventually is 'mature' enough to give up that self-aggrandizing martyr's role. She accepts that Tridib 'gave himself up' — he sacrifices himself. It is this 'true' understanding of Tridib which finally raises May's account of Tridib's death over Robi's experience of it, and which unites the narrator and May.

V

The male characters of *The Shadow Lines* all in some way or the other make their peace with one another and with the world. The narrator finally feels an empathy even with Nick; a male bonding brought about by the 'inverted' power relationship he sees enacted between Ila and Nick:

> Looking at him, I tried to think of the future, as it must have appeared to him: of helpless dependence coupled with despairing little acts of rebellion. I wanted to get up then and hold him, chest to chest, his shoulders to mine (189).

The 'despairing little acts of rebellion,' of course refer to Nick's infidelity to Ila, which is somehow justified by the 'helplessness' Nick is faced with, confronted as he is with his economic dependence on his wife.

The woman characters, on the contrary, find no similar peace — the grandmother dies lonely after sickness, a victim of her own middle-class work ethic — her grandson was not informed of her death because his parents did not want to disturb him as his exams were so close. Ila retreats into a masochistic relationship, a vicious cycle of hate and love and revenge based on lies and self-deception. After confronting Nick's infidelity, she exercises her economic power over him, then hides behind a façade of misunderstanding and reconciliation.

Throughout the text, Ghosh also represents the female characters as isolated from each other, either misunderstood or as perpetrators or victims of misunderstanding. The conventional 'sisterhood' of female bonding is non-existent, and instead the spirit of male 'brotherhood' dominates the novel. None of the women find comfort or solace with each other like the men do — Ila and the grandmother never got along, and the grandmother's last act is a poisonous one directed against her grandson and Ila. Ila doesn't understand May — they have nothing to do with each other. It is once again, only May, the 'outsider' who finds some measure of comfort with the narrator, but in that final union, whereas the narrator 'becomes Tridib' his uncle, May herself somehow disappears.

VI

A reading of the representation of gender in a text therefore looks at how both genders are represented, in terms of their attitudes, characteristics and reactions to various situations. The inscribing of certain attributes, either 'negative' or 'positive' to gender roles does not have to be a conscious bias or position. Very often both authors and readers subconsciously or unconsciously subscribe to various mainstream notions of gender positions and roles, in ways that we assume are 'natural' or 'common-sense.' Uncovering the unconscious biases and political positions inscribed in these 'natural' roles however does help in uncovering the bias against women that seems to permeate even progressive and radical texts.

The narrative voice of *The Shadow Lines* is one that does seem to recognize and acknowledge its own biases and prejudices, however it remains privileged and seems to offer a definitive view of reality. The colouring of our reactions and perceptions of the characters is therefore almost inevitable. We see Ila and the grandmother, Tridib and May, and the entire structure of society through the eyes of the narrator, evaluating and accepting his point of view as sane, logical and sensitive. The alternative views of history and freedom provided by him give us invaluable insights into a different kind of 'maleness' and courage. However, the representation of the female characters and of the gendered behaviour and attitudes, which the text seems to implicitly portray, remain disturbing in all their implications.

Notes and References

1. Susan Mills, *Feminist Stylistics* (London: Routledge, 1995), 162.
2. Amitav Ghosh, *The Shadow Lines*, (Delhi: Ravi Dayal, 1988), 11. All subsequent quotations from the text refer to this edition.
3. The grandmother's promotion from a school teacher to the headmistress of her school is mentioned casually, almost as a 'natural' progression in a career, not worthy of special mention. But the father's promotions, however insignificant, are duly communicated albeit through the grandmother, to the readers.
4. Robin Lakoff in an extract from "Language and Woman's Place, Dominance and Difference in Women's Linguistic Behaviour," in Deborah Cameron (ed.), *The Feminist Critique of Language — A Reader*, (London: Routledge, 1990), 228.
5. Meenakshi Mukherjee, "Maps and Mirrors: Co-ordinates of Meaning

in *The Shadow Lines*," Amitav Ghosh, *The Shadow Lines*, Educational Edition, (Delhi: OUP, 1995).

6. *Ibid.* 262.
7. Suvir Kaul, "Separation Anxiety: Growing up Inter/National in *The Shadow Lines*," *op. cit.* 275.

12

A Post-colonial Interpretation of *The Shadow Lines*

PROMILLA GARG

In her essay "Crossing *The Shadow Lines*," Silvia Albertazzi pays a glowing tribute to Amitav Ghosh when she says that *The Shadow Lines* is probably 'the most important fictional work to have appeared in South Asian literature in the last decade.' And she goes on to explain that it voices almost all post-colonial concerns of our period, namely, 'the search for identity, the need for independence and the difficult relationship with colonial culture, the rewriting of colonial past, an attempt at creating a new language and a new narrative form and the use of personal memory to understand communal past.'[1]

In my essay, I shall particularly deal with the issues of 'identity,' 'freedom' and 'cross-cultural interactions,' in the backdrop of communal violence. I shall try to understand the implications of these significant issues by analysing the attitudes and motives of both Indian and British characters in the novel, as they emerge in the context of different situations they are confronted with. Towards the end I shall also try to project a general scenario of post-colonial writers and try to see where Amitav Ghosh belongs.

In an essay published in 1995, Ghosh stated that he got inspiration to write this book from the anti-Sikh riots of '84 in Delhi. He says: 'It became a book not about any one event but about the meaning of such events and their effects on the individuals who live through them.'[2]

Against such a violent scenario and in the context of cross-cultural interactions, the author seems to express his own views through Tridib. He considers the world as 'a global village' of men and women where they should be trying to reach towards one another, irrespective of their culture and race. Like Fielding in Forster's *A Passage To India,* Tridib believes that it can best be done with goodwill and understanding. He does not revel in the ethnicity of India; instead, he invents the West for himself and for the boys from Calcutta streets through his imagination, and his childhood experience of staying with the Prices in London. But, later in the novel, when Tridib wrests initiative from May to save the old uncle of the grandmother in the riot-torn Dhaka, he unintentionally proves that his culture is not in any way less idealistic than the English culture. It will be a sad mistake to assume that the western culture can displace thousands of years of our Indian civilization, as it gets embodied, say, in a moment of greatness that Tridib clinched. Again, it is he who opened the world to the wondering eyes of the narrator and taught him to invent places through active imagination, reflecting the prophetic streak in him. His vision transcends the limitations of time and space, as he expects us to reach forth towards 'the other' — be it an aspect of physical reality or a human being. But, on yet another plane, Ghosh presents a limited vision in terms of higher middle-class people, who work in foreign missions and agencies and have contacts abroad. Some of these characters may seem to feel concerned for Indians — for instance, when Mayadebi's husband talks to the narrator's mother about the shortage of kerosene and the high price of fish in Calcutta, but then, it is only a part of his polite posturing. It creates the impression as if he is really interested in people's welfare. Unlike R.K. Narayan, the author's vision is not rooted in ethnic India. The novel is more a study of cross-cultural relationship between India and England than anything else.

I

The racist Empire stood on the presumption that 'humanity is not one,' while the post-colonial writers insisted that both belong to 'the same world and not absolutely other.'[3] Amitav Ghosh in *The Shadow Lines* seems to conform to this view as his protagonist Tridib, an Indian, falls in love with May; and Ila-again an Indian, marries Nick Price, an Englishman. The unnamed narrator, of course, is friendly with May.

The interaction between these characters reveals the aspirations, defeats and disillusions of the colonized people when they try to carve out their place in the world. The action of the novel revolves round these characters who, really, belong to the two worlds. In their case the barriers seem to be breaking, though there are problems also. For instance, Mrs. Price is very cordial towards Mayadebi's husband. She addresses him as the Shaheb. She welcomes the young narrator and Ila to her home, treating them as equals. And her children, May and Nick, associate with Indians, apparently without any self-conscious effort. Yet, this interface does not really bring happiness to most of them.

The anglicised gaze of the educated Indians like Ila, Tridib and the narrator points to the fact that independent India is culturally colonized still. The desire of the anglophils like Arun Mehra in Vikram Seth's *A Suitable Boy* is to be construed as pursuing European plenitude. It is nothing but their ardent desire to own the coloniser's world. Arun Mehra exults over the joys of Hamley's Toy Shop; he claims to know its exact location on the Regent Street in London. When Haresh, the homegrown young man asks humbly when Mehras were last in the Imperial capital, it is discovered that they have never been there. Vikram Seth's satire on Mehra's exploits indicates the oriental's longing for its conquering other, though there is pathos in Arun's anglomania, which re-echoes in Tridib's and Ila's longing for the West. Even the young boys from Calcutta streets flock to Tridib to know more about the West. On one such occasion, he tells the boys at the street corner that he had been to London to meet his English relatives by marriage. As the boys were listening to him spellbound, the narrator shouts that Tridib was in Calcutta itself and that he had met him the other day in his room. Tridib like Arun remains unfazed and tells 'If you believe anything people will tell you, you deserve to be told any thing.'[4] Similarly, Ila tells the narrator about her sexual exploits in London to impress upon him that the West offers her a lot of freedom. Later she laughs and tells him that she is as chaste as any other Indian girl of her age. Now, it is foolish on her part to ape the western manners and mannerisms and wear foreign dresses and dance to the sound of pop music, in the fond hope that it will guarantee her social recognition and acceptability in the English society.

The native's desire to own the colonizer's world is often accompanied by disowning the colonized world. To disown India, Ila shocks her people, particularly the grandmother by her western dresses, and, subsequently, she shocks Robi and the narrator by her uninhibited behaviour in a hotel in Calcutta, where she wanted to dance with a stranger. When her uncle Roby, does not permit her to do so, she cries out, 'Do you see why I have chosen to live in London? [...] It's only because I want to be free [...]. Free of your bloody culture' (88).

Hegel's note on *Lordships and Bondage* indicates that human beings acquire identity and self-consciousness only through the recognition of the other. Each self has before it another self, in and through which it secures its identity. Initially, there is antagonism and enmity between these two confronting selves, as each aims at the cancellation and death of the other, while proper end requires that they shed these negative attitudes and get closer to each other. When the narrator in the novel tells Ila, 'you can't be free of me, because I am within you [...] just as you are within me' (89), he seems to be expressing an ideal position.

II

In post-colonial societies even the colonizer's attitude undergoes a change. They try to understand the colonized culture and take care not to offend those who subscribe to that culture. To illustrate this, we may cite the following incident. When May Price comes to Calcutta, she greets Tridib on the railway platform by hugging and kissing him, but she soon realises her mistake, as people around them jeer at them by chanting 'Once more.' It is good that she realizes the importance of the 'other.' But when she denounces Queen Victoria's statue exclaiming, 'It shouldn't be here [...] it is an act of violence. It is obscene,' she seems to be expressing her sound conviction. When Tridib says, 'this is our ruin and this is where we meet' (170), he means that the 'ruin,' associated with Raj, will serve as their meeting place to promote love and understanding between them. When May was in Delhi, India frightened her. She did not understand it a bit and she reminded herself that she came to India out of curiosity, to know what lay beyond West Hampstead and not exclusively to meet Tridib. Subsequently, she realised that she was in love with him. But, despite her good intentions and best efforts, she is unable to understand the colonial psyche and brings disaster on Tridib, unwittingly.

The narrator's visit to England twenty years later shows that the English have changed. They try to please Indians by treating them as equals, even partying with them; still, the two cultures cannot really meet. Probably, multicultural and cross-border friendships are desirable, but we find that Ila's international contacts with the friends from her International school, particularly, with the adulterous Nick, cause humiliation and pain only.

III

The representation of the colonizer and the colonized in the post-colonial literature can be seen as an explication of Hegel's master-slave relationship. In Hegel's paradigm, the slave must turn away from the master to forge the meaning of his existence in labour. In *The Shadow Lines* the narrator returns to India after interacting with the West and understanding it better. Fanon believed that decolonization was a significant period in the history of any nation, which was a part of the European Empire. When the colonized people could not accept foreign values any longer, they started mocking their values, which had enabled the West to stay in power so long. The grandmother's anxiety in *The Shadow Lines* to protect her grandson from Ila's corrupting western influence is a case in point. She thinks that Ila is misguided and that she loves the west for wrong reasons (permissive culture and freedom to do whatever one likes, etc.). The grandmother admires the West for its spirit of nationalism, sacrifice and courage, which the younger generation fails to understand. The grandmother — when she is critical of the western culture, echoes the voice of the 60's and early 70's, which is marked by anti-colonial sentiments, associated with international black consciousness. She wants India to achieve a cultural nationalism which would at once speak for and forge a national identity. To give a practical shape to her ideas, as the headmistress of her school, she initiates her students to cook food of different states of India so that they become aware of the diversity and unity of Indian culture. The grandmother wanted that Indians eschewed their perverse and self-defeating longing for the European culture.

And yet, there was a contrasting trend — what, for the English, could be a course of pride and a confirmation of their great civilization became for the colonized a kind of yardstick to which they must conform. For instance, when Mary forces Tridib to help her in putting an end to the pain of a seriously injured dog by killing it, or when she goads Tridib to save the old uncle of Tha'mma in the charged atmosphere of the riots, she tries to display the superiority of western values. And she expects that Tridib would emulate her. But, while trying to emulate her, he gets killed. Or, shall we say, he embraced death on his own; 'it was a sacrifice.' But the fact is that the two cultures cannot meet, they remain apart. This post-colonial desire to assess one's own culture by the standards of the western culture is evident in the young narrator's effort to size himself up in relation to Nick Price in the 'mirror.'

The decolonised people, with all their complexities and traumas, caused by the protracted colonial rule can never meet the colonizer on equal terms. The colonized people try to associate with the erstwhile colonizer to boost their own ego and try to embrace their world, which seems to them not only glamourous but places them above the common natives. Basically, it is a desire to run away from a society, which is striving to define its own identity. The writer shows the futility of such efforts when Ila marries Nick Price, not for the express love of him but for the licence it will give her to live in London. Their union is stillborn, though she refuses to admit it even to herself. Similarly, Tridib's desire to love and marry May Price leads him to his untimely death.

IV

With the emergence of the new nation-states, the colonized show a tendency to forget the colonial past. They try to avoid any reference to the bullying and treachery of the colonizer throughout the rule of the Empire. The desire to forget the past in the post-colonial era is symptomatic of the colonized people's need to make a new start and to erase the painful memories of colonial subordination. Jameson feels that post-coloniality is actually an ability to successfully imagine and execute a decisive departure from the colonial past. Albert Memmi, a prominent Tunisian anti-colonial revolutionary, believed that we, in the colonial aftermath, are deluded if we think that a new world will magically emerge from the ruins of colonialism. Both Memmi and Edward Said insist that the colonial aftermath does not yield the end of colonialism, hence the self-willed historical amnesia. There is a deliberate unwillingness to remember what Homi Bhabha describes as 'painful and humiliating memory of history of a race and racism.'[5] It may be noted that in *The Shadow Lines* there is hardly any reference to the colonial India. Even while talking about the riots of Calcutta and Dhaka, in which Tridib lost his life, Ghosh does not talk about the partition of India which led to such riots, and he does not blame the colonial regime for the mess they created by partitioning India.

V

The Imperialists extolled their literature as great for its imputed power to convey universal values. 'The concept of universalism became a part of the technology of the Empire.' The post-colonial writers like Fanon and Achebe challenged this myth of universality for its basic (false) assumption that European culture symbolised universal values. They questioned the myth that when we talk of universal experience we talk of cultural responses that have been shaped by the western tradition. These writers questioned the cogency of such ideas and found them worthless, as they were contrary to the experience of the people. Fanon anticipates another condition beyond Imperialism and finds that, despite the shared experience of colonialism, the cultural realities of the post-colonial societies may differ vastly. Most of the western critics ignore the cultural differences, as they are indifferent to the sensibilities of others. In this connection, I may cite the critic Mark Van Doren who thinks that great love stories have no time and place and that love is the most common theme of literature. Leslie Fiedlar challenged this by observing that there is at least one whole section of the world, where love story is virtually non-existent. Thus, he emphasizes the fact that what is universal for the Europeans might not be so for the post-colonial societies. Further, there is a lack of concern about death in European fiction. The European reader might miss the significance of death in the African novels. One wonders if two people as different as European and African will ever be able to appreciate fully one another's literature and understand it. What is true of life is no less true of fiction; and Amitav Ghosh's text says it, implicitly. Despite the fact that May is keen to understand India, she is unable to do so, and her effort brings only disaster. Ila's effort to be a part of the western civilization also meets with disaster.

To conclude, *The Shadow Lines* shows two types of postcolonial understanding. One is that of higher social elites like Mayadebi and the Shaheb, and, second, is that of characters like Ila who still live in close contact with the West. They do not have roots in the home country and want to be a part of the colonizer's world. Such characters have no desire even to think of the colonized world, they are happy imitating the West. Ila's mother, for instance, sits like 'Queen Victoria.' The grandmother, on the other hand, shows the other side of post-colonial understanding. She is enlightened and self-sufficient and ardently proud of being an Indian. She wants India to forge her own identity. Though she admires the nationalism and patriotism of the English, she feels it is time for Indians to act and achieve their own identity and not waste time in apeing the West.

The post-colonial writer is using the colonizer's ways — his language and culture. Despite his protests to the contrary, he knows that he can attract attention by clinging on to the colonial master's culture and bearings, and it is reflected in his writings.

Is he not posturing when he claims that he is the voice of the voiceless natives? Is his whole endeavor not just a burning desire to impress his erstwhile colonial masters and be counted among the genuine spokesmen of the world culture? It is for this purpose that he combines the earthy nativity of the colonized and the high avant-garde savouries of the metropolitan cultural market place. Kwame Anthony Appiah says that such post-colonial writers 'meditate the trade of cultural commodities of the world capitalism at the periphery.'[6] Had he been writing in the colonized state, speaking of the colonized mind, he would not have just made his work look 'chic.' As for his complaints and protestations of the West, they are basically hollow because he knows that his value lies in not being embroiled in the rustic idiocies of tribalism, engendered by the shackled psyche of the colonized. Most of the time the post-colonial writer does not value life as it is actually lived; it has value for him only when it gets entangled and disentangled in relation to the West. He seems to write with a squinted eye, which is, consciously or unconsciously, aware of the hidden eye of the West.

Notes and References

1. Silvia Albertazzi, "Crossing *The Shadow Lines*," University of Bologna: http//w.w.w.lingue.unibo.it/postcolonial-studies-centre/postcolonial-linee d ombra. Htm.
2. Amitav Ghosh, "The Ghost of Mrs. Gandhi," *The New Yorker*, July 17, 1995.
3. Neil Kortenar, "How the Center is Made to Hold Things" in *Things Fall Apart, Contemporary Critical Essays*, ed. Michael Parker & Roger Starkey (London: Macmillan Press, 1995), 32.
4. Amitav Ghosh, *The Shadow Lines* (New Delhi: OUP, 1995), 12. Subsequent references are to the same edition, and are included in the parentheses.
5. Homi Bhabha, *Signs Taken for Wonders: The Location of Culture* (London & New York: Routledge, 1994), 174.
6. Kwame Anthony Appiah, in his book, *In My Father's House: Africa in The Philosphy of Culture* (London: Methuen, 1992).

13

VIOLENCE IN *THE SHADOW LINES*: NATIONALIST RHETORIC AND HISTORICAL SILENCE

RUDRASHISH CHAKRABORTY

> The organising principle of any society is war. The authority of the state over its people resides in its war powers.
>
> —Oliver Stone's *JFK: A Film On Cold War*

Anthony Giddens, in his epochal work *The Nation State and Violence* makes a seminal observation that state-power is perpetrated and perpetuated by 'the consolidation of centralised control of the means of violence' (5). He traces the evolution of 'nation-states' from the 'traditional states' of Greece and Rome, through the Renaissance absolutist state to the modern nation-state, especially in the context of the official patronage to violence. Violence is not always physical or tangible; it can be unleashed through powerful discursive practices with the purpose of circulating the dominant ideology through the body-politik. Such an intensely political and theoretical grounding can form a suitable entry-point to a seemingly apolitical narrative of Amitav Ghosh's *The Shadow Lines* — a text which is international in scope but very local in spirit.

Homi K. Bhabha, in his introduction to *Nation and Narration* (1990) rightly observes:

> Nations, like narratives, lose their origins in the myths of time and only fully realise their potential in the mind's eye. Such an image of the nation — or narration — might seem impossibly romantic and excessively metaphorical,

> but it is from these traditions of political thought and literary language that the nation emerges as a powerful historical idea [...] an idea whose cultural compulsion lies in the impossible unity of the nation as a symbolic force (Bhabha, 1).

Bhabha seems to corroborate Ernest Renan's observation in the latter's essay 'What is a Nation?' Renan says:

> I would even go so far as to say historical that error is a crucial factor in the creation of a nation, which is why progress in historical studies often constitutes a danger for the principle of nationalism (*Nation and Narration*, 11).

It should be clear that 'nation' to Renan and Bhabha becomes a 'construct' rather than a concrete reality, having more shadow than substance. As a logical corollary to this is the idea of 'nationalism' which is fallacious — a propaganda exercise, full of gaps and fissures. Ernest Gellner seems to drive home this point in *Thought and Change* (1964):

> Nationalism is not the awakening of nations to self-consciousness: it invents nations where they do not exist (Gellner, 169).

Tha'mma finds herself in between the extremes of the existent and non-existent realities. Her subject position is precarious: on the one hand, she advocates the militant nationalism of revolutionaries like Khudiram and Bagha Jatin, and, on the other, she does not conform to the socialist ideas of those revolutionaries as is evident through her contemptuous attitude towards the refugees living in shanties on the outskirts of the city. Her nationalist fervour, during her college days, against the colonial rule sharpened her sense of nationhood. She extends that antagonistic logic to the formation of the Indian nation-state in the post-independence context — a nation, whose borders are confirmed in war. War is an instrument of the state to legitimise its claim to be the sole agent and authority of violence; it unites the country against a common enemy, ratifies the territorial boundaries and deepens the ideological and international opposition necessary to shape a cohesive national identity. It is in this light one may understand

Tha'mma enthusiastically telling her grandson about the British history of bloodshed: 'War is their religion. That's what it takes to make a country.' As physical strength is a prerequisite for any aggressive military action, she insists that her grandson take physical exercises daily: 'you can't build a strong country [...] without building a strong body.' Her ecstasy at contributing to the War Fund is symptomatic of her tenuous situation *vis-à-vis* the nationalist rhetoric which thrives only in a national crisis, be it Indo-Pak or Indo-China war: 'We have to kill them before they kill us; we have to wipe them out.'

The motif of violence looms large throughout *The Shadow Lines*. As a matter of fact, it forms the end-points of the actual narrative. The narrative begins in 1939 — the year of the outbreak of the Second World War — and essentially ends in 1964 with the eruption of riots in Dhaka and Calcutta. Tridib's boyhood experiences of war-torn London in 1939 and his violent murder 25 years later by a rioting mob in Dhaka constitute the end-points of the main narrative. These two instances of the destructive force of violent nationalism mark not only the actual time span of the novel but also probe the legitimacy of the nation-states. This scrutiny becomes much more significant in the light of the 'looking-glass' metaphor located precisely at these very markers of the novel, namely: Tresawen's description of nationalist jingoism in Germany, though in a 'grotesque' way, during the Second World War; and Tha'mma's disappointment with the Indo-Pak border on her trip to Dhaka when she could not spot a tangible difference, a physical demarcation between the two nations. Her nationalist faith gets a severe jolt at such an absence, which actually rips apart her whole ideology: "What was it all for then — partition and all the killing and everything — if there isn't something in between?"

Tha'mma's nationalist vocabulary is couched in the language of modernity, which, particularly in its colonial derivation, requires the syntax of good citizenship and an exclusive national pride. But as her grandson rightly points out, her tragedy is the tragedy of the entire middle-class:

> All she wanted was a middle-class life in which, like the middle-classes the world over, she would thrive believing

in the unity of nationhood and territory, of self-respect and national power; that was all she wanted — a modern middle-class life, a small thing, that history had denied her in its fullness and for which she could never forgive it.

Tha'mma's precise class location is surely that of a '*Bengali bhadromohila*' (lady). However, one major component missing in this prognosis is that she is a rootless refugee from East Pakistan, suddenly thrown into a financial crisis owing to the partition. Consequently, she gets declassed, much against her wish. Her predicament is that of countless Bengali Hindu refugees in post-independence Bengal, who had been rendered penniless — in stark contrast to their erstwhile financial edge over the Muslim peasants and workers in the unified Bengal province. Tha'mma's class-consciousness never allows her to identify herself with the plight of the refugees living in unhygienic slums on the outskirts of the city. Following the same logic, she is contemptuous of her relatives who too belong to the same category. She is not ready to accept the fact that she has been rendered 'homeless' like others till she has undertaken her trip to Dhaka. She cannot relate to Calcutta as her home; nor can Dhaka satisfy her construct of a home. 'Home' is now forever a memory for her, a fond recall which she can share with her grandson. To borrow Paul de Man's words, memory for Tha'mma is the retrospective recording of her failure to overcome the power of time. Born in Dhaka, but separated from her birthplace by a history of bloodshed and lines on a map, Tha'mma loses her grammatical coordinates as evident in her confusion about 'coming' and 'going' home. Her strictly disciplinarian and regimented mind seems unable to understand 'how her place of birth had come so readily at odds with her nationality.' She suffers from a post-partition 'angst' typical of the East Bengalis, rendered 'immobile' *vis-à-vis* their homeland. Like a typical character from an absurd play, she is an alien, a stranger, unable to come or go. This angst precisely accounts for her pathological hatred for her erstwhile neighbours in Dhaka during the war of 1965; as for her, the theatre of war cleanses the messy mob violence of streets of which she had been a witness.

In such a volatile situation, no wonder cartography forms a

recurring symbol in the text — with maps, lines and borders driving home the contradiction between national culture and universal civilisation. The narrator is precariously positioned between a staunch nationalist grandmother and a defiant Tridib (his uncle), who actually opens to him new avenues of ideas, though insisting on 'imagination with precision.' Tridib is the polar opposite of Tha'mma owing to his quality to transcend barriers of the mind. He is a man without a nation, a Tristan incarnate, in love with a woman-across-the-seas (an image typical in Bengali fairy-tales). May misses the point when she interprets Tridib's murder as a 'sacrifice': it is actually a defiance of nationalist rhetoric, a refusal to accept the state-imposed boundaries which close human mind and denigrate humanitarian values. Tridib's killing while trying to rescue the senile old man — one who had been their arch-enemy in a family feud — was compounded by the death of Khalil in the same incident. Their death underlines the essential fallacy in all rhetoric of nationalism and the separatist political logic of the nation-state, since these cannot enforce cultural difference on people. There is always some 'other thing' — whether a bus journey or a cricket match — that connects Calcutta to Dhaka, a Bengali to a Bangladeshi, Lahore to Amritsar, Srinagar to Muzzaffarabad in Pakistani-occupied Kashmir, as images in a mirror. Even the mutuality of riots in both Dhaka and Calcutta over the disappearance of the prophet's hair in Srinagar nullifies all claims of exclusive national identity. Ironically, it is through self-destructive violence that the sub-continental commonality is asserted.

However, as A.N. Kaul rightly says, 'Ghosh's proclamation of the death of nationalism is premature.' Realities cannot be wished away just because one calls them illusions, and *The Shadow Lines* bears testimony to this without being conscious of this paradoxical position. The narrator, despite his imaginative explorations beyond boundaries, cannot think beyond his own locale in Calcutta. During his college days in Delhi (beyond the scope of this Tha'mma's vigilance) he used to visit whores — an act which violates the propriety of a Bengali middle-class *bhadralok*. He can fantasise relationships with Ila or May, who are figures of desire owing to their 'foreignness.' These fantasies provide an outlet for the narrator, who typifies the sex-starved provincial Bengali youth. Again, the incident of the Grand Hotel — where Ila is restrained from dancing with a stranger by Robi and the narrator — underlines the gender (in)sensitivity of the Bengali youth, who are apparently cosmopolitan in their sensibility but are enforcers of national difference and patriarchal authority when it comes to women. Ghosh's treatment of the precarious, tensed community relationship in India also conforms to exclusive national identity and cultural symbols: *vermilion* for Hindus, *burkas* for Muslims. He expresses the same even through his non-fiction *In An Antique Land*:

> But I was never able to explain very much of this (riots) to anyone in Nashawy. The fact was that despite the occasional storms and turbulence their country had seen, despite even the wars that some of them have fought in, theirs was a world that was far gentler, far less violent, very much more humane and innocent than mine. I could have never expected them to understand an Indian's terror of symbols (92).

In an interview to *India Today* in April 2000, Amitav Ghosh has declared that his early novels, including *The Shadow Lines*, are about 'the castaways of history.' Ghosh however creates ambiguity with respect to the nature of the so-called 'castaways,' especially in their class-character and cultural rootlessness. The degree of marginalisation needs to be scrutinized: whether it is Tha'mma forced to stay away from Dhaka, or the mechanic Saifuddin, being uprooted from Motihari. Saifuddin is doubly marginalised — firstly, as an uprooted Muslim compelled to migrate to East Pakistan; and secondly, a non-Bengali 'Mohajir' who, in the charged context of 1964, was at the receiving end of the cultural and linguistic nationalism spearheaded by the Bengalis in East Pakistan. A classic example of this problematisation of exclusive national and cultural identities is the meeting between Tha'mma and her senile uncle when she visits her ancestral residence in Dhaka in 1964. The incident which begins as a mere domestic gathering, eventually snowballs into a showdown between different ideologies working at cross-purposes. Saifuddin's desperate attempt to dispatch the senile old man to 'India' on the pretext of security is negated by the rickshaw-puller Khalil's staunch support for the old man's stay in the house. The 'Two-Nation Theory' fails hopelessly in this context since religious commonality is overcome by linguistic affinity as evident in the Khalil-Saifuddin showdown. Khalil's allegation that Saifuddin intends to capture the whole house has a very serious political sub-text: it echoes the fear psychosis generated among the Bengali populace of East Pakistan owing to the dominance of Urdu-speaking West Pakistanis in all spheres of their life. More importantly, in historical terms, Ayub Khan's military regime patronised the sweeping take-over of all leading political, cultural and economic institutions of the Bengalis in East Pakistan by West Pakistanis as a part of his policy to homogenise the theory of Pakistan and also to suppress the growing discontent among the Bengali majority in the East. Khalil's anger is that of a Bengali who resents the presence of a Non-Bengali like Saifuddin in the house, the latter being a political and economic threat to his identity. Khalil develops a cultural bonding with a Bengali Hindu, namely, Tha'mma's old uncle, thus nullifying all claims of a homogenous Muslim nationality. The language movement in 1952 which was launched to accord the status of national language to Bangla along with Urdu sowed the seeds of Bengali Nationalism. This eventually prospered into a full-fledged political and cultural movement in 1960s, leading to the formation of independent Bangladesh in 1971.

Saifuddin's presence in this context is a brutal eye-opener for liberals like Tridib who have never countered any such figure. The one-sided biased accounts of history circulated by chauvinists like Tha'mma tend to discriminate between communities and cultures. Saifuddin's marginalisation is a bitter reminder of the fact that the riots have spared none — neither Hindus nor Muslims. Saifuddin's case is worse: unlike Tha'mma who could at least settle in India after the partition, Saifuddin becomes an outsider even in the promised 'land of the pure' (Pak-i-stan) because of another fissure in his society on the issue of language. His social and psychological insecurity can well be understood by his desperate bid to hold on to the house; he reels under a serious minority complex which compels him to manipulate. Tridib's cosmopolitan and internationalist temperament cannot comprehend the enormity of Saifuddin's situation. Hence Tridib can only respond to him by rushing out of the room — an action revealing his utter helplessness to rationalise the situation. It is ironical that Ghosh deals with this highly tensed situation in a very cursory, non-serious manner. In fact, this perfunctory attitude towards serious historical issues is typical of Amitav Ghosh, especially in *The Shadow Lines*, where he indulges himself in not writing of history, but *writing off history*. There seems to be an attempt, willingly or unwillingly best known to the writer, not to probe deep enough issues of historical importance. This must have been done to avoid unpalatable realities which would have demolished pre-conceived notions of history. The narrator's efforts to piece together the fragments of suppressed history in the form of Calcutta riots in 1964 was more an act of a personal vindication rather than a concrete political awareness.

Prof. A.N. Kaul observes that *The Shadow Lines* is a metaphor for evading rather than exploring political realities. This may be attributed to the absence of any cogent analysis of political realities responsible for the streak of violence in the text. Ghosh can be defended against this charge on two grounds: First, he is a creative writer and not a chronicler, hence it is not his job to give an account of historical facts. Two, and more importantly, he seems to work out the Jamesonian concept of 'the political unconscious' whose covert presence is to be exposed by the readers themselves. According to Fredric Jameson, the rifts and discontinuities in a text, and especially the unsaid elements are symptoms of the repression by ideology of the contradiction of 'history' into the depths of the political unconscious. The content of this repressed history, Jameson asserts, is the revolutionary process of 'the collective struggle to wrest a realm of Freedom from a realm of Necessity.' History is not a text but an 'absent cause' to be reconstructed from a 'prior ideological historical subtext.' Hence the Marxist critic has to rewrite the text's unspoken (because repressed and unconscious) awareness of the ways it is determined not only by current ideology but also by the long-term process of 'true' history. Ghosh has been a student of social anthropology; and his narrator is a student of history. Hence it is implausible that both Ghosh and his narrator are unaware of the context of the sub-continent which in fact contributed to the 'Two Nation theory.' In Bengal during 1930s and 1940s, a lop-sided agrarian structure and the raw deal meted out to the peasants and the working class (most of whom, incidentally, were Muslims) gave impetus to the separatist ideology of different communities, leading to the eventual partition. The same logic holds true in the struggle for Bangladesh when the aggrieved Bengali populace in East Pakistan revolted against the atrocities and exploitation perpetrated by the Urdu-speaking West Pakistani tyrants. Amitav Ghosh's generalisation of riots and violence deliberately avoids harsh political and historical realities. In fact, he overlooks the most quintessential argument that religious and cultural separatism became secondary when confronted with serious socio-economic threats. Ghosh leaves it to his discerning readers to read between the lines and reinvent history, which in Foucauldian terms, is not linear but disjunctive, bound together by successive power-structures. There is no absolutist readings to *The Shadow Lines*; the text is full of gaps, fissures rifts that mark the sites of personal and national trauma. They are not contingent or accidental but are entry points to probe and interrogate the alternative narratives hidden in the sub-text.

Works Cited

A.N. Kaul, "A Reading of *The Shadow Lines*" (New Delhi: Oxford Paperback, 1999).

Amitav Ghosh, *In An Antique Land* (Delhi: Ravi Dayal, 1991).

Anthony Giddens, *The Nation State and Violence: Volume Two of a Contemporary Critique of Historical Materialism* (Cambridge, UK: Polity Press, 1985).

Ernest Gellner, *Thought and Change* (London, 1964).

Ernest Renan, "What is a Nation?" trans. Martin Thom. *Nation and Narration*. ed. Homi Bhabha (London: Routledge, 1990).

Fredric Jameson, *The Political Unconscious: Narrative as a Socially Symbolic Act* (Ithaca: Cornell University Press, 1981).

Homi Bhabha ed., *Nation and Narration* (London: Routledge, 1990).

Meenakshi Mukherjee, "Maps and Mirrors: Co-ordinates of Meaning in *The Shadow Lines*." (New Delhi: Oxford Paperback, 1999).

14

The Bengalee in *The Shadow Lines*

MINOTI CHATTERJEE

The Eastern State of Bengal is still racked by memories of two partitions, one in 1905 and the other in 1947. Amitav Ghosh's *The Shadow Lines* reminds us of the trauma of both times, though it is, mainly, about the post-partition riots of 1964. The private turmoil of the narrator of the novel is reflective of the public turmoil, principally, around strife-centred areas, namely, Dhaka of erstwhile East Pakistan (now Bangladesh) and Calcutta of India. The *Bengalee* belonged to both the East and West Bengal but an artificial, calculated divide was created. As a rent in heart Ghosh in his novel deals with memories of an undivided Bengal, together with the forces of nationalism, which create the shadow lines of division between people.

Rabindranath Tagore's political message was clear. There is an in-built critique of nationalism in his work and refusal to recognize the nation-state as the organizing principle of Indian civilization and as the last word in the country's political life. Ghosh makes his historical concerns blend with his narrative vision and his story-telling ability, essentially echoing the sentiments of the futility of drawing lines across nations. For him all such demarcations are arbitrary, forced and invented.

Amitav Ghosh experienced Bengal deeply and substantively and writes of his actual and imaginative experiences through Tridib's and Grandmother's eyes so that the past comes to life and acquires immediacy for him and for us. How can one divide memory? There is a generation of Bengalees whose collective memory still makes them believe that borders have a tenuous existence and that not even a history of bloodshed can make them real and impermeable. But as time moves on, the inheritors of this legacy, slowly but surely recognize that partition is indeed a part of their history. Amitav Ghosh has put his finger precisely on this pulse. He says:

> I grew up believing in the truth of the precepts that were available to me; I believed in the reality of space, I believed that distance separates, that it is a corporeal substance; I believed in reality of nations and borders. I believed that across the border there existed another reality. The only relationship my vocabulary permitted between those separate realities was war or friendship.[1]

A flood of nostalgia and memory overtook me as a *Probashi* (The Bengalee who lives outside Bengal) and a strange yearning for my culture and roots overtook me, as I raced through the book. *Probashis* are indeed Calcutta-centric; we have no home but in memory, and thus have learnt to be skilled in the art of recollection.

Tha'mma is the epitome of the displaced generation. She is dreamy about Dhaka, about the terrorist nationalist movement of 1905 in Bengal, about secret societies like *Anushilan* and *Jugantar*, which carried on clandestine activities, making bombs and targeting British officials. Despite this, these societies had the support of the common people for their cause. The history of revolutionary terrorism in Bengal is extraordinary and the history of repression by the British even more horrific. Arrests, deportation, executions were the order of the day. Many a patriot went to the gallows with a song on his lips. An innocent-looking boy who studied in *Tha'mma's* class in Dhaka was actually a revolutionary. The revolutionaries exercised in gymnasiums, learnt to use pistols and make bombs, smuggle messages and ran errands. This boy was assigned the first mission. It was to assassinate the English magistrate of Khulna district, but the police found out. He was tried and deported to the infamous Cellular jail in the Andaman and Nicobar islands. Even before this incident, the grandmother had remained fascinated by the heroism of Khudiram Bose, the sad death of Bagha Jatin who was hunted down the banks of the Buribalan

River, betrayed by traitorous villagers bought over by the British. It is not difficult to believe that the womenfolk in East Bengal were a great support to revolutionary terrorists like Surya Sen alias *master da* during those turbulent times. They cooked and washed for the revolutionaries and even helped them in hiding whenever the situation so warranted. Fired by such times, *Tha'mma* wished she could have been with her classmate and had gone to Khulna and

> stood at his side with a pistol in her hands, waiting for the English magistrate [...]. I would have been frightened, she said. But I would have prayed for strength, and God willing, yes I would have killed him. It was for our freedom: I would have done anything to be free (39).

Those turbulent times of Bengal reflect the essence of various facets of Indian nationalism. The partition of Bengal in 1905 forms its first political constituency. The partition was like a convulsion that gripped Bengal and galvanized the masses into action. The romanticism and adventure of the terrorist movement and its militancy constitute a major part of Indian nationalism. But a fall out of this violent thinking finds reflection in strained Hindu-Muslim relations, which undoubtedly varies in different periods, but the situation was never so complicated and dismal in and around the times of the partition of Bengal in 1947.

Both the communities had been living together with minor skirmishes now and then, but the differences had never been acute. Bengali-Hindus and Bengali-Muslims shared a mutual goodwill and brotherhood, and the rich heterogeneity of their lives was never seriously threatened. The Hindus were the worshippers of many *Pirs* and Muslims participated in Hindu festivals. Both the communities shared common spaces in *Haats* and *Bazars*. A homogenous group speaking the same language, having the same dietary habits, and wearing the same clothes were separated for political or so-called administrative reasons by the British. Ironically, even as they moved apart, they yearned for one another at the same time. They came closer than ever before because of this partition:

> The simple fact that there had never been a moment in the four thousand year old history of that map, when the places we know as Dhaka and Calcutta were more closely bound to each other than after they had drawn their lines — so closely bound to each other, that I in Calcutta had only to look into the mirror to be in Dhaka: a moment when each city was the inverted image of the other, locked into an irreversible symmetry by the line that was to set us free — our looking-glass border (233).

That indivisible sanity, which binds people to one another, independently of their governments, is illustrated in the history of Bengal.

Subsequently, the simple explanation of the organized communal politics in Bengal came to be clearly formulated: the dominant upper caste Hindu *Bhadralok*, politically organized under the Congress, sought to protect and preserve the rights and privileges of the Zamindari and intermediate tenure holding renter interests. Whereas, Muslim leaders of Eastern Bengal, relying on the support of the Muslim *Praja*, sought to uphold the rights of *raiyats* and were placed in opposition to the Congress. This was the basic foundation of communal divide in organized politics in Bengal, which finally convinced the new Muslim leadership of Eastern Bengal for the need of an independent political organization.

Some parts of the novel are played out against this canvas of sweeping historical events — the freedom movement, and the rise of insurgency and communalism in Bengal. However, in recent writings any consideration of 19th and 20th century Bengal at any level, almost invariably tends to make nationalism its nucleus. Amitav Ghosh's *The Shadow Lines* is no exception.

The grandmother's memories of Dhaka of her childhood are so sharp and vivid that her grandson can easily visualize it all for himself — through another kind of imaginative reconstruction of reality. When she attempts to recall and retrieve the memories, she seems to be acting like any displaced person who had to leave her/his ancestral home in Dhaka and settle down in Calcutta after partition. She returns to Dhaka, her homeland, in 1964. But Dhaka of her memories is different; it remains as real for her as ever. This idyllic vision of the ancestral home is shattered by political events like communal riots in both India and Pakistan in 1964. Her home in Dhaka, which was like a heavenly retreat, has got associated with death and destruction.

The partition played havoc for the East Bengali psyche, as the Bengali had to move to West Bengal; he was dislocated. Displaced, alienated in an adopted land, he felt closer to those whom he had left behind in the villages of East Bengal, Hindus and Muslims alike. The novel, essentially, rejects the very concept of partition. Both the Bengals are historically, culturally and geographically alike and the partition was not a solution to Hindu-Muslim malevolence. But it is curious that people on both sides who were willing to lay down their lives for one another became enemies overnight.

Returning to the grandmother, she cannot understand why she cannot, like in the past, travel from Calcutta to Dhaka freely. She is severed from her old roots and is groping for a new kind of stability and identity; she wanted to know whether she would be able to see the border between India and East Pakistan from the plane.

> When my father laughed and said, why, did she really think the border was along a black line with green on one side and scarlet on the other, like it was in a school atlas, she was not so much offended as puzzled (151).

She tries to explain her viewpoint thus:

> No that wasn't what I meant she said. Of course not. But surely there's something trenches perhaps, or soldiers, or guns pointing at each other, or even just barren strips of land. Don't they call it no-man's land? (151)

If the borders were not visible, it would be like the good old days when she could freely travel from Dhaka to Calcutta and back. 'What was it all for then — partition and all the killing and everything — if there isn't something in between?' (151). When it was explained to her that border started right from inside the airport, where she would have to declare her place of birth, which ironically happened to be Dhaka, she was simply puzzled.

'[...] At that moment she was not able to quite understand how her place of birth had come to be so messily at odds with her nationality' (151).

At the cost of displeasing those that credit *The Shadow Lines* as a book which transports one to many spaces, Ghosh's repeated allusions to the close ties between the two Bengals would make one want to believe that it is Bengal which is the focus of the book. This is not to say that there is an effort on his part to whip up Bengali chauvinism, but let us face it, despite his anonymity, the narrator of *The Shadow Lines* is a firmly rooted *Bengalee.*

The *Bhadralok* in Bengal was ostensibly created by the British for running the colonial state — he was usually an educated and language-proud pen pusher. There is ample in the novel, which reflects the *bhadralok's* decadence and obsession with trivia. The grandmother called her brother-in-law, Mayadebi's husband the *Shaheb* — he was so much Europeanized 'that his hat would not come off his head' (34). He was more English than the English.

> It was my grandmother's theory that the Shaheb's wardrobe was divided into sets of hangers, each with its own label: Calcutta Zamindar, Indian Diplomat, English gentleman, would be Nehru, South Club tennis player, Non-Aligned Statesman and so on [...] yet in Calcutta the fall of the dhoti was always perfect — straight and starched — the top button of his kurta open in an exact equilateral triangle [...] (34).

On the other hand, there was the *Bhadralok's* inordinate respect for academic work of any kind recognizing 'research as a life-long pilgrimage which ended with a named professorship and a marble bust in the corridors of Calcutta University or the National Library' (7). Along with this, the specific desire of the Bengalee middle-class family to educate their children in an anglicized manner, which could be a post-colonial hang over, is true of the narrator as well. The middle-class is indeed confronted by an opposition in their value system — the traditional versus the modern, or even the deviant. The *Bengalee Bhadralok* and nationalism are embodied in Tha'mma:

> All she wanted was a middle-class life in which like the middle-classes the world over, she would thrive believing in the unity of nationhood and territory; of self-respect and national power: that was all she wanted — a modern middle class life, a small thing that history had denied her in her fullness and for which she could never forgive it (78).

The *Bhadralok* background of the narrator's family, the middle-class that starts at the lower rung of the ladder and slowly gains upward mobility, with connections in the higher echelons of society, is described in some detail in the book. The movement from the flat in Gole Park, to a house in Southern Avenue, with the gentry at Gariahat road thrown in for good measure, virtually chalks out the narrator's journey from childhood to adolescence.

Meenakshi Mukherjee in her essay "Maps and Mirrors: Co-ordinates of Meaning in *The Shadow Lines*"[2] has analyzed the narrator's cultural milieu. The Bengalee's passion for travel is the central theme in many works of fiction. Mukherjee observes that any casual tourist would confirm that Bengalees outnumber travellers from any other part of India and that they do not always come from social classes for whom travel is an easily affordable luxury. This is a typical Bengalee trait. The child narrator is told that in the *Raibazar* house near Calcutta, the rainforests are imported from Brazil and Congo. This global reference may at first appear to be unusual for the story of an ordinary Bengalee boy, who is taught to hang on to the values of middle-class gentility by studying hard and performing well in exams. However, the introduction of children to fantasies and tales of travel from the world over, is a typical Bengalee trait and helps to situate the narrator very firmly in his specific cultural milieu.

With amazing lucidity, the author evokes the colonial past, critiques it and narrates the cultural fractures, traumas and anxieties, with his Bengali background. The house metaphor is worked out relentlessly, by tying it up with the division of Bengal. The overdoing of nostalgia is perhaps the dominant note in most partition fiction of West Bengal, but Ghosh seems wary of it and has provided some elements of humour in the novel, which sounds extremely catchy, especially in his chosen lexical Bengalee.

The ease with which the narration moves back and forth in time is stunning indeed. The fond recall of Dhaka by the grandmother and then the reconstruction of Tridib's death in Dhaka are experiences at variance with each other. But there is a kind of stability about her memories of Tridib being 'a loafer and a wastrel' and of Ila leading a kind of Bohemian life. She cannot come to terms with their concept of freedom and insists that freedom was what her generation struggled for.

Her memories of Dhaka are recreated by the narrator very fondly at times, '[...] they consisted of some unique alchemical mixture of sounds of the dialect and the smell of fast, mile-wide rivers, which alone had the power to bring upon her that comfortable lassitude which we call a sense of home-coming' (193). A rude shock awaits her when she sees a completely changed *Dhanmundi*. 'But this is for foreigners, where is Dhaka? And Tridib could not resist the malicious pleasure of pointing out: But you *are* a foreigner now, you're as foreign as May — much more than May, for look at her, she doesn't even need a visa to come here' (195).

Apart from sheer semantics of words like 'coming home' to Dhaka or 'going away' from it, the final moment of reckoning is to be found in the author's assertion. 'Every language assumes a centrality, a fixed and settled point to go away from and come back to, and what my grandmother was looking for was a word for journey that was a search for precisely that fixed point which permits the proper use of verbs of movement' (153).

Tha'mma's Dhaka had long since vanished into the past. For that matter the *Jethamoshai* in Dhaka, the so-called east Bengalee has more method in his madness, when he says:

> [...] I don't believe in this India-Shindia. It's all very well, you're going away now, but suppose when you get there they decide to draw another line somewhere? What will you do then? Where will you move to? No one will have you anywhere. As for me, I was born here, and I'll die here (215).

The senile old *Jethamoshai* seems to have a grasp of the ambiguous and tenuous nature of geographical boundaries. The narrator, through him, refers to lines of separation and the invisible links, which bind people. The author says: 'As always there were innumerable cases of Muslims in East Pakistan giving shelter to Hindus, often at the cost of their own lives and equally in India of Hindus sheltering Muslims' (229-30). These men and women demonstrated that their bonding was something quite outside and independent of their governments, which claim to have a monopoly over people and even decide their relationships.

The events of 1945-47 tragically proved that in the context of India the price of independence was an encouragement of divisive forces, culminating in yet another partition of Bengal. Who could imagine that a peaceful transfer of power would be accompanied by an unimaginably bloody communal carnage? Bengal reeled under the shock of its second partition and was numbed into silence. But the discourse in Ghosh's novel is not just about partition and sorrow, his sense of humour prevails almost through the entire novel, in the choice of words in Bengalee which are thoroughly enjoyable and carry the flavour of Calcutta. Ghosh gives a very vivid and detailed account of some salient aspects of his place of birth, where he spent his adolescent years. He has a sense of history and a firm grasp of his socio-cultural and historical material relating to the times. In order to depict such history, Ghosh uses Modern English wedded to an essentially Bengalee sensibility.

The narrator in the context of Tridib gives a vivid account of the street side *addas* and other meeting places. Tridib, we are told was 'happiest in neutral, impersonal places — coffee houses, bars, street-corner *addas* — the sort of place where people come talk and go away without expecting to know each other further' (92). He spends much of his time, gossiping with young "wastrels" at street corners and tea-stalls. (Anyone who has participated in *adda* sessions would know that frequenting them becomes compulsive and addictive). Tridib is a quintessential middle class Bengalee, living a routine life in Calcutta and looking after his grandmother and doing research for his doctoral degree. The apparently simple quality of Tridib's life attracts the narrator very much.

Calcutta of the 60's, with scattered shacks at Gariahat road, refugees from the East huddling around shanties and posh areas of Gole Park, and the literary and cultural atmosphere of Calcutta teashops — all this is evoked and is easily recognizable. The smoke of the cigarettes, heaps of ash and the proverbial Bengalee engaged in some kind of intelligent conversation — these are normal sights in Calcutta. Tridib is no exception; he is 'a familiar figure within the floating talkative populations of students and would-be footballers and bank clerks and small time politicos and all the rest who gravitated towards that conversation [...]' (8).

Playing chess and ludo, listening to the 'afternoon radio,' a happy past time of a Bengalee housewife, and listening to a very popular programme called *Anurodher Aashor* (listeners' choice) broadcast by the All India Radio, or even dishing out of omlettes 'a leathery little squiggle studded with green chillies' (5) and serving and eating masterly tidbits like hot *shingaras* (Samosas), stuffed with mince meat and raisins or eating crisp *dalpuris* — these are an essential part of Bengalee culture.

Dakshineswar, the famous *Kali* temple surrounded by a swarm of *pandas*, 'the traffic coming to a virtual halt, vast crowds circulating in the courtyard of the temple, like floodwaters sweeping through a garden' (44). And, the gates of the railway crossing at *Dhakuria* always being down so that one was kept 'waiting in the mid-day heat for half an hour before they were lifted.' Narrow roads with 'shacks on both sides, ramshackle structures some of them built on low stilts with walls plaited bamboo and roofs that had been patched together somehow out of corrugated iron. A ragged line of concrete houses rose behind the shacks, most of them unfinished' (131). All this depicts a common scene. But it has changed so much for the grandmother that she exclaims: 'when I came here ten years ago, there were rice fields looming alongside the road, it was the kind of place where rich Calcutta people built garden houses. And look at it now — filthy as a *babuis* (weaverbird) nest. It's all because of the refugees flooding in just like that' (131).

A visit to the *Victoria Memorial* in Calcutta is a must for Bengalees; there is nothing better than to eat 'chaat' and ice cream there. The huge black statute of Queen Victoria '[...] we found ourselves staring up [...] like Maharajas at a durbar.' The colonial mindset of the Bengalees is humorously projected here. Strangely, Ila's mother was named Queen Victoria 'because she just sat so, with her hands planted regally on the arms of her chair, clutching her tea-cup like a scepter.'

Ghosh in *The Shadow Lines* makes a liberal use of Bengalee words. For instance, he uses Tha'mma *i.e. thakurma* for the paternal grandmother, and the word *loafer* used by Tha'mma to describe Tridib means a 'wastrel.' The word *fail-cases* means no-gooders who attend *addas* and are not going to succeed in their lives. *Mairi* used usually at friendly *addas* is a colloquial Bengalee slang meaning 'swear.'

Later in the book, in an enclosed courtyard ringed with coconut palms and papaya trees, the cook is slaughtering a chicken, chanting '*Joi-Ma-Jagad-Janani*,' very much in line with a *Bali* or a sacrifice made to the Goddess Kali in Bengal. Of course all this is said in a much lighter vein. Queen Victoria ordering her servant *Muro-it* meant 'off with the head,' in this case, of thala-goya.

Durga Puja is celebrated to evoke the Goddess Durga. The narrator in his novel has captured the beginning of the festival on the sixth day of *Navratas*, which is *Soshti*. It is a perfect Puja day with the back lanes of Calcutta, all lit up with bright *pandals* and awnings 'some not yet finished and others with images installed and their loudspeakers already humming' (33-34). Women on this occasion wear white sarees with red borders. There is a reference to the narrator's first recollection of Ila. She wore a western dress then; but, on another occasion, he was disappointed to see her dressed in a simple white saree with a red border, like any other *Bethune College* girl on her way to a lecture. (*Bethune College*, incidentally, has a history of women who have contributed towards India's freedom struggle.)

At Dhaka, it was still the typical Bengalee joint-family. The house was very old and had grown like a honeycomb because every generation was making its own additions and alterations until the house was extending beyond its capacity and looking warped. 'Inhabited by so many branches of the family that even the most knowledgeable amongst them had become a little confused about their relationships' (121).

The head of the family was Jethamoshai, Tha'mma's father's elder brother who was the stereotyped stern patriarch. His presence was formidable and it is only when he left for the district courts did the house relax. (The word *cadaverous* has been used to describe Jethamoshai. Few Bengalees know that this word is actually English. It is used very frequently by people of all classes, knowingly or unknowingly, to describe a despicable person.)

Even today in Bengal, children, both urban and rural, pick up their rapid readers or the Bengali grammar book and say their lessons loudly, swinging their heads back and forth in a mechanical manner — more so to be seen and heard than to be actually studying. Being rapped on the knuckles with an umbrella is nothing new for them. An umbrella, incidentally, is an inseparable part of the Bengalee patriarch's identity.

When Mayadebi was married, 'her mother gave her strict instructions not to forget to send her aunt about half a dozen sarees from Calcutta.' Incidentally, handloom weavers of Bengal, known as *taanth,* are very popular amongst women. We may recall that the grandmother had not forgotten to gift a *saree* for the wife of Saiffudin, the mechanic, who was the present occupant of the old house in Dhaka. As for the eatables, the narrator, helped by her Tha'mma's narration could readily visualize 'Kanu-babu's sweet shop at the end of the lane, could imagine [...] the pink *chamchams,* the freshly pressed *shandesh* heaped in orderly mounds beneath the cracked glass' (194).

There are brilliant descriptions of urban and rustic aspects of Dhaka in the novel. The house of Mayadebi at Dhaka had a *pukur* (pond) outside the wall at the back. Usually a quiet pond, it turned stormy during monsoons after flooding the driveway and streets. And when that happened, how the cook Nityanand would scoop up the fish that floated up and kept them in an earthenware pot, to be used later. And Robi who had learnt to suck the watery nectar from the stems of canna lilies, and to catch dragonflies and climb mango trees. Seeing Robi climb the tree on one occasion, *Tha'mma* wished she could do just that, because may be she would be able to see Dhaka from up there. All these are touching reminiscences of the narrator.

Shadorbazar, the Royal Stationery Store, Naresh Babu's jewellery shop [...] the grandmother's eyes search for all these once familiar sights on her return to Dhaka. She in vain wanders in the backyard looking for the lime trees her mother had planted. The backyard was now being used as a garage where there were now pools of grease and sets of twisted handlebars of motorcycles. But just in case we forget, 'Nostalgia, she hates and counts as a weakness, a waste of time, that everyone's duty is to forget the past and look ahead and get on with building the future [...]' (208).

Later in the book, the narrator's sense of 'Deja-vu' in London's Brick Lane, an area where most Bangladeshis live, is perceived in the manner of his grandmother's recall, though this is another reality. Bengalee neon signs above the shops that lined Brick Lane, display windows lined with the latest Bengalee film magazines, anti-racism posters obviously pasted by some members of a left wing party, along with a riot of posters of Hindi films, people hurrying about speaking many dialects of Bengalee like shoppers at *Gariahat* on a cold morning. The narrator is amazed at the number of Bengalee dialects being spoken in the streets of London — dialects, which he had never heard even in Calcutta. 'The sniff of *rosogolla*s exactly like the sweet shop at the corner of *Gole Park*, the same laminated counters and tables — except that there was no *paan*-shop at the corner or a Nathu Chaubey' (100).

There is a Bangladeshi restaurant called *Maharaja* in Clapham where Ila sometimes goes to eat. Once when she goes there accompanied by Robi and the narrator she says that her mother's *chochchori* and *bhaath* (special Bengalee preparation of mixed vegetables and rice) was unbeatable. The owner was one Rehman Saheb who spoke Bengali, with a nasal *Sylhet* accent, and who prided himself in being a Bangladeshi and a citizen of England, insisting that his sweets were better than what one gets in Calcutta. I may here mention that some

Bangladeshis try to pull away from Calcutta/Dhaka culture. Even Robi says that all he remembers of Dhaka is that his brother Tridib was killed there — not so far from where his mother was born.

This then is the paradox of Bengal as depicted in the novel. The partition, the pain and trauma of the divide is summed up poignantly when the narrator declares that the memories pertaining to Tha'mma's Bengal cannot be divided, and yet the ghastly reality that stares one in the face is, you never know when violence flares up. 'It is a fear that comes of the knowledge that normalcy is utterly contingent that spaces that surround one, the streets that one inhabits, can become suddenly and without warning, as hostile as a desert in a flash flood. It is this that sets apart the thousand million people who inhabit the sub-continent from the rest of the world — not language, not food, not music — it is the special quality of loneliness that grows out of fear of the war between oneself and one's image in the mirror' (204). The two Bengals will always share this agony.

Needless to say that every individual has the right to perceive reality, in her/his own way. The author himself has done it through his novel and I have attempted to explore his fictional world to perceive the 'reality' he has created; and I find that none of Amitav Ghosh's political insights, as manifest in his novel, impede his wonderful quality of storytelling and the *Bengalee* in him.

Notes and References

1. Amitav Ghosh, *The Shadow Lines* (Delhi: Ravi Dayal Publishers, 1988), 219.
2. Meenakshi Mukherjee, "Maps and Mirrors: Co-ordinates of Meaning in *The Shadow Lines*" in *The Shadow Lines*, educational edition (Delhi: OUP, Fifth impression, 1998).

   I have benefited from the following works: Meenakshi Mukherjee, ed., *The Perishable Empire* (Delhi: OUP, 2000); Azim Zaman, Hussain, ed., *Colonial and Postcolonial Encounters* (Delhi: Manohar, 2000); Niaz Zaman, *A Divided Legacy: The Partition in Selected Novels of India, Pakistan, Bangladesh* (Delhi: Manohar, 2000); Viney Kirpal, ed., *The New Indian Novel in English: A Study of 1980's* (Bombay: Allied Publisher, 1990); E. Nilufer Bharucha & Nabar Vrinda, ed.,

Mapping Cultural Spaces: Postcolonial Indian Literature in English (New Delhi: Vision Books, 1998); P.K. Dutta, "Studies in Homogeneity: A Reading of Two Recent Indo-Anglian Novels" in *Social Scientist*, No. 202, Vol. 18, March 1990; Sumit Sarkar, *The Swadeshi Movement in Bengal 1903-1908* (Delhi: Peoples Publishing House, 1973).

PART III

15

The Shadow Lines in Context

ADITYA BHATTACHARJEA

This essay examines *The Shadow Lines* in relation to Amitav Ghosh's other writings, both fiction and non-fiction. It begins in Section I with brief summaries of the plots and structures of four of his other books, for the benefit of those who have not read them. In the course of this, I draw attention to Ghosh's versatility in handling very different genres, as well as some of the themes, techniques and autobiographical details that recur in his work. I, then, highlight some of these themes, and argue in Section II that some of the criticism that has been directed against *The Shadow Lines* is misplaced. Section III, however, suggests that some of its weaknesses can also be seen in his other books.

I

Ghosh's first novel, *The Circle of Reason*, although published in 1986, was written in the early 1980s, in the afterglow of the tremendous success of Salman Rushdie's *Midnight's Children*. Although Ghosh does not go overboard with the more fantastic elements of magical realism and hybrid 'Hinglish' vocabulary, Rushdie's influence is apparent in the profusion of bizarre characters, many of them severed from their roots and marked by peculiar eccentricities and obsessions. We also observe here traces of Rushdie's non-linear narrative technique, with frequent digressions, recollections, and stories within stories. (Critics have observed that this strategy, adopted by several other Indian writers in English, lays claim to the heritage of the *Panchatantra* and thereby validates the authors' identities as Indians despite their use of an 'alien' language.)

The Circle of Reason begins in rural Bengal in the late 1960s, where a village schoolteacher with a passion for phrenology (the 'science' of predicting a person's character from the bumps on his head) and for killing germs, adopts his orphaned nephew Alu and has him trained as a master weaver. The narrative is interwoven with flashbacks to the teacher's days in Presidency College in the 1930s, where students worship science and rationality with an absurd determination not very different from the blind religious faith they are trying to question. The influx of refugees from East Bengal (later Bangladesh), and the emergence of a corrupt village politician, leads to a police raid and an accidental explosion that wipes out most of the characters who populated the first third of the novel. Alu is forced to flee, with Jyoti Das, an unlikely police officer who likes painting birds, in pursuit. Alu makes his way first to Kerala and then across the Arabian Sea to al-Ghazira, a fictional sheikdom on the Persian Gulf, where he is thrown together with several other colourful Indian migrants and Arabs. Their stories make up the next third of the novel, disrupted once again by an assault by the local police which kills several of them and forces the survivors to flee across North Africa to a remote outpost in the Sahara desert, where the novel's denouement is set.

I presume that anyone reading the volume in which this essay is included is already familiar with *The Shadow Lines*, and does not need a plot summary. However, readers might be interested to know that in an essay published in 1995, Ghosh traced the origins of the novel to his personal experience of the 1984 anti-Sikh riots in Delhi and their aftermath:

> Within a few months, I started my novel, which I eventually called *The Shadow Lines* — a book that led me backward in time, to earlier memories of riots, ones witnessed in childhood. It became a book not about any one event but about the meaning of such events and their effects on the individuals who live through them.[1]

A clue to these earlier riots is provided in one of his later books, to which I return below. On other aspects of *The Shadow Lines*, I shall only point out that in moving from his first to his second novel, Ghosh adopts a more tightly controlled narrative style with a limited number of characters. From *The Circle of Reason* he retains the non-linear format, the interpolated stories, the fascination with exotic locations, the characters' ability to move easily across national borders, and the innovation (innovative in Indian English fiction, at any rate) of dispensing with inverted commas in direct speech.

As if tired of experimenting, Ghosh does use inverted commas in his later books, but the blurring of borders remains an enduring characteristic of his work, despite the very different forms he adopts. *In an Antique Land* (1992) can scarcely be called a novel. It interweaves Ghosh's personal experiences as an anthropologist doing field-work in two Egyptian villages with his hunt for information about the life and times of a twelfth-century Jewish trader from Africa, his several Arab and Indian friends, and in particular two Indian slaves, one of whom he supposedly married, while the other became almost a part of his family. As if reliving their experience, Ghosh similarly becomes virtually a member of his Egyptian host's family (without of course getting enslaved or married!). The quest takes Ghosh to libraries and historians around the world, and to the places where his twelfth-century subjects lived (Cairo, Aden, Mangalore). In the process he recreates a harmonious medieval world with no borders, either in the mind or on the ground, in opposition to the accounts of 'Muslim invasions' enshrined in History (a word which he capitalizes to emphasize its hegemonic significance). Along the way, he investigates syncretic religious sects and visits shrines that are sacred to both Hindus and Muslims, or Jews and Arabs.

An autobiographical aside in this wide-ranging book provides a clue to how Ghosh's personal memories helped shape *The Shadow Lines*, and also helps to understand the passing reference to 'riots witnessed in childhood' in the 1995 essay quoted above. The author recalls how, when he was seven years old, his father was posted to the Indian diplomatic mission in Dhaka, and in 1964 a large number of Hindu refugees took shelter in their house, which was then surrounded and almost overrun by an angry mob. He discovered only many years later through old newspapers that 'mirror-image' riots took place at the same time in Calcutta as well, in which many innocents were killed, but others were saved by their neighbours. The reflection of this personal experience in *The Shadow Lines* should be obvious to anyone who has read the novel. *In an Antique Land* is thus simultaneously an anthropologist's field diary, a historical novel, a detective story, a research monograph (with sources meticulously cited in the copious end-notes, and excerpts published in the influential *Subaltern Studies* series), a travelogue, a memoir, and ultimately (like *The Shadow Lines*) an essay protesting against irrational divisions between people based on ethnicity.

The Calcutta Chromosome (1996) is similarly difficult to classify. It is partly a work of science fiction (it won the coveted Arthur C. Clarke Prize), set in the near future, with computers that can project objects and people from anywhere on earth as holographic images in the user's living room, and with tremendous information retrieval capability. (In one case it reconstructs an e-mail message erased twenty years earlier from its electronic signature in the ionosphere!) It can also be read as a detective novel, while one chapter could easily stand alone as a chilling ghost story. This appears to be very different from the first three books, but the anthropological angle remains, with members of a strange cult reappearing mysteriously as the plot unfolds; and the conflict between science and superstition is also foregrounded. We are again in a borderless world, with effortless communication. Also familiar from the earlier books is the protagonist's obsessive search for a version of the past that is radically different from accepted History. In this case, he insists on proving that Ronald Ross's celebrated discovery in 1898 of how malaria is transmitted by mosquitoes was manipulated by members of a ghoulish sect who immortalize themselves by transmitting their personalities into new bodies via the malarial parasite. The narrative once again moves back and forth in time, between the future, the 1890s, and the 1990s, with the same easy fluency Ghosh displayed in the earlier books.

Ghosh's latest effort, *The Glass Palace* (2000), is again on the surface a completely different kind of novel. Covering more than a century (1885 to 1996) with a more or less linear narrative, it is a saga of three generations of three families, tied together by friendship, marriage and business dealings, against the background of the ascendance and dissolution of British imperialism in India and South-east Asia. The story takes off from a little-known historical fact. As every schoolchild knows, the last Mughal emperor of India was deposed and exiled to Burma after the defeat of the 1857 Revolt. What few people know is that the last king of Burma was deposed and exiled to Ratnagiri in India after the British conquest of 1885, and he too died in exile. The three families chronicled in the novel are those of Rajkumar, a poor orphan from East Bengal who grows up to become a successful timber merchant in Burma; Saya John, an ethnic Chinese businessman; and Uma Dey, a middle-class Bengali widow who becomes a nationalist politician. I shall not attempt to summarize the multiple plots of this novel of 550 pages, but I shall refer to it frequently below. For the moment, let me just note some flashes of *The Shadow Lines*: an ethnic riot, observed from a car, in which an innocent rickshaw-puller is killed; people being saved by their friends of the 'other' community; the easy crossing of borders; and a different version of that 'special quality of loneliness that grows out of the fear of the war between oneself and one's image in the mirror' —in this case, the acute dilemma faced by men of the British Indian army when they consider going over to the INA in the Second World War.

In the Acknowledgments at the end of *The Glass Palace*, Ghosh mentions that his father, to whose memory the book is dedicated, was an officer in the Indian Army during the Burma campaign. His parents were originally from Dhaka, and an uncle was a businessman in Burma. His childhood was spent in the area of Calcutta that figures in *The Shadow Lines* as well as *The Glass Palace*, and he went to St Stephen's College in Delhi, which appears anonymously in the former. I have already mentioned two places where he records his personal memories of communal riots, and how *Antique Land* is based on his experiences as a social anthropologist in Egypt. There is thus a significant autobiographical element in his work.

II

Apart from the common themes I have noted in the course of these extremely compressed summaries, which scarcely do justice to the rich complexity of Ghosh's novels, I would like to highlight a few others. As Meenakshi Mukherjee noted in her brilliant essay on *The Shadow Lines*,[2] Ghosh has the knack of unobtrusively inserting meticulously researched details of the times and places in which he locates his story. The same ability is displayed in the other four books as well, as if the author has taken as his credo Tridib's injunction to use his 'imagination with precision' (24). They are not conventional historical novels, for all of the books, with the possible exception of the first, show an abiding interest in details of events, regions and people who have been marginalized by purveyors of mainstream History. The narrators or main protagonists are researchers who have a personal motive for digging into the past. Like the narrator of *The Shadow Lines*, they insist on their own version of history, often in the face of criticism and ridicule from those who think they know better.

Apart from this engagement with History, Ghosh's works also contain a wealth of almost encyclopedic information on other subjects. If in *The Circle of Reason* we find ornithology, phrenology, the technology of handloom weaving, the etymology of cotton, and episodes from the history of science, *The Calcutta Chromosome* has microbiology, genetics, linguistics and computer science. *The Glass Palace* shows familiarity with teak logging, elephant lore, rubber plantations, photography, jungle warfare and regimental traditions in the army, while changing automobile models mark the passage of time. These elements are introduced smoothly into the narratives: there is no pedantry or showing off, just the joy of discovering and sharing knowledge.

The easy crossing of borders, in practice as well as in the imagination, with tales of far-off places, is a hallmark of Ghosh's writings. It is unfair to dismiss this, as some eminent critics of *The Shadow Lines* have done, as an effort to escape from India's harsh social realities, or as a mindless celebration of the cultural 'hybridity' promoted by globalization. (I argue at the end of this essay that there is an escapist element in Ghosh's work, but it does not take him abroad.) Nor should the prominence given to the Price family, or Tridib's penchant for tales of exotic lands and his intimate familiarity with London *circa* 1940, both of which are inherited and internalized by the narrator of *The Shadow Lines*, be simplistically read as an escape from difficult questions of nationalism and freedom or as betraying a fascination for all things English.[3] Rather, as Professor Mukherjee points out, this represents a longstanding tradition in Bengali literature, which Ghosh has transplanted into Indian English fiction. Besides, if one reads all of Ghosh's novels, one finds the same careful attention to period details for Aden and Cairo in the twelfth century, Mandalay in 1885, Ratnagiri in the early years of the twentieth century, and Rangoon in 1941. If anything, the English characters in *The Shadow Lines* are rather pathetic in comparison to the Arab, Jewish, and Indian characters of the other novels. And wherever else they may roam, all the novels with the exception of *Antique Land* are firmly anchored in the neighbourhoods of south Calcutta, and the sensibilities, foibles and insecurities of Bengali *bhadralok*.

Ghosh's peregrinations do however have a deeper purpose than either gratuitous exoticism or laying claim to the mantle of Bengali fiction. He wants to remind us of the longstanding emotional and economic ties between India and its neighbours to the east and west. In *The Shadow Lines*, the central image is the compass-and-atlas exercise that shows that Srinagar and Dhaka are far apart and yet so closely tied together. This connection has primarily negative associations, for the grandmother's fond memories of the Dhaka of her childhood are overshadowed by the killing of her uncle and nephew there many years later. The other novels, especially *Antique Land*, speak of much happier ties, although as I have noted elsewhere, the author's artistic licence takes him a bit too far in erasing the nastier aspects of twelfth-century history.[4] *The Glass Palace* takes a balanced view. The contribution of ethnic Indian businessmen to the economy of Burma and Malaya is highlighted, as are their friendships with the locals, but so also is the dark underside of the Indian presence. It is the Indian army that conquers and maintains the empire on behalf of the British, and Rajkumar's rags-to-riches story is built on the indentured labour he imports from India.

However, if one has any misconceptions about Ghosh's alleged loyalty to the English cause, then *The Glass Palace* should cure it. The rulers' racism is unsparingly portrayed: the Indian officers and businessmen are shabbily treated in the colonial clubs, and when the Japanese invade Burma they are excluded from evacuation trains and forced to trek to India on foot, and that too by the harder routes. As Professor Mukherjee declares in her recent review, '*The Glass Palace* will remain for me memorable mainly as the most scathing critique of British colonialism I have ever come across in fiction.'[5] This anti-imperialist strain can be glimpsed even in one of the stories embedded in *The Circle of Reason*, which recounts the bullying and treachery with which first the British and then an unnamed oil company and their local collaborators took over the fictional principality of al-Ghazira.

Two aspects of Ghosh's treatment of cross-cultural ties deserve special mention. The first is his unique perspective on exile. The 'exile-heroes' of the earlier generation of Indo-Anglian authors, or the more recent flotsam of the Indian diaspora portrayed by authors like Jhumpa Lahiri, find themselves in Europe or America, where they suffer acute alienation and loneliness. Antar in *The Calcutta Chromosome* may seem to be a futuristic projection of the same sad continuum, for cooped up in his Manhattan apartment he communicates with the world only through a computer (named Ava, perhaps to suggest that it provides him a surrogate for female company). To my mind, however, Antar's predicament is a warning about the effects of being exiled in Cyberia rather than in another country, reminiscent of a short story by another author not known for his science fiction: "The Machine Stops," by E.M. Forster. The exiles of Ghosh's other novels, in contrast, make themselves quite at home, whether they are Indians in the Middle East or Southeast Asia, or a north African Jew or deposed Burmese royalty in India. The merging of the apparent binaries of home and away, of coming and going, which play such an important role in *The Shadow Lines*, occurs in the other novels as well. Towards the end of *The Glass Palace*, there is a poignant moment when Indians who had to leave Burma —the only home they knew —during the Second World War meet in a Buddhist temple in Calcutta, in order to reminisce about the old days, to hear Burmese being spoken, and even to prostrate themselves in the traditional Burmese manner before the old king's daughter, who has lived in India far longer than they have. Who is the native here and who the exile?

The second notable feature I would like to mention is Ghosh's version of the melting pot, throwing together disparate characters from diverse ethnic backgrounds. In this respect *The Shadow Lines* is something of an exception. Ila's multi-national contacts, from the friends in her international schools to the adulterous Nick, cause humiliation and pain. In all the other novels, beginning with the motley boatload of emigrants in *The Circle of Reason*, and their interactions with Arabs and East Africans in al-Ghazira, multi-cultural and cross-border friendships are a source of great strength. I have already outlined the nature of these friendships in the later novels, but apart from developing the relationships between his major characters, Ghosh makes it a point to highlight the cosmopolitan character of the places where he locates their stories, whether Aden, Mangalore or Mandalay. Contrary to his critics, Ghosh is celebrating a tolerant, inclusive multiculturalism far removed from that of the Western metropolis, and established long before the hybridizing cosmopolitanism promoted by the cultural logic of globalization under late capitalism. There is an explicit allegation in two of the later novels that European imperialism was in fact responsible for destroying these idyllic Asian societies. In *Antique Land*, the end of the old order is heralded in 1509, when 'a transcontinental fleet, hastily put together by the Muslim potentate of Gujarat, the Hindu ruler of Calicut, and the Sultan of Egypt was attacked and defeated by a Portuguese force,' a defeat that the author blames on 'the rich confusions that accompany a culture of accommodation and compromise' (288). In *The Glass Palace,* one of the characters mourns for 'the old loyalties of India, the ancient ones—they'd been destroyed long ago, the British had built their Empire by effacing them' (441).

Another aspect of Asian solidarity in Ghosh's novels also compels attention. Unlike the messy relationships between Ila and Nick, or Tridib and May, love in the tropics is uncomplicated, and effortlessly transcends barriers of class and ethnicity. The Jewish trader in *Antique Land* marries a former slave (quite improbably, a Nair), while in *The Glass Palace,* a Burmese princess marries a Maratha coachman, and Rajkumar travels from Burma to Ratnagiri to woo and later marry one of the princess's servants, whom he saw fleetingly some twenty years earlier when they were both children. Later, the offspring of the novel's three central families get romantically involved with each other as if it was ordained by nature. There is also a suggestion in the novels that, along with romantic love, class solidarity (amongst migrant workers in *The Circle of Reason*; among business associates in *Antique Land* and *The Glass Palace*) can easily triumph over ethnic divisions. If only it were that simple.

III

Ghosh makes it seem so easy—to use a sporting metaphor, he gives common humanity a walkover—because he deprives his characters of any meaningful caste or religious identity. They have purely nominal affiliations, but religion plays no role in their lives. It sometimes gets them killed, and determines how their funerals are performed, but it does not inform their value systems and practices, and they remain untouched by any trace of loyalty or animosity based on the group they were born into. This is a notable void in Ghosh's work, and to my mind it cramps his steadfast espousal of a universal humanitarianism. If fiction in the realist mode is to serve the cause of overcoming ethnic hatred, it must look it squarely in the face by portraying three-dimensional subjects with 'politically-incorrect' views, rather than locate it in the occasional faceless mob or untraceable rumour. This would bring out the role of social conditioning, and of manipulation of group identities for political or economic advantage. For Ghosh, unfortunately, ethnic hatred is something like the infectious diseases that figure in *The Circle of Reason*: almost in the air we breathe, erupting occasionally into a deadly epidemic. (That over-used journalistic phrase, 'communal virus,' similarly makes human beings into passive carriers and deprives them of agency and thereby responsibility.) His remedy, to adapt a motif from the same novel, seems to require only that the milk of human kindness is always Pasteurized. He regards the disease as an exclusively South Asian malady, for he writes in *The Shadow Lines* that it 'sets apart the thousand million people who inhabit the subcontinent from the rest of the world' (204); and again in *Antique Land* his sojourn in an Egyptian village convinces him that the Middle East 'was a world that was far gentler, far less violent, very much more humane and innocent than mine' (210). Here his understandable despair at the riots he repeatedly witnessed since childhood surely overcomes his sense of history. Other recent novelists (Bhisham Sahni's *Tamas*, Vikram Seth's *A Suitable Boy* and even Arundhati Roy's *The God of Small Things* come to mind) have been much bolder in confronting the hate that does not speak its name, and consequently more effective.

Finally, it is probably this same despair, and his unsentimental documentation of various social horrors, that leads Ghosh to end every one of his five books on a note of unfounded hope. In the three middle works, this sentiment acquires a quasi-religious dimension. *The Shadow Lines* concludes with the narrator finally learning the real reason for Tridib's death, and spending the night with his former girlfriend, grateful for what he calls 'the glimpse she had given me of a final redemptive mystery.' Then, in the epilogue of *In an Antique Land*, Ghosh discovers archival documents that enables him to surmise that the friendship between the Jewish merchant and his Indian 'slave' continued until the end of their lives, validating his belief that a better world existed eight hundred years ago. The relevant page of the documents contains only a mundane set of accounts, but Ghosh charges it with emotive meaning because of a passing mention of the former slave. The setting of this discovery—a subterranean vault, in which the parchments rest in 'cabinets that rise out of the floor like catafalques'—and the author's sense of almost religious fulfilment, are strongly reminiscent of a pilgrim in the presence of a holy relic. Even the sci-fi thriller, *The Calcutta Chromosome*, ends with the successive discoverers and inheritors of the mysterious Chromosome being helped 'across' by their predecessors, to transmigrate into another body and thereby attain immortality and a reprieve from the disease, loneliness or oppression that mark their lives. All this makes it seem as though the author, having deprived his characters of the solace that organized religion occasionally provides, is forced to come up with his own substitutes.

The ending of *The Glass Palace* is more down to earth, yet ultimately more uplifting. We first get a glimpse of the inspiring figure of Aung San Suu Kyi, whose dignified and courageous resistance to Myanmar's military regime holds out hope for her unfortunate country. Then, in a bizarre but moving scene that concludes the novel, two of the central characters who personify diametrically opposed personal and political values end up in bed with each other in their old age. This represents the possibility of real reconciliation, unlike the union with May with which the narrator concludes *The Shadow Lines*, which is more in the nature of his claiming the last bit of Tridib's legacy. (Perhaps the 'redemptive' quality of this encounter should be interpreted in secular rather than religious terms, as in 'reclamation'?) Earlier in *The Glass Palace*, one of the characters, a young army officer, is forced to consider where his loyalties lie when his men revolt to join the INA. There are no easy answers:

> Loyalty, commonalty, faith — these things were as essential and as fragile as the muscles of the human heart; easy to destroy, impossible to rebuild. How would one begin the work of recreating the tissues that bound people to each

> other? [...] It was a labour that would last not one year, not ten, not fifty — it was the work of centuries (441).

Ghosh seems to be acknowledging in this latest novel that he no longer believes that a remedy for the world's ills can be found by escaping into a world of imagination where all lines between human beings are merely shadow lines; or into a reconstructed past, as in *Antique Land*; or into a transcendental state of immortality, as in *The Calcutta Chromosome*. Instead, he returns to the open-ended possibilities of his very first novel, *The Circle of Reason*, which ends with the enigmatic line 'Hope is the beginning,' after Alu has been displaced under tragic circumstances for the fourth time.

Many readers will find these endings unbearably mawkish. But here, for my own ending, I invoke the spirit of a very worldly philosopher, the great twentieth-century economist John Maynard Keynes, who once raised a toast proclaiming economists to be 'the guardians, not of civilization, but of the possibility of civilization.' I doubt that economists are worthy of this honour; we might as well hand it over to intelligent and sensitive novelists like Amitav Ghosh.

Editions Cited

The Circle of Reason: Roli Books International, 1986.

The Shadow Lines: Educational Edition, Oxford University Press, 1995.

In an Antique Land: Ravi Dayal, 1992.

The Calcutta Chromosome: Ravi Dayal, 1996.

The Glass Palace: Harper Collins, 2000.

Notes and References

1. Amitav Ghosh, "The Ghosts of Mrs. Gandhi," *The New Yorker*, July 17, 1995.
2. "Maps and Mirrors: Co-ordinates of Meaning in *The Shadow Lines*," in *The Shadow Lines Educational Edition*, OUP, 1995. All page references to the novel are also from this edition.
3. This range of criticisms comes from, among others, Harish Trivedi, "Epilogue/Epitaph" and Tapan Basu, "Writing Of(f) History," both in *The Fiction of St Stephen's*, edited by Aditya Bhattacharjea and Lola

Chatterji (New Delhi: Ravi Dayal Publisher, 2000); as well as A.N. Kaul, "A Reading of *The Shadow Lines*," in *The Shadow Lines Educational Edition.*

4. See my "Privileged Fiction: The Stephanian Novelists and (Their) Others," in *The Fiction of St Stephen's.*

5. *The Indian Review of Books*, October 2000.

Chronology in *The Shadow Lines**

ARVIND CHOWDHARY

Year	Event	Age	Page Nos.
1925	Narrator's father born in Mandalay.		124
1931	Death of Grandmother's parents.	N's father 6	126
1935	Narrator's Grandfather dies of pneumonia in Burma.	N's grandmother 32, N's father 10	125
1936	Grandmother starts teaching in a school in Calcutta (Bhowanipore).	N's grandmother 33	125
1939	Tridib's visit to England, accompanied by his parents. They go there in connection with Tridib's father's medical treatment.	Mayadebi 29,Tridib 8; N born 13 yrs. later	3
25 Sep. 1940	Tridib's 9th Birthday. He receives Tristan-Iseult story from Snipe as a gift.		182
29 Sep. 1940	Death of Alan Tresawsen (Nick's Uncle).		55-56
1 Oct. 1940	Bombing of Lymington Mansions (two floors damaged).		56
1943	Mike reported dead, figures in the casualty list in *THE TIMES*.		103
1947	Partition (Dhaka becomes the capital of East Pakistan).		125
1959	Beginning of Correspondence between Tridib and May.	Tridib 27 , May 19	17
1960	Ila's visit to Calcutta from London for Durgapuja. Visit to old family house at Rai	Ila / N 8 approx.	32

Year	Event	Age	Page Nos.
	Bazar (invents London for the Narrator; Nick becomes a spectral presence for the narrator's 'looking -glass' Magda/Ila rescued by Nick from a tormentor. Robi beats a bully at his school.	Nick 12 Robi 12	49 36
1961	Tridib's conversations with the narrator and others at the street-corner-addas. (His 'made-up' story about May etc.)	Tridib 29-30; N 8–9	7-11
1962	Ila's visit to Calcutta from Colombo (narration of thala-goya incident). Retirement of N's Grandmother (after 27 yrs. of service). N's father becomes G.M. of his firm; they move to a new house on Southern Avenue.	Ila 10 Grandmother 60, N 10	25 114 119
1962 Winter	Grandmother meets Minadi and learns from her that her cousin, Nidhu Babu (Jethamoshai 's son) and his family are living in Calcutta. Subsequently, visits the relatives conducted by Mrinamoyee and accompanied by her son, daughter-in-law and grandson; discovers that Jethamoshai is alive and wrote to his daughter-in-law a month back from Dhaka in response to the news that Nidhu Babu had died. (He had written quite a few months after his son's death.)		135
Oct. 1962	India's war with China.		218
Late 1962	May receives her fourth letter – a pornographic one – from Tridib.		138
March 1963	The news disclosed by the N's father that the Shaheb has been posted as Counsellor in the Deputy High Commission in Dhaka.		148
June 1963	Trunk call for the N's grandmother from Mayadebi from Delhi		

Year	Event	Age	Page Nos.
	informing her about her departure for Dhaka a couple of days later and an invitation for her to visit Dhaka.		149
Late 1963	Narrator meets May Price for the first time in Calcutta. May's visit to Rai Bazar family house, and her taking note of a large unused table, bought in 1890's from England and her visits to Queen Victoria Memorial, Diamond Harbour, accompanied by Tridib and the narrator.	Tridib 31 approx.; May 23 approx.	13 48
27 Dec. 1963	Disappearance of Mu-i-Mubarak (a sacred relic of the Prophet Mohammed) from its place in the Hazratbal Mosque.		225
29 Dec. 1963	Demonstrations in Srinagar against the disappearance of Mu-i-Mubarak; and riots, target government property and police and not people.		225
2 Jan. 1964	A letter for Grandmother from Mayadebi confirming that Jethamoshai was alive and being looked after by a Muslim family.		189
3 Jan. 1964	Departure of Grandmother, Tridib, Robi and May to Dhaka by plane.		150
4 Jan. 1964	Recovery of Mu-i-Mubarak. Riots in Khulna (East Pakistan). Few people killed.		226
6 Jan. 1964	Fourteen die in frenzy off Khulna.		228
Thursday Jan. 1964	Grandmother, Mayadebi, Tridib, Robi and May visit Jethamoshai. Tridib dies a sacrificial death trying to save Jethamoshai; the latter also gets killed along with Khalil (the rickshaw-puller) in the race riot in Dhaka.		243-46 250-51
8, 9 Jan. 1964	Rumors afloat in Calcutta, of mass killing of Hindus in East Pakistan.		229
9 Jan. 1964	Twenty-nine killed in riots in Khulna.		223

Year	Event	Age	Page Nos.
10 Jan. 1964	Calcutta riots (10 dead, 15 wounded). Kunderan's day in Madras (unbeaten 170 against England). Sacred relic reinstalled at Hazratbal Mosque.		224
11 Jan. 1964	Army called out from Fort William to check the riots in Calcutta.		229
End of 1964	Riots fade from the pages of the newspapers.		230
1965	Grandmother gives her necklace to the war fund (India-Pakistan war), after about 1 ½ year of Tridib's death.		236
1966	Ila's visit to Calcutta ; tears out a page (of photographs) from the Year book which shows her as an alien in England; the narrator knew about this fact.	Ila 14	23
1968	Ila's visit to Calcutta, flies in from Indonesia ('a Bethune college girl').	Ila/narrator 16	18
1969	Ila meets Nick last before they meet again in London in 1979	Nick 19	54
Mid 1970's	Grandmother precariously ill. Robi, Ila and the narrator together in Calcutta during their vacation (Ila joins them from London). The Grand Hotel incident in Calcutta when Robi did not permit Ila to dance with a stranger there and the former had left them in a fit of fury. Narrator's B.A. final year exam. two months away; returns to Delhi. Grandmother's death after a few days of his departure. Narrator mourns her death – rides bus no. 210 from Maurice Nagar to Secretariat and back, aimlessly. Dean of his college calls him to his office, with the intention of rusticating or expelling him, after receiving a three-line letter from the latter's grandmother to the effect that he had been visiting prostitutes in houses of ill-repute in Delhi and		80 91 92 93

Year	Event	Age	Page Nos.
	that he be sent back to Calcutta (the letter was penned down by her a day before her death).		
1978-79	Narrator's London Visit on a year's research grant for getting material from the India House Library for his Ph.D.	N 27 approx.	13
Oct./Nov. 1978 ?	Narrator meets May for the first time in London after the concert in the Festival Hall.		
Dec. 1978	Christmas Eve party at Mrs. Price's house (44 Lymington Rd.), attended by the Narrator, Ila, Nick and May. Blizzard blowing outside. The narrator, May and Ila have to stay back.		105
Feb.-March 1979 ?	Ila's Wedding (6 months after the narrator came to London in September 1978).		154
	The narrator dead drunk. May persuades him to come and stay with her at her Islington residence. May successfully resists his physical advances towards her but forgives him. Next day he accompanies her on her rounds for collecting money for her worthy causes.		156
Sep. 1979	Robi's stop-over in England. He talks about his nightmarish experience of Tridib's death for the first time in a Bangladeshi restaurant, after they – namely, Robi, the narrator and Ila – had been to see Mrs. Price.		243-47
	Narrator visits Mrs. Price 3 days before his departure to Delhi, accompanied by Ila. In the cellar, she confides with the narrator about her unhappy married life because of Nick's unfaithfulness.		187
	Narrator visits May a day before his departure to Delhi, where he shares her epiphanic experience regarding Tridib's death, also her physical intimacy.		247, 249-52

Year	Event	Age	Page Nos.
Late 1979	Narrator establishes a connection between his nightmare bus ride from school in Calcutta and the events that befell Tridib and the others in Dhaka in Jan. 1964, with the help of material evidence from Teen Murti Library archives in New Delhi.		218
Late 1979 / early 1980?	Learns a new meaning of space – spaces related to one another through mutual concern or mutual indifference of people – in the hostel room in Delhi.		231-33

N: Narrator

*Tabulation by Shagun Chaudhary, a student from ER and DCI, Noida.

A Family Tree: Indian Characters*

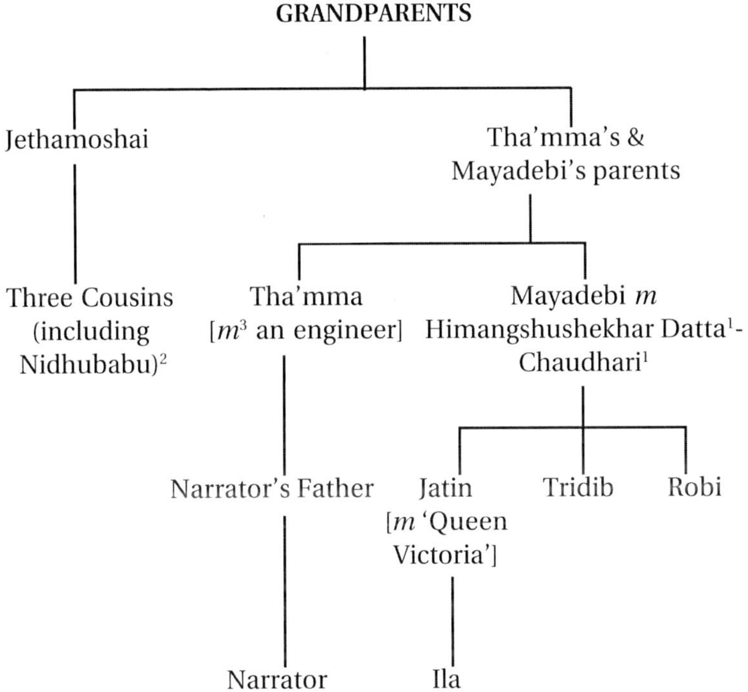

Note

1. The Shaheb
2. Garia relative (Nidhubabu)
3. m: marries

*Prepared by Angelie Multani

Index*

---

*Prepared by Manjula Saxena.